E X P L O R A T I O N S

From Sentence to Paragraph

Virginia Williams
Hillsborough Community College

Carl David Blake

HarperCollins*Publishers*

to E. V. Williams, the inspiration for the explorations

Sponsoring Editor: Jane Kinney
Development Editor: Sue Baugh
Project Coordination, Text and Cover Design: PC&F, Inc.
Cover Photo: Marcus Brooke, FPG International
Production Manager: Michael Weinstein
Compositor: PC&F, Inc.
Printer and Binder: Courier Corporation
Cover Printer: The Lehigh Press, Inc.

Explorations: From Sentence to Paragraph
Copyright © 1992 by HarperCollins Publishers Inc.

Library of Congress Cataloging-in-Publication Data

Williams, Virginia (Virginia L.)
    Explorations. From sentence to paragraph / Virginia Williams,
  Carl David Blake.
       p.   cm.
    Includes index.
    ISBN 0-06-047139-5 (student ed.) -- ISBN 0-06-500545-7 (inst. ed.)
    1. English language--Rhetoric. 2. English language-
  -Grammar--1950-   I. Blake, Carl David. II. Title.
  PE1408.W597 1991
  808'.042--dc20   91-24739
                                               CIP

91 92 93 94   9 8 7 6 5 4 3 2 1

Photo Credits

Pg. 1, U.S. Department of the Interior, National Parks Service, Edison National Historic Site; Pg. 18,
Bibliothèque Nationale, Paris; Pg. 33, British Museum; Pg. 117, Tom Stack & Associates; Pg. 129, The
Metropolitan Museum of Art, New York, Wolfe Fund, 1906. Catharine Lorillard Wolfe Collection.
(06.1234); Pg. 144, The Cousteau Society; Pg. 174, Nina Leen, LIFE Magazine © 1965 Time Warner Inc.;
Pg. 329(*left*), Bibliothéque Nationale, Paris; Pg. 329(*right*), Ralph Nelson, Jr., 1983 LUCASFILM LTD.; Pg.
345, The Louvre/Giraudon; Pg. 396, The Escher Foundation © 1992 Cordon Art-Baan Holland

Contents

UNIT FIVE

Chapter 24

Chapter 25

Chapter 26

Preface

Explorations: From Sentence to Paragraph is a developmental English text that will help students improve and refine their writing skills. This innovative text guides writers through the transformation from the early stages of the generation and organization of ideas to the arrangement of words into coherent, interesting sentences. The text provides practical fundamentals, giving writers a foundation upon which to base newly learned skills of sentence writing, paragraph development, and lastly, those "polishing" skills of revising, editing, and proofreading.

Students will explore not only the English language from sentence to paragraph but also the nature of the creative process itself: a process of discovery and invention. Students will learn more about the world around them through creative, imaginative, and thought-provoking writing assignments and through an interdisciplinary approach to the design of interesting exercises centered around the images of discovery, invention, and exploration.

Features

The text has been carefully constructed. Each new unit is introduced by graphics tied to the main concept. Special care has been taken to create a text that is both informative and interesting while merging innovative concepts of the writing process with a practical approach to English syntax.

In Unit One, the comprehensive coverage of prewriting methods—such as freewriting, brainstorming, listing, and mapping—enables students to develop creative ideas and organize them into a logical sequence.

Units Two and Three contain a clear and thorough presentation of the grammar rules that govern the syntax of the English language. Skills are emphasized through work in sectional exercises and then put to use in the writing assignment at the end of each chapter. Writing assignments take students through the complete recursive process of writing: from prewriting to writing to rewriting. In step 3 of each writing assignment—"Revising, Editing, and Proofreading"—students focus specifically on the skill learned in that particular chapter as they practice the writing process.

The topic of Unit Four is the process of writing a paragraph. The elements of paragraph structure are considered in some detail, and 12 strategies for paragraph organization are presented. The skills in paragraph development learned in this unit will serve as a foundation for essay composition in the second book, *Explorations: From Paragraph to Essay.*

Unit Five introduces revision and editing techniques not thoroughly explored or completely presented in any other developmental text. Topics include logical arrangement of ideas, sentence variety, and sentence combining. This unit gives students immediately useful tools for revising and editing.

The extensive use of student papers in examples and exercises makes the text more applicable and realistic. Seeing other students' use of the skills taught in this textbook gives readers confidence in their own ability to learn and apply these same skills.

With its unique approach to the coverage of writing and grammar, *Explorations: From Sentence to Paragraph* is a valuable tool for classroom teaching, laboratory writing, or independent study.

Acknowledgments

We are grateful for the guidance we received from Jane Kinney, acquisitions editor; Anne Smith, English editor; Patricia Rossi, developmental editor; Kimberly Neat, editorial assistant; and the HarperCollins staff. Barbara Cinquegrani, senior marketing manager, provided the starting point for this book. L. Sue Baugh, developmental editor, shaped the manuscript; Susan Freese, copyeditor, refined it; and Louise A. Gelinas, Managing Editor at PC&F, Inc., polished *Explorations: From Sentence to Paragraph.*

We would like to thank the following reviewers, whose comments were important to the writing of this book:

Charles Coleman, York College, CUNY; Martha French, Fairmont State College; Brad Hayden, Western Michigan State; Rosemary Hunkler, University of Wisconsin—Parkside; Martha Kuchar, Illinois Technical College; Kathleen Lazarus, Daytona Beach Community College; Linda Leeds, Bellevue Community College; Judith Longo, Ocean County College; Lucy Tribble MacDonald, Chemeketa Community College; Gretchen Niva, Western Kentucky University; Geraldine Rosen, Rockland Community College; Audrey Roth, Miami-Dade Community College

We would also like to acknowledge the following people for making *Explorations: From Sentence to Paragraph* a reality:

For their support—Robert J. Morgan; Sonni and Steve Roth; Henrietta W.

Delk; Bernice T. Williams; Lucy Payne; Mary Williams; Ray H. Doyle, Jr., communications consultant; and Joey Szabo.

For their encouragement—professors from Florida State University, Dr. Azzura Givins, Modern Language Department; Dr. Eugene J. Crook, Dr. John J. Fenstermaker, and Dr. Fred L. Standley, English Department. Dr. David V. Sheehan, the University of South Florida; and Dr. Janet M. Fisher, Jacksonville University.

For their friendship—Dr. Diana Ferriera, Dr. Bob Beaman, and Dr. Leo Diaz, Hillsborough Community College.

The existence of this book is due to the contributions, interest, and encouragement of our students.

This book is dedicated to my father E. V. Williams with love and admiration.

Virginia Williams
Carl David Blake

U|N|I|T O|N|E

Prewriting: Invention and Discovery

"Genius is one percent inspiration and
ninety-nine percent perspiration."

—Thomas A. Edison

*Thomas Alva Edison
(1847–1931)—one of
the greatest inventors of
all time, with over one
thousand patents issued
to his name—never
ceased exploring the
possibilities held by the
world around him.*

"Writing is easy; all you do is sit staring at a blank sheet of paper until the drops of blood form on your forehead."

—Gene Fowler

It is late at night. You are seated at your desk. You hold your head in your hand, while leaning on your elbow, and tap your pencil idly on the paper. Crumpled papers are strewn on the floor surrounding your chair. The clock ticks ominously as you struggle to write your college paper due in eight short hours. It was difficult enough to write in high school, and it seems even more so now that you are in college. Does writing have to be this painful?

A thought forces its way through the gloom. You write half a sentence before your internal critic snaps to attention. You pick up the paper and stare at your words. They are trite, incoherent, and stupid! You crumple the paper and toss it to the floor, where it adds to your efforts to "recarpet" your room in paper.

You are not alone in thinking that writing is difficult. William Styron, a contemporary American author, stated quite simply, "Writing is hell." And after all, who are you to disagree with a Pulitzer Prize–winning author? It took Mark Twain eight years to develop the plot for *Huckleberry Finn.* Even when he finished it, he thought it was trash. But you are not writing the Great American novel. You are just writing a paragraph for English class. Nevertheless, you have contracted that often experienced, always dread-ed disease: writer's block.

How can you overcome this barrier, a wall of words that you cannot penetrate, and start the creative process flowing? You tap your pencil and wait for divine inspiration: a muse[1] to sit on your shoulder and dictate profound, eloquent words into your ear. But it is not going to happen that way. Jack London, the American author who wrote *The Call of the Wild,* knew the secret: "You can't wait for

[1]The muses were the nine beautiful daughters of the Greek god Zeus, who inspired literature, the arts, and the sciences.

inspiration. You have to go after it with a club." In short, you need a plan to follow and some tools to do the job. The techniques taught in this unit are time-tested devices that will help you overcome writer's block and create original ideas to develop through the process of writing.

So many writers, from their earliest experiences on, assume that writing is a one-step process. But how can any *process* contain only one step? Writing is a skill that you can master by learning the three stages of the writing process. Once you know and understand them, you will discover that writer's block can be controlled. It will become easier and easier to create and organize your ideas, step 1, in preparation for writing your paragraph, which is step 2 of the writing process. You will find that the time for the inner critic to assert itself will not be when you are first beginning to write, but rather during the third stage of the process, when you edit and revise your writing to produce a cohesive, unified, and interesting final draft. At any time, you can move forward or backward to any of the three stages of the writing process to amend or clarify what you have written including adding or deleting ideas, and checking spelling, grammar, or punctuation. If you start writing and find that you do not have enough ideas, you can always go back to the first step in the process and begin again.

You will learn from this book that writing is a process of (1) invention, discovery, and organization; (2) writing; and (3) revising, editing, and proofreading. As you master this process, your writing will improve.

Unlocking Your Creativity

Let's return to our student suffering from writer's block. Since last we observed him, more time has elapsed, and more crumpled paper has been added to the floor. Our writer has reached a total impasse. He stares at the blank piece of paper and the pen beside it. He is in the full throes of writer's block.

Is all of this suffering necessary? Aren't there ways to generate interesting, original material for compositions without this agonizing? How is it possible that some writers have reached a point where writing is a process of discovery and exploration, an almost magical experience when ideas merge and the words flow onto the page?

Stephen King, the popular author of *The Shining* and *The Stand,* is the man to answer our questions. King is such a prolific writer that when his editors told him that his books were flooding the market, he started writing under the pseudonym Richard Bachman. King has worked on four novels at the same time, each waiting for him on a different computer. Yet even King stated in a recent interview that he, too, sometimes falls prey to writer's block. If Stephen King is an occasional victim, it is certainly no wonder that the rest of us suffer from the "disease."

In her paragraph "My Back Is against the Wall," student Judith Gable describes some of her encounters with writer's block:

> I am taking an English composition class. My problem is I can never think of anything to write about. As soon as I pick up a pen and paper, my mind becomes a total blank. They say this malady is called "writer's block." I call it "hell!" I have tried everything to overcome this curse. One time, I made a batch of Cajun popcorn and paced the

```
floor. On more than one occasion, I have eaten my

favorite chewy, nutty, chocolate candy. Another

time, I did the laundry. A few times, I have gone

antiquing. Then I tried rearranging the furniture

in the living room. I have even tried sitting in

different parts of the room. I thought watching my

favorite soap opera would give me some ideas. In

desperation, I have turned to my family, with no

luck. Our dog even runs now when she sees me coming

with pen in hand. Panic has set in. How do I over-

come writer's block? I'm going to take a deep

breath, find a nice comfy chair, and settle in with

a pound of my favorite chocolate nuts and chews. The

solution will come to me sometime. It always does.
```

Of course, a part of the creative process is waiting: for the critical insight, the special idea, the perfect topic. But if you have been waiting for hours, even days (and for some writers, even months), it is time to apply some of the remedies detailed in this chapter and get to work. The remedies we will discuss are freewriting, focused freewriting, brainstorming, listing, asking questions, mapping, and keeping a journal.

Freewriting

The first and best technique to start the flow of words is called **freewriting.** This technique was first developed by Peter Elbow, the author of *Writing without Teachers* and *Writing with Power: Techniques for Mastering the Writing Process.* With freewriting, you do not have any particular subject in mind. You write rapidly, without stopping, until the designated time period has elapsed. You turn off that internal critic inside your head and write down whatever comes into your mind. You do not worry about grammar, punctuation, or spelling, nor do you stop to proofread or edit. If you get stuck, you simply write the same word or sentence over and over again until another idea comes into your mind.

Using this method guarantees that you will get words down on paper because you have shut down your internal critic, the voice inside you that is useful in revision because it criticizes every word but not helpful during the creative process. You do not stop to analyze anything that you have written until the writing exercise is over. At that time, your internal critic will come to life to see if any of your ideas could be developed into a composition.

In her ten-minute freewriting exercise, Dawn Hernandez describes a typical morning at her home. Dawn has underlined her favorite passage of the exercise:

> My morning started at 6:00 A.M. It was time to wake two of my children so they could get ready for school. First I woke Jorgie up. He is my oldest, he is eight years old. He proceeded to climb out of bed. While he was wiping the sleep out of his eyes, I went into my daughter's room. Her name is Jennifer, we call her Jenny. She is six years old. I then went to the kitchen to fix them each a bowl of Captain Crunch cereal with a glass of orange juice, and a vitamin. I then took my youngest, Jamie, who is two years old, to my room. I do this so the older kids won't wake him up.
>
> After the kids eat breakfast, we begin arguing about what they want to wear to school. <u>My son wants to wear his Batman shirt with a pair of jams (shorts). My daughter wants to wear her favorite Sunday school dress. Trying to explain to the kids why I won't let them wear these items gets very difficult. I eventually get frustrated and tell them they can't wear those clothes because I'm the mommy.</u> Well they finally finish getting ready and I shove them out the door to catch the bus. Now it's my turn to get ready.

You may have noticed some errors in Dawn's paragraph (namely, comma splices, missing punctuation). Remember that this exercise was written during a freewriting session, which means that it has not been edited or revised. Dawn simply wrote without worrying about mechanics or style.

Dawn's reaction to the freewriting exercise:
"I enjoyed writing. I felt very lighthearted. I enjoyed thinking about my kids and our typical routine."

Dawn's reaction to the ideas generated by freewriting:
"I could probably write more on the interaction among me and my children."

EXERCISE

Write without stopping for ten minutes about any topic or idea that comes to mind. Do not stop to make any judgments about the quality of what you have written. Do not make any corrections. Do not put your pen down until the ten minutes have elapsed. Just write everything and anything that occurs to you.

_____

_____

_____

_____

_____

_____

_____

_____

_____

_____

_____

_____

_____

_____

_____

_____

_____

_____

_____

_____

_____

_____

What is your reaction to the experience of freewriting?

_____

_____

_____

_____

Now read what you wrote during the freewriting exercise. Go back and underline anything *in the exercise that you like.*

  Write down any ideas generated in freewriting that you could develop later into a composition.

_____

_____

_____

_____

Focused Freewriting

A variation of freewriting is **focused freewriting.** *Focused* means that you choose one subject on which to center your attention as you freewrite. You do not write about any other topic except the one you have chosen.

You can try focused freewriting for a shorter period of time than you did the unfocused exercise. Three-to-five minutes should be sufficient. You may want to try one focused freewriting of three minutes or three separate runs of three minutes each on the same topic with a short pause between each session.

This focused method of freewriting will help you to see new aspects of a topic about which you might not be clear. It will also help you to narrow down a large topic to one aspect that you can sufficiently cover.

Here is Tony King's three-minute focused freewriting exercise on the topic *exploration:*

```
    Exploration is something I would love to be

able to do, but are there any more places to

explore? Just think how fascinating it would be to

go where no one has ever gone before or accomplish

something no one has ever accomplished. Lewis and

Clark must have had a blast but many times were

scared. They survived though and today are famous.

I guess there are many other areas to explore:

science, literature, ourselves, and associating

with others.
```

EXERCISE

Freewrite for three minutes on the topic exploration.

_____

_____

_____

_____

_____

_____

_____

_____

_____

Reread what you wrote during focused freewriting. Underline anything *in the exercise that you like.*

Write down any ideas generated in your focused freewriting that could be developed later in a composition.

_____

_____

_____

_____

_____

Brainstorming

Brainstorming is a prewriting activity that would appear, at first, to be different from freewriting. Namely, you work in a group, not by yourself, and you talk instead of write. But beyond these differences, brainstorming and freewriting are very similar in that they are both means of generating ideas about which to write. In brainstorming, the group discussion becomes a springboard for ideas, as one person's idea prompts another person's idea and so on. Once things get going, brainstorming is usually lively and highly creative. You should not be afraid to speak out. Everyone has something to contribute.

This give-and-take approach to offering new solutions to old problems, creating new concepts, and seeing situations differently is often used in the business world. Some corporations hire innovative employees to form a "think tank," a group that does intensive research or problem solving. Creative and unusual ideas can emerge from brainstorming sessions.

Brainstorming can also work well in the classroom. The entire class can work together, with one student or the instructor serving as the moderator, or the class can break into small groups, brainstorm the same topic, and then reassemble to discuss the ideas that have been generated in the individual groups. Whether you work in a small group or with the entire class, as the brainstorming session takes place, tape record the discussion or jot down notes.

To brainstorm, work in one large group or several small groups. Generate as much material as possible. The focus is on *quantity.* Do not allow anyone's internal critic to censor a relevant idea that may seem too insignificant or stupid to mention. Bounce ideas off each other. Do not make fun of anyone's comments. Quantity is more important than quality. After the brainstorming session has been completed, use the material gathered to develop ideas for your composition. This technique is especially useful when the entire class has been given the same assignment.

EXERCISE

Brainstorm, as a class or in small groups, one of the following topics:

In what ways can you help save the environment?
At what age should drinking alcoholic beverages be legal? Why?

What are the benefits of having a college education?
What fictional character do you admire? Why?
Should we continue to explore outer space? Why?
Should popular songs be censored? Why?
What is the last great movie that you saw? Why was it great?

Write down any ideas that were generated during the brainstorming session that could be later developed in a composition.

_____

_____

_____

_____

_____

Listing

You have made lists before: bills to pay, items to study for a test, groceries to buy at the store, and presents to buy friends and relatives at Christmas. These are a few examples of the kinds of lists that most people make as a matter of habit. We use lists to jog our memories and keep us organized. **Listing** can also be a valuable prewriting technique. It is a great method to help you discover new and interesting ideas to write about and investigate or to show how much you already know about a topic. After making a list about a particular subject, you will be able to review the items and draw together a complete picture of your subject. What's more, you will discover how the items on the list can be sorted into distinct categories and be used to organize a composition.[1]

Sheron LeGrant is interested in writing about one of her favorite subjects, Leonardo da Vinci, the Renaissance artist best known for his painting *Mona Lisa.* Here is the list Sheron generated based on her research of da Vinci's life:

Listing: Leonardo da Vinci
> *Mona Lisa*
> *The Last Supper*
> Theory of painting
> Sculptor
> Scientist
> Dissections
> Anatomy

---

[1]Chapter 2, "Organizing Your Ideas," will cover this process in detail.

Engineer
Parachute
Flying machine
Divine proportions
Italian
Died in France
Grave lost when church was torn down
Artist
Teacher
Architect
Hired by royalty
Believed sight was most important sense
Theory of architecture
Book on mechanics
Book on anatomy
Left-handed
Research and drawings on water and air currents
Born in 1452
Died in 1519
Illegitimate yet raised in father's home as legitimate
Never married
Called "the ideal Renaissance man"
Pen-and-ink sketches
Scientific illustrations
Born in Florence
Mechanical drawings
Used mirror writing

In order to generate the list, Sheron focused on the general subject *Leonardo da Vinci*. She included everything she could relate to her subject no matter how insignificant or unimportant it seemed. She did not include anything in the list that did not relate to da Vinci.

As Sheron listed, she wrote as fast as possible, jotting down single words or phrases, whatever entered her mind about Leonardo da Vinci. She made notes in random order as thoughts occurred to her; she was not judgmental about what she included. At this point in the prewriting stage, no detail is too insignificant to include.

When Sheron finished listing, she had a lot of details about Leonardo da Vinci. You will see her list again in Chapter 2 when she goes through the process of adding new items, dropping unimportant ideas, and clustering and rearranging items into related groups. This organization of ideas is still a part of prewriting and will ensure that she is logically prepared for the second part of the writing process, writing the paragraph.

Often with this method of prewriting, you will be amazed at how many ideas about a subject you can generate. While some of the ideas will be worthless later on, as you glance down your list you may discover some that will be pure gold among the rest of the rubble.

Before you practice a listing exercise, note that listing is similar to brainstorming because you generate as much material as possible about your subject without being judgmental. Of course, you can readily see the obvious differences between brainstorming and listing: Brainstorming takes place in a group and is spoken while listing is a solitary activity and is written.

EXERCISE

Choose a topic from the list below, and use it for the title of your list. Write about the topic as rapidly as possible, writing fragments, not sentences. Include any detail about your subject no matter how insignificant. Jot down your ideas in any order; you will organize them later.

Sample Topics: *A favorite movie and why you liked it*
                The ideal vacation
                Your best career choices
                Favorite recording artists
                Places you would like to visit
                Important inventions
                Important discoveries

Your Title: _____

Your List: _____

_____

_____

_____

_____

_____

_____

_____

_____

_____

_____

_____

Asking Questions

Journalists ask six questions to develop newspaper articles. **Who? What? Where? When? Why?** and **How?** You can use these questions to generate content for your compositions. Answering them will provide you with a review of all the essentials you need to cover the subject.

If you have trouble with any one of these questions, recheck your material to find additional information. Whether you are writing about your own experiences or some particular historical event, this method is a sure way to verify that all the important details and facts are included.

For instance, a writer who wants to generate ideas about the invention of the lightbulb could answer the questions as follows:

Who?　　Thomas Alva Edison
What?　　Invented the incandescent lightbulb
Where?　His laboratory in Menlo Park, New Jersey
When?　October 1, 1879
Why?　　To create a safe, inexpensive electric light to replace gaslights
How?　　Searched for 14 months to find a suitable filament that would stay lit for more than a few seconds. Carbon filament was finally chosen.

EXERCISE

Answer the six questions for one of the following topics:

An important event in your life
A discovery you have made about yourself (Example: I discovered when I went to work that I have a great memory.)
A recent event in world history

Use the space below to answer the six questions:

Who?　　_____

What?　　_____

Where?　_____

When?　_____

Why?　　_____

How?　　_____

Mapping

Mapping is the most creative of the prewriting techniques. It involves literally drawing a plan, or map, of your ideas, showing the relationships among them. It is similar to the old method of outlining but less inhibiting; the writer is free to think creatively and associate ideas, representing them in a sketch. Think of it as a map to a territory that you want to explore in your composition.

Students have found mapping to be the best method for generating ideas for paragraphs and later for entire essays that are written under test conditions or time restraints. You will be amazed to find that once you master this technique, you will generate an entire map for a composition within five to ten minutes. Since mapping is more visual than the other prewriting techniques, it is a great method of generating ideas for students who suffer from writer's block.

To begin mapping, write your *subject* in the middle of a sheet of paper, and draw a circle around it. Now draw a line out from the encircled subject, and draw another circle at the end of that line. Inside that circle, write the name of a *major* subdivision of your subject. From that circle, branch out to further subdivisions of that major subdivision. Connect specific ideas and details related to the subdivisions with circles and lines.

When you have mapped out as much as you can about that major subdivision, go back to the encircled subject at the center. Now start the same process again with another major subdivision. Continue with this mapping process until you run out of ideas. Remember as you work to add anything that occurs to you that is appropriate to any section of the map. You do not have to work on just one subdivision at a time.

Example:

The student has chosen the *horse* as her subject. She begins by writing *Horse* in the center of the page and drawing a circle around it.

Next, she develops her map by adding the first major subdivision: *Investment value.* That major subdivision is further divided, showing types of horses that have *Investment value: Trotters, Race horses,* and *Jumpers.*

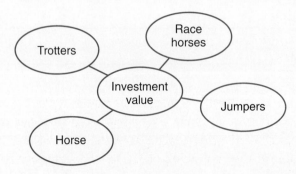

She continues to add major subdivisions until the mapping process is complete. The technique has generated five major subdivisions branching out from the subject: *horse.* Here is the completed map:

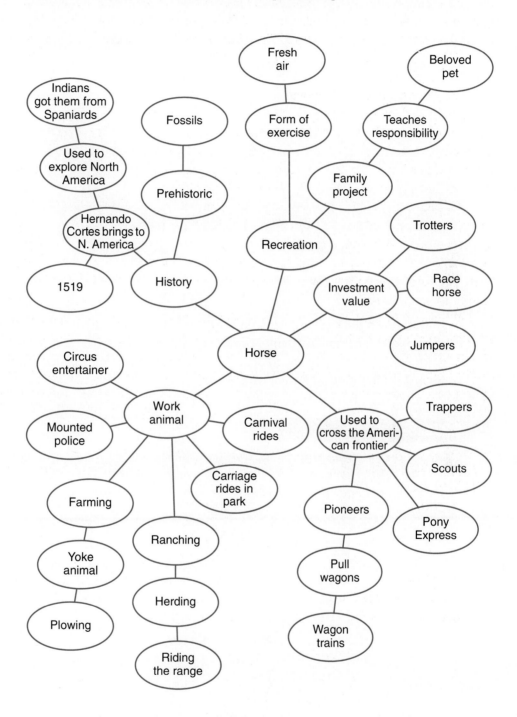

After looking at her map, the student decides that she wants to cover only three of the five major subdivisions: *History, Used to cross the American frontier,* and *Work animal.* She drops the subdivisions *Recreation* and *Investment value* as they are unimportant to this composition. The student has now

Cortes used the horse in his exploration of North America and Mexico.

narrowed down the topic to focus on how the horse was instrumental in the history, exploration, and settlement of North America.

Mapping is a simple way to deal with what can sometimes be a cumbersome task: generating and organizing ideas.

EXERCISE

Complete the following map below, working with the subject Types of movies. *One of the subdivisions has been filled in for you. Add others, along with examples of each. Add more lines or circles to the map if you need to do so.*

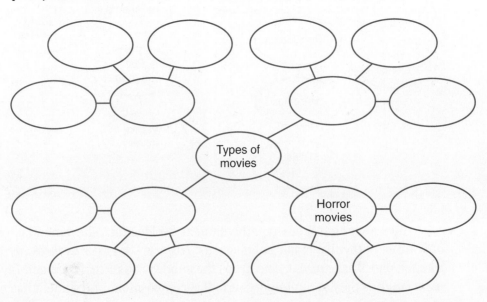

EXERCISE

Complete the following map below, working with the subject Team sports. *One of the subdivisions has been filled in for you. Add others, along with examples of each. Add more lines or circles to the map if you need to do so.*

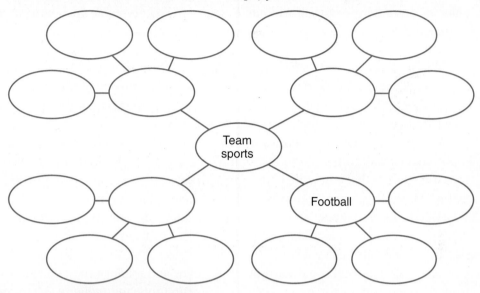

EXERCISE

The subject has not been provided in the following map. Choose one of the topics listed below, or choose your own. Complete the map with major subdivisions and examples of each. Add more lines or circles to the map if you need to do so.

Topics: *Types of transportation*
          Types of books
          Electronic inventions
          Uses of the automobile

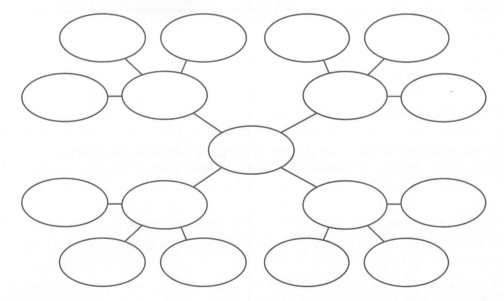

Keeping a Journal

Writing is a *skill*. As such, you need to practice it in order to improve. A good method for practicing the skill of writing is keeping a journal. Writing on a regular basis for no one but yourself will make you more comfortable with writing. In a journal, it does not matter what you say or how you say it; there is no pressure to perform. Keeping a journal can sometimes help students overcome writer's block.

A journal is also an excellent way to keep a record of the events and details of your life. At some future date, that material may provide you with ideas for a composition. It does not matter whether you use the material again; keeping a journal will help you sharpen your skills of observation.

You may use anything you want for the actual journal: an elegant leather-bound diary or a spiral-bound notebook with a picture of Batman on the cover. It does not matter what you write in as long as you write, write, write! Some students prefer to keep their journal entries on their personal computers.

What will you write about in your journal? The answer is, quite simply, anything you want. Look at the suggested exercises at the end of this section, but essentially, the journal is yours.

Keeping a journal is a great way to discover and explore the external world around you as well as the inner world of your thoughts and feelings. Many years ago, when I was a student at the University of Paris in France, I made a daily entry of everything that happened each day: where I went, who I saw, what I ate, what I wore, what I studied, and so on. Today, I can pick up my journal, read an entry, and find the past revived before my eyes. A favorite page is the description of visiting King Louis XIV's palace at Versailles with a close friend. Many entries hold special memories for me. I always tell students who are planning to take a trip to keep a journal of their experiences. Years later, what they have written will be priceless to them.

But you do not need to travel far from home to keep a journal. In 1845, Henry David Thoreau moved two miles away from Concord, Massachusetts, to live beside Walden Pond in a one-room hut. For the two years and two months that he lived there, he kept a journal of his activities and thoughts. After leaving Walden Pond, Thoreau spent five years reworking the material from his journal. In 1854, his book *Walden* was published.

What is ironic about Thoreau's view of his own writing style is particularly appropriate to this chapter on prewriting. Thoreau labored at writing and never thought he was a great writer. He died of tuberculosis at the early age of 44 and was never shown otherwise. It was not until the 1930s that critics realized *Walden* was an American masterpiece. Thoreau, the man, lives and breathes again in the pages of his book, his thoughts and feelings captured forever. Yet the work was begun in journal form by a man who did not think he could write well.

Perhaps there is a lesson here: Never underestimate your power to create through the written word. You may have locked within you a talent far greater than you realize.

EXERCISE

Write in your journal each day. Use the suggested topics below as a starting point.

1. Describe interesting people you meet.
2. Discuss important daily events.
3. Go to a place you enjoy (mall, restaurant, garden, sports field), and record all the sights and sounds you see and hear in one hour's time.
4. Discuss something you have discovered about yourself.
5. Retell a humorous or amusing event you have observed.

2 *Organizing Your Ideas*

Now that you have a list of what appear to be brilliant ideas, what will you do with them? Are you ready to write the first draft? No.

After completing the prewriting exercise, most writers rush into writing the first draft. They make a mistake, however, because at this point their ideas are in no particular order and have no structure. Many writers do not even have enough topics or information to begin writing.

The second phase of the prewriting process consists of the following steps:

1. Expanding prewriting ideas
2. Selecting or dropping ideas
3. Clustering similar ideas
4. Narrowing selected topics
5. Rearranging topics in logical order

Expanding Prewriting Ideas

Ideas gleaned from the prewriting techniques will need to be expanded if the topic requires additional information or clarification. Use the same techniques you used to create your original groups of ideas to expand any topic that seems incomplete.

Example:

The subtopic *artist* was generated from the main topic *Leonardo da Vinci* by Sheron LeGrant using the listing prewriting technique as described in Chapter 1. Sheron decided that she did not have enough information relating to da Vinci's art career. She again used the listing technique to expand this subtopic, adding the following items:

Subtopic: Artist

        17 paintings in existence today

Madonna Benois (1474–75)
Portrait of a Young Lady (1475–78)
Adoration of the Magi (1481, unfinished)
St. Jerome (1480)
Virgin of the Rocks (1483–85)

EXERCISE

Take one of the prewriting ideas that you developed in Chapter 1 and generate at least five additional ideas for that topic.

Subtopic: _____

1. _____

2. _____

3. _____

4. _____

5. _____

Selecting or Dropping Ideas

You now have your first group of ideas and have expanded some of those thoughts even further. Next, select only the best ideas for your writing assignment. Weed out those thoughts that do not belong, particularly those that seem irrelevant or vague.

Example:

Sheron dropped the following ideas from her list on the subject *Leonardo da Vinci.* She did not consider them important to her main subject.

Mona Lisa
The Last Supper
Theory of painting
~~Sculptor~~ —————————————— DROP (She is interested only in his paintings.)

Scientist
Dissections
Knowledge of anatomy
Engineer
Parachute
Flying machine

Divine proportions

~~Italian~~ —————————————— DROP (This fact is too well
known to be interesting.)

Died in France
Grave lost when church was torn down
Artist
Teacher
Architect

~~Hired by royalty~~ —————————— DROP (She is not interested in
his work for members of
the royalty.)

~~Believed sight was most important sense~~ DROP (She is not going to
discuss his theories
about sight.)

Theory of architecture
Book on mechanics
Book on anatomy

~~Left handed~~ —————————————— DROP (She doesn't consider
this fact important.)

Research and drawings on water and air
    currents
Born in 1452
Died in 1519

~~Illegitimate yet raised in father's home as~~
~~legitimate~~ DROP (She is not discussing
the details of his personal

~~Never married~~ —————————— DROP life.)
Called the ideal Renaissance man
Pen-and-ink sketches
Scientific illustrations
Mechanical drawings

~~Used mirror writing~~ ———————— DROP (She did not consider
this fact to be essential to
the main topic.)

EXERCISE

Your main subject is Water sports. *Drop ideas from the following list of topics, explaining briefly why you did so.*

Boating
Swimming
Getting a great tan
Diving
Sunglasses

Surfing
Having great fun
Giant wave
Playing volleyball
Fishing
Fishing tackle
Driving to the beach
Wind surfing
Water polo
Speedboat racing

Topic	*Reason dropped*
_____	_____
_____	_____
_____	_____
_____	_____
_____	_____
_____	_____

Clustering Similar Ideas

You must organize your thoughts before you can write. Consider your list of ideas. It may be great. But is the information in a hodgepodge order? At this point, group those ideas that relate to the same topic.

In the example below, Sheron grouped her ideas under the subtopics *Artist, Engineer, Personal facts,* and *Scientist,* which cover different aspects of da Vinci's life.

Example:
Subtopic: Artist
17 paintings in existence today
Theory of painting
Divine proportions
Pen-and-ink sketches
Teacher
Mona Lisa
The Last Supper
Madonna Benois

> *Adoration of the Magi*
> *St. Jerome*
> *Virgin of the Rocks*

Subtopic: Engineer
Parachute
Flying machine
Theory of architecture
Book on mechanics
Mechanical drawings

Subtopic: Personal facts
Died in France
Grave lost when church was torn down
Born in Florence
Born in 1452
Died in 1519

Subtopic: Scientist
Anatomy
Dissection
Book on anatomy
Scientific illustration
Research on water and air currents

EXERCISE

Your topic is Pollution. *The following list contains ideas relating to three different subtopics:* Water pollution, Air pollution, *and* Ground pollution.

Car exhaust emissions
Sewage
Recycling
Factory smokestacks
Too much garbage
Ozone
Factory controls
Chemical spills
Oil spills
Improper hazardous waste disposal
Carbon monoxide
Tin
Paper
Fluorocarbons
Glass
Waste oil
Strong perfumes

Drought
Forest fires
Inefficient solid waste disposal

Group, or cluster, similar ideas under each of the appropriate subtopics.

Water pollution	Air pollution	Ground pollution
_____	_____	_____
_____	_____	_____
_____	_____	_____
_____	_____	_____
_____	_____	_____
_____	_____	_____
_____	_____	_____
_____	_____	_____
_____	_____	_____

Narrowing Selected Topics

Once you have clusters of related ideas, you need to focus on those ideas about which you would like to write. You will limit each cluster of ideas to only those that relate directly to your focused subtopics.

Example:

Sheron has chosen four subtopics on which to focus: *Artist, Engineer, Personal facts,* and *Scientist.* Since the assignment is to write one paragraph, Sheron has too much material; thus, one or more ideas under each subtopic must be dropped.

Subtopic: Artist

For this subtopic, Sheron decided to write on the progression of da Vinci's artistic ability from his pen-and-ink drawings to the complex paintings for which he is most famous. She dropped the paintings that are not as well known to the public. She also decided that the entry *Teacher* did not relate clearly to the subtopic *Artist*.

Theory of painting
Divine proportions
Pen-and-ink sketches
~~Teacher~~ ———————————— DROP
Mona Lisa
The Last Supper
~~*Madonna Benois*~~ ———————————— DROP
~~*Portrait of a Young Lady*~~ ———————————— DROP
~~*The Adoration of the Magi*~~ ———————————— DROP
~~*St. Jerome*~~ ———————————— DROP
Virgin of the Rocks

Subtopic: Engineer

Under the subtopic *Engineer,* Sheron eliminated the entry *Theory of architecture* since all of the other entries in this category are concrete proof of da Vinci's ability as an engineer.

Parachute
Flying machine
~~Theory of architecture~~ ———————————— DROP
Book on mechanics
Mechanical drawings

Subtopic: Personal facts

All of the following are pertinent to the *Personal facts* subtopic.

Died in France
Grave lost when church was torn down
Born in Florence
Born in 1452
Died in 1519

Subtopic: Scientist

Under this subtopic, Sheron decided that da Vinci's investigations and reports on the human body were the most important facts and thus eliminated the last two entries.

Studied anatomy
Dissection
Book on anatomy
~~Scientific illustrations~~ ———————————— DROP
~~Research on water and air currents~~ ——— DROP

In a final analysis, Sheron finally decided to limit her paragraph to three topics—*Artist, Engineer,* and *Scientist*—thus eliminating the subtopic *Personal facts.*

EXERCISE

Your topic is Air pollution. *The following list includes ideas relating to this topic. Limit the topic by crossing out (dropping) ideas that are not important or that do not clearly relate to the other ideas or to your focused topic.*

Subtopic: Air pollution
          Car exhaust emissions
          Factory smokestacks
          Lack of government controls
          Acid rain
          Carbon monoxide
          Ozone
          Forest fires
          Fluorocarbons
          Drought
          Strong perfume

Which ideas did you drop? Why did you eliminate them?

_____

_____

_____

_____

Rearranging Topics in Logical Order

Let's return to the major clusters on da Vinci. Under each of the subtopics, the individual ideas are not arranged in order of importance. Sheron must now determine the order of her ideas from least to most important.

Example:

Artist:

The numbers to the side of each entry indicate the order in which the ideas will be arranged. Sheron decided that the logical sequence should be to discuss da Vinci's work, beginning with simple pen-and-ink sketches and ending with his complex paintings. The paintings are arranged in order of least famous to most famous.

Theory of painting	3
Pen-and-ink sketches	1
Divine proportions	2
Mona Lisa	5
The Last Supper	6
Virgin of the Rocks	4

Scientist:

Sheron found in this subtopic that her information was already arranged in a logical sequence. That is, da Vinci studied anatomy by dissecting bodies and then wrote a book on his findings.

Studied anatomy
Dissected bodies
Wrote book on anatomy

Engineer:

Again, the numbers to the side of each entry indicate the order in which the material will be arranged. Sheron's analysis is based on the fact that da Vinci created mechanical drawings in order to illustrate his designs for the parachute, a flying machine, and other mechanical devices. Later in life, he wrote a book on mechanics.

Parachute	2
Flying machine	3
Book on mechanics	4
Mechanical drawing	1

The three major subtopics (*Artist, Scientist,* and *Engineer*) can now be listed in order from least to most important. Sheron decided to arrange these subtopics as follows:

Engineer
Scientist
Artist

Sheron decided that the most important aspect of da Vinci's diverse talent was his ability as an artist so she saved this topic for last. Of the two remaining topics, Sheron felt that da Vinci's studies of the human body were more important than his contributions to engineering; thus, she put *Engineer* first (as the least important subtopic) and *Scientist* second.

Sheron is now ready to begin the first draft of her composition. Not only has she generated ideas about which to write, but she has also arranged her topics in an organized, logical manner.

A. Engineer
1. Mechanical drawing
2. Parachute
3. Flying machine
4. Book on mechanics

B. Scientist
1. Studied anatomy
2. Dissected bodies
3. Wrote book on anatomy

C. Artist
1. Pen-and-ink sketches
2. Divine proportions
3. Theory of painting
4. *Virgin of the Rocks*
5. *Mona Lisa*
6. *The Last Supper*

UNIT TWO

Writing: Exploring the Basic Parts of English

The discovery of the Rosetta Stone in 1799 provided the key to a once incomprehensible language and the fascinating culture of ancient Egypt.

Language constitutes a formal system of communication whereby complex messages can be built out of simple components. The Rosetta Stone, the Dead Sea Scrolls, and other ancient discoveries provide a window into the mysterious past.

Many adventurous individuals tried to break the code of the unique Egyptian hieroglyphs, but until the discovery of the Rosetta Stone, this ancient language remained a mystery. The Egyptian language was last written in hieroglyphs in August A.D. 394. Less than 60 years later, the demotic script, the most cursive of the Egyptian scripts, also fell into disuse. For 1,370 years, the ancient Egyptian language was lost. Then in 1799, Napoleon's soldiers discovered the Rosetta Stone in the city of Rashid, known to the Europeans as Rosetta.

The black basalt stone is composed of three sections each containing a different language. A team of specialists, led by the Lieutenant of Engineers, Pierre Bouchard, quickly realized that one of the inscriptions was written in Greek and could also possibly be the translation for the other two sections. The stone was transported to Cairo where it generated intense interest from the body of learned men Napoleon had taken with him to Egypt. The script was copied by inking the surface with printer's ink and then using rollers to transfer the image to paper. These relief copies were sent to scholars in many parts of Europe.

The French scholar Jean François Champollion drew up a classified list of hieroglyphs, identified the names of many Egyptian kings, and formulated a system of grammar and general decipherment; thus, he is known as the Father of the Decipherment of Hieroglyphs. Champollion used the investigations of other scholars and his own ingenuity and intuition to lay the vocabulary and grammatical foundations on which present knowledge of ancient Egyptian language is based. Understanding the structure of the Egyptian language helped Champollion and other language specialists decipher the meaning of the many hieroglyphic inscriptions that had been discovered.

With written language, it is impossible to interpret what is being said when you do not understand how the parts of the language function. It took Champollion years to decipher the riddle of the ancient Egyptian grammar.

Formal written English will be "decoded" by your audience as they read it. To ensure that your "code" will be understood, you must follow the correct grammatical structure. Incorrect structure will obscure your thoughts and confuse your reader. Improving your writing skills through knowledge of how English grammar works will become increasingly important.

You will use the skills learned in this book not only as part of your school classes but also in your personal and business life. Everyone, at some point, will write a letter, either to that long-lost friend, a favorite relative, or the bungling repairman who "fixed" your still broken refrigerator. In your career, you may have to write reports, business letters, proposals, synopses, résumés, and pamphlets. Your writing skills will be an important consideration when you interview for jobs, as well.

In preparation for writing, Units Two and Three provide you with the information about grammatical structure necessary to write clear, correct sentences. In Unit Four, you will learn about arranging sentences into paragraphs and about the different types of paragraphs. Unit Five will present the skills of revising, editing, and proofreading.

The three-part writing process taught in this book allows a writer to move back and forth according to his or her needs. Do you need more ideas or fresh thoughts? Go back to the prewriting techniques of Unit One. Are you having trouble with sentence structure? Check Unit Three, "Writing: Exploring Sentences." Revising, editing, and proofreading are explained in Unit Five. While you are proofing or revising, you can return to Unit One to expand an idea or to Unit Three to check a grammar problem.

You will learn to decipher the English language by reviewing the parts of speech, progressing to writing a sentence, and ending with writing a paragraph. You will explore the English language and make new discoveries about how to use it correctly and vividly.

Neither Egyptian hieroglyphics nor English letters and words can be decoded without knowledge of the basic grammar rules of each language.

3 | *Overview of Parts of Speech*

In modern English, words can be divided into eight categories called **parts of speech.** Our review of the parts of speech will be particularly helpful for quick reference as most of these terms will appear throughout the book. Learning the names and definitions of grammatical terms will not automatically make you a better writer, but by understanding sentence structure, you will improve your writing skills.

The eight parts of speech are nouns, pronouns, adjectives, verbs, adverbs, prepositions, conjunctions, and interjections. Each will be discussed in turn.

Nouns

A **noun** is the name of a person, place, thing, or idea. There are four types of nouns: proper, common, concrete, and abstract.

A **proper noun** names a particular thing or person and is always capitalized.

Examples:

the Atlantic Ocean, Jacques-Yves Cousteau, Paris

EXERCISE

In each of the following sentences, underline the proper noun(s).

1. Alexander Graham Bell and Thomas Alva Edison were born in the same year, 1847.

2. The Niger River is the third longest river in Africa.

3. The Pueblo Indians have permanent villages in Arizona and New Mexico.

A **common noun** is not capitalized because it does not refer to a specific thing or person. Common nouns name kinds or groups of things.

Examples:

ocean, explorer, city

EXERCISE

In each of the following sentences, underline the common noun(s).

1. Prehistoric people lived in caves for protection from a hostile world.

2. The alligator has been known to attain a length of 20 feet and can live up to 75 years.

3. An alphabet is a set of characters intended to represent the sounds of spoken language.

A **concrete noun** labels something that can be perceived by one or more of the five senses.

Examples:

a map, an archaeologist, a scream

An **abstract noun** refers to what cannot be perceived through the senses, such as ideas, qualities, and concepts.

Examples:

love, curiosity, hatred, courage, truth

EXERCISE

In each of the following sentences, underline the concrete noun(s) and circle the abstract noun(s).

1. World famous explorers possess curiosity, determination, and courage.

2. Soccer, the most popular sport in the world, causes much rivalry and hatred among spectators.

3. The Colosseum was a huge, oval stadium in Rome that once held 45,000 people.

Pronouns

A **pronoun** takes the place of a noun; it is substituted so that we do not have to keep repeating the same noun. It must always be clear, however, what noun the pronoun stands for. Just as a noun can serve as the subject or object of a sentence, so can the pronoun.[1]

Examples:

I looked at Bill.

Baseball is a game *that* looks easy to play but is quite difficult.

Who is at my door?

EXERCISE

Circle the pronoun(s) in each of the following sentences.

1. Who was Alexander the Great, and why is he so famous?

2. Aristotle was his teacher.

3. Alexander took a group of scholars along with him to study the cultures of Asia.

Adjectives

An **adjective** modifies (describes or limits) a noun or pronoun.[2]

Examples:

a *strong* storm

the *largest* pyramid

a *silver* sword

Usually, an adjective appears in front of the noun it modifies or after a linking verb.

Examples:

Cleopatra wore a *beautiful gown.*

Her gown *was beautiful.*

[1]Chapter 4, "Pronouns," examines the types of pronouns.
[2]See Chapter 5, "Adjectives and Adverbs."

In each of the following sentences, underline the adjective(s).

1. Sir Lancelot was the most famous of King Arthur's knights.

2. The giant statues of Easter Island are a fascinating mystery.

3. While panda bears look adorable, they can be very aggressive.

Verbs

Verbs express an action, a state of being, or the condition of the subject as well as the time of action (past, present, or future). Verbs can be divided into three general classes: action, linking, and helping.[3]

Action verbs express the action that the subject performs.

Example:

Jim *throws* the ball to Ted.

In each of the following sentences, underline the action verb(s).

1. Richard the Lion-Heart led his forces on a crusade to Jerusalem.

2. Prince John ruled as a tyrant during Richard's absence.

3. The barons forced Richard's brother, King John of England, to sign the

   Magna Carta in A.D. 1215.

Linking verbs, such as *is* and *feels,* express no action. Rather, they join the subject with an adjective or a noun that follows to describe or identify the subject.

Examples:

Sylvester Stallone *is* popular.

Sylvester Stallone *looks* tough.

In each of the following sentences, underline the linking verb(s).

1. Richard the Lion-Heart was the son of Henry II and Eleanor of Aquitaine.

[3]Chapters 6–12 discuss verbs in detail.

2. *The Lion in Winter* is a movie about the lives of Henry II and Eleanor of Aquitaine.

3. Peter O'Toole and Katharine Hepburn are the stars of the movie *The Lion in Winter.*

Helping verbs, such as *can* and *has,* show past, present, or future time. They are used exclusively with another verb that follows, called the ***main verb.*** Helping verbs are also called **auxiliaries.**

Examples:

I *have* submitted my manuscript on time.

Ray *has* learned to dance.

We *have* gone to the movies.

Some of us *have been* watching too much television.

EXERCISE

In each of the following sentences, underline the helping verb(s) and the main verb(s).

1. The nobles had issued the Magna Carta in 1215; then, 20 copies were sent to be read in England's major cities.

2. A reader can find eight elements of the Magna Carta in the United States Constitution, including trial by jury, due process of law, protection of private property, and the protection of the rights of all citizens.

3. The British government has preserved the Magna Carta for over 800 years.

Adverbs

An **adverb** modifies a verb, an adjective, or another adverb. Adverbs generally answer questions, such as where, when, how, or to what extent.[4]

Examples:

Arsenio Hall smiled *broadly.*
(modifies the verb *smiled*)

[4]See Chapter 5, "Adjectives and Adverbs," for more information about adverbs.

Her hairspray made her hair *very* stiff.
(modifies the adjective *stiff*)

She yelled *quite* loudly.
(modifies the adverb *loudly*)

EXERCISE

In each of the following sentences, underline the adverb(s).

1. Most species of bats have very good vision.

2. River dolphins cannot see well.

3. Porcupines mate carefully.

Prepositions

Prepositions connect nouns or noun substitutes to the rest of the sentence.

Examples:
Rambo walked *into* the room.

I will meet you *at* midnight.

He is *without* hope.

Prepositions are combined with nouns to form **prepositional phrases.** A prepositional phrase always has at least one noun or pronoun as the **object of the preposition.** Prepositional phrases function in the sentence as adjectives or as adverbs.

Commonly Used Prepositions

about	beneath	in	to
above	beside	into	toward
across	between	like	under
after	beyond	of	underneath
against	by	off	until
along	despite	on	up
among	down	over	upon
around	during	past	with
at	except	till	within
before	for	through	without
below	from	throughout	

EXERCISE

In each of the following sentences, underline the preposition(s).

1. The largest octopus has an armspread that can measure over 12 feet.

2. The anaconda is one of the largest snakes and can move over land or in water and climb into trees.

3. The Komodo dragon is the largest lizard in the world and can reach a weight of 300 pounds; it is found on the island of Komodo in Indonesia.

Conjunctions

Conjunctions join words, phrases, and clauses. There are three major types of conjunctions: coordinating, subordinating, and conjunctive.

Coordinating conjunctions join words or sentences of equal value. There are seven coordinating conjunctions: *and, but, for, or, nor, yet,* and *so.*[5]

Examples:

She ate ham *and* eggs.
(*and* joins the words *ham* and *eggs*)

She ate ham and eggs, *but* he ate oat bran cereal.
(*but* joins the two sentences)

EXERCISE

Underline the coordinating conjunction(s) in each of the following sentences.

1. "Utopia" means "no such place," but there are legends about such an ideal community called "Shangri-La."

2. The location of Shangri-La is not on any map, yet some legends place it on the Tibetan side of the Himalayas.

3. Some legends state that Shangri-La may be in western China, and others state that it is in the mountains of Mongolia.

---

[5]See Chapter 17, "Coordination," for more on this part of speech.

Subordinating conjunctions join a dependent clause and an independent clause to form the complex sentence pattern.[6]

Frequently Used Subordinating Conjunctions		
after	if	whenever
although	since	wherever
as	unless	whether
because	when	while

EXERCISE

Underline the subordinating conjunction(s) in each of the following sentences.

1. Whenever we think about a utopia, the concept of Shangri-La comes to mind.

2. Although such an earthly paradise may not exist, it is a dream that many explorers have pursued.

3. Because Shangri-La has never been found, adventurers will continue the search for it.

Adverbial conjunctions (conjunctive adverbs) join two or more sentences to form a compound sentence.[7] Used correctly, they are preceded by a semicolon and followed by a comma.

Frequently Used Conjunctive Adverbs			
consequently	however	nevertheless	therefore
furthermore	moreover	otherwise	thus

EXERCISE

Underline the adverbial conjunction(s) in each of the following sentences.

1. Shangri-La may be a legend; however, it continues to excite the imagination.

2. Perhaps it is better that Shangri-La does not exist; otherwise, everyone would want to live there.

[6]See Chapter 18, "Subordination."
[7]See Chapter 17, "Coordination."

3. Some may not believe in the existence of a paradise on earth; nevertheless, many will continue to hope that one does exist.

Interjections

An **interjection** is a word used to show strong emotion, such as sorrow, surprise, joy, or anger. Usually, an exclamation mark follows the interjection when it stands alone; it may be connected to the sentence following it by a comma.

Examples:

Wow! Batman was a great movie.

Oh! Here comes Vicky Vale.

Aw, this chapter is over.

EXERCISE

Underline the interjection(s) in each of the following sentences.

1. Oh! Look at that mountain.

2. Hey, isn't that a Porsche?

3. Aha! I know who did it.

WRITING ASSIGNMENT

A utopia is an ideal society; unfortunately, it exists only in the minds of people. The legendary Shangri-La is one example of a utopia.

Step 1: Prewriting

Using two of the prewriting techniques explained in Chapter 1, focused freewriting and mapping, develop the concept of your own utopia.

Develop a social structure for your ideal society. Describe the citizens' interaction with one another. How is your utopia unique?

Example:

My utopia is unique because there are no concepts of hate or war.

Step 2: Writing

Using the ideas you generated by the prewriting exercise, write a paragraph describing your utopia.

Step 3: Revising, Editing, and Proofreading

After completing your paragraph, reread it and label the nouns, verbs, and adjectives. Also check your spelling.

4 *Pronouns*

Pronouns, like verbs, have come to us from Old English, the form of English used until about A.D. 1150. Old English was very much like German in grammar and pronunciation; the two were derived from the same family of languages, the Indo-European group. Obviously, both languages have evolved into modern forms that are quite different, but similarities to the old forms remain.

For instance, modern English pronouns are still nearly as complex as Old English pronouns. We have come from *ic* to *I,* from *hine* to *him,* and from *hi* to *her.* The *I* was capitalized not because of egotism but because the lower-case *i* standing alone was likely to be overlooked by the reader. Until about the fifteenth century, English used the *th-* forms for second-person singular (*thee, thou, thy*) and the *y-* forms for plural (*ye, you, your*). The *th-* forms indicated intimacy and were used with close friends and family; the *y-* forms indicated a measure of formality or respect and were used with everyone else. In losing this distinction for second person, English lost a useful device.

Old or new, pronouns give versatility by allowing us to refer back to or replace a noun. It would be awkward if we had to write: *John took John's car to John's mechanic.* It sounds much better to write: *John took his car to his mechanic.*

To make sense, however, pronouns must be used properly. In this chapter, you will learn not only the correct use of pronouns but also how the use of pronouns can improve your writing style.

Types of Pronouns

Pronouns can be used as substitutes for nouns or to refer back to other nouns or pronouns. Pronouns can be personal, reflexive, intensive, indefinite, demonstrative, interrogative, relative, or reciprocal.

PERSONAL PRONOUNS

Personal pronouns refer to people or things. Personal pronouns are the most commonly used type of pronoun.

Personal Pronouns

	Singular	Plural
First person	I, me, my, mine	we, us, our, ours
Second person	you, your, yours	you, your, yours
Third person	he, him, his, she, her, hers, it, its	they, them, their, theirs

Example:

He wrote *his* book using *her* computer.

REFLEXIVE AND INTENSIVE PRONOUNS

Both reflexive and intensive pronouns are formed by adding *-self* or *-selves* to a personal pronoun.

Reflexive and Intensive Pronouns

Singular	herself, himself, myself, itself, yourself
Plural	ourselves, themselves, yourselves

Reflexive pronouns refer back to the noun or pronoun that is the subject of the sentence.

Example:

I wrote the report by *myself.*

Explanation:

The reflexive pronoun *myself* refers back to *I* and shows that the speaker wrote the report without the help of anyone else. The pronoun completes the meaning of the sentence.

Intensive pronouns are *not* a necessary part of the sentence but emphasize the noun or pronoun to which they refer.

Example:

I *myself* wrote the report on Stonehenge.

Explanation:

The intensive pronoun *myself* could be dropped from the sentence without changing the meaning.

EXERCISE

Write the correct pronoun in the blank for each of the following sentences.

1. Merlin was not only a magician; _____ was also a prophet.

2. Merlin, by _____, carried the baby, Arthur, to his foster father, Lord Ector.

3. _____ used _____ mystical powers to see the future for King Arthur.

4. Merlin fell in love with Nimue, the Lady of the Lake, who tricked _____ into revealing secrets about _____ magic.

5. When Nimue gained enough knowledge, _____ sealed Merlin in a rocky tomb.

INDEFINITE PRONOUNS

Indefinite pronouns do not refer to specific nouns. Rather, they often refer to unnamed people or things.

Common Indefinite Pronouns	
Singular	another, anybody, anyone, anything, each, either, everybody, everyone, everything, much, neither, nobody, no one, nothing, one, somebody, someone, something
Plural	both, few, many, several
Singular or plural	all, any, most, none, some

Examples:

Someone took my biochemistry study guide.

Many are called, but *few* are chosen.

DEMONSTRATIVE PRONOUNS

Demonstrative pronouns are used to point out or identify specific nouns.

Demonstrative Pronouns	
Singular	this, that
Plural	these, those

Example:

These are Tracy's physiology notes.

INTERROGATIVE PRONOUNS

Interrogative pronouns are used to ask questions: *what, which, who, whom,* and *whose.*

Examples:

Who is your favorite painter?

What are you taking to the party?

RELATIVE PRONOUNS

Relative pronouns are used to introduce and to relate dependent clauses to the rest of the sentence. They include: *that, what, whatever, which, whichever, who, whoever,* and *whom.*

Examples:

Nancy is the one *who* can speak five languages.

That is her greatest talent.

EXERCISE

Write the correct relative pronoun in the blank for each of the following sentences.

1. Dian Fossey, _____ majored in occupational therapy, was chosen by Dr. Louis Leakey to study the mountain gorillas.

2. Dian wanted to continue Dr. George Schaller's study of the mountain gorillas _____ he had conducted from 1959–1960.

3. Gorillas were feared until Dian's reports showed _____ she had actually held hands with a gorilla.

4. The gorilla with _____ Dian held hands was named Peanuts.

5. No one knows _____ killed Dian Fossey, but her work to save the mountain gorilla is continued by the Mountain Gorilla Project.

RECIPROCAL PRONOUNS

Reciprocal pronouns are used to express mutual relation, as follows: *each other, each other's, one another,* and *one another's.*

Example:

We got to know *one another* really well on our trip to the Salvador Dali Museum.

Cases of Pronouns

Case is a noun or pronoun form that indicates its use in a sentence. There are three cases in the English language: nominative, objective, and possessive.

The **nominative** case is used for subjects and predicate nominatives. The **objective** case is used for direct objects, indirect objects, objects of prepositions,[1] and objects of verbals. The **possessive** case is used to show ownership.

Pronoun Cases		
	Singular	*Plural*
Nominative case	I, you, he, she, it	we, you, they
Objective case	me, you, him, her, it	us, you, them
Possessive case	my, mine, your, yours, his, her, hers, its	our, ours, your, yours, their, theirs

Examples:

My friend and *I* decided to visit Disneyland on New Year's Eve.   (nominative)

Teaching *him* to freewrite is easy.   (objective)

The scientist reached for *his* computer as he made the final calculations.   (possessive)

Incorrect Example:

Ricardo lent his English notes to Victor and *I*.

CORRECTED EXAMPLE:

Ricardo lent his English notes to Victor and *me*.

Explanation:

The object of the preposition must be in the objective case (see Chapter 3).

EXERCISE

Circle the correct pronoun to complete each sentence below. Write an N *if the pronoun is in the nominative case or an* O *if the pronoun is in the objective case.*

1. ____ Mrs. Fernandez assigned the report on Mozart to Barbara and (I, me).

2. ____ She and (I, me) enjoy Music Appreciation 1010.

[1]Consult the following chapters for specific discussions of the following topics: subjects, Chapter 14, "Subjects and Verbs"; predicate nominatives, direct objects, and indirect objects, Chapter 13, "Sentence Formats"; and objects of prepositions, Chapter 3, "Parts of Speech."

3. ____ Will Brian or (I, me) bring the tape player to class?

4. ____ Brian and Mary teamed up with Barbara and (I, me) to play in a quartet.

5. ____ The report will be presented by either Barbara or (I, me).

PRONOUNS USED IN COMPARISONS

Pronouns can be used in making comparisons and usually follow the words *as* or *than*. In doing so, not all the words needed to make a comparison sound grammatically correct are stated. Namely, the verb is not repeated.

Examples:

Carl is better at math than I (am).

Tom likes Betty more than (he likes) me.

Explanation:

In each sentence, the word(s) in parentheses is not stated, yet the meaning of the sentence is still clear. Errors occur when the proper case of the pronoun is not used. In the first example, the pronoun *I* is in the nominative case because it is the subject of the understood verb *am*. In the second sentence, the pronoun *me* is in the objective case because it is the object of the understood verb *likes*.

To determine the proper case of the pronoun, finish the comparison silently to decide if the pronoun should be in the nominative case or in the objective case.

EXERCISE

Circle the correct pronoun to complete each sentence below.

1. I can type faster than (he, him).

2. Computer terminology is easier for me to understand than for (she, her).

3. I liked the movie *Batman* better than (he, him).

4. I dislike office work much more than (she, her).

5. Mary brought more science fiction books than (I, me).

6. When Luke Skywalker fought Darth Vader, Luke was stronger than (he, him).

7. That color looks better on Maria than (I, me).

8. Indiana Jones is much braver than (I, me).

9. My best friend is four months older than (I, me).

10. Sheron can remember facts better than (she, her).

Pronoun-Antecedent Agreement

A pronoun substitutes for and refers to another noun or pronoun. The noun or pronoun to which a pronoun refers is called its **antecedent,** which means "coming before."

Example:
Rob said that *he* was hungry.
Explanation:
The pronoun *he* refers to *Rob. Rob* is the antecedent of *he.*

Example:
Tracy and Chris have been good friends since *they* were in college.
Explanation:
The pronoun *they* refers to *Tracy and Chris.* The compound subject *Tracy and Chris* is the antecedent of *they.*

Example:
She and I worked late last night, but *we* still have a little more work to do.
Explanation:
The pronoun *we* refers to *She and I. She and I* is the antecedent of *we.*

EXERCISE

Underline the antecedents and circle the pronouns in each of the following sentences.

1. René Descartes (1596–1650) was a famous mathematician and physicist; he was also a brilliant philosopher.

2. Although René Descartes was a brilliant man, he was not always accurate with his theories.

3. Marie Curie (1867–1934) and Pierre Curie (1859–1906) were famous physicists; they won the Nobel Prize for Physics in 1903.

4. The cyclops in Greek mythology were nasty beasts, and Odysseus despised them, particularly one named Polyphemus.

5. George Armstrong Custer (1839–1876) underestimated the American Indians, whom he wanted to force onto government reservations.

VAGUE PRONOUN REFERENCE

A pronoun should always refer clearly to a specific noun or pronoun, the antecedent. If the reference is unclear, you end up with a problem called **vague pronoun reference.**

Example:

I went to college yesterday, and *he* said I should take physics in the fall.

Explanation:

Who is *he*? *He* is an example of a vague pronoun reference.

CORRECTED EXAMPLE:

I went to college yesterday with my friend, *Bob,* and *he* said I should take physics in the fall.

Do *not* add a pronoun directly after its antecedent. The pronoun would then be redundant.

Example:

My mother, she said never to add a pronoun directly after its antecedent.

Explanation:

You do not need the pronoun *she* because the subject, *my mother,* is clearly stated.

CORRECTED EXAMPLE:

My mother said never add a pronoun directly after its antecedent.

EXERCISE

Rewrite the following sentences to avoid the problem of vague pronoun reference or redundancy.

1. My sister, she did not like her astronomy class.

_____

2. Bill and Ted went on an excellent adventure, and he got lost in time.

   _____

3. He told him that he was tired of her.

   _____

4. My favorite comedians, Eddie Murphy and Richard Pryor, they starred in *Harlem Nights.*

   _____

   _____

5. Ginger and Sara walked all the way to English class, and she forgot her book.

   _____

   _____

GENDER, PERSON, AND NUMBER

A pronoun must agree with its antecedent in **gender, person,** and **number.**

Example:
> *Sheron* wrote *their* research paper on Chaucer's *Canterbury Tales.*

Explanation:
> The third-person plural possessive pronoun *their* does not agree in number with the antecedent, *Sheron.*

CORRECTED EXAMPLE:
> *Sheron* wrote *her* research paper on Chaucer's *Canterbury Tales.*

Example:
> The *student* may bring *their* applications to admissions on Tuesday.

Explanation:
> The third-person plural possessive pronoun *their* does not agree in number with the antecedent, *student.*

CORRECTED EXAMPLE:
> The *students* may bring *their* applications to admissions on Tuesday.

Example:
> *You* may do *your* report on Dante's *Inferno.*

Explanation:
> The possessive pronoun *your* and the subject *you* are both indefinite in gender, second person, and indefinite in number. This example is correct.

EXERCISE

Fill in the correct pronoun in each of the following sentences.

1. Joan found the reports that _____ had lost last week.

2. The boys brought _____ guitars to class.

3. The explorer floated down the river on _____ inflatable raft.

4. Raccoons can learn to open _____ cages.

5. I'm giving you a pass to the amusement park for _____ birthday.

6. Joan and Bill completed the model airplane that _____ had built.

7. Pedro and his friends turned in _____ papers.

8. You and Stacy should study for _____ test.

9. Dr. Chang and his graduate students finished _____ research.

10. You and I should finish _____ biology project.

COLLECTIVE NOUNS AND THEIR PRONOUNS

Pronoun-antecedent agreement becomes more difficult when a **collective noun**—such as *class, jury,* or *committee*—is the antecedent.

Example:

The humanities *class* gave *its* teacher a party for her birthday.

Explanation:

The collective subject *class* is singular; thus, the pronoun must also be singular (*its*).

INDEFINITE PRONOUNS

Indefinite pronouns may be singular or plural.

Indefinite Pronouns	
Singular indefinite pronouns	anybody, anyone, anything, each, either, everybody, everyone, everything, neither, nobody, no one, nothing, one, somebody, someone, something
Plural indefinite pronouns	both, few, many, several.

Example:

Each of the employees gave *his* or *her* report during the meeting.

Explanation:

The possessive pronouns *his* or *her* agree in number with the indefinite pronoun *each*.

Example:

After the restoration, *several* of the paintings lost *their* dull appearance.

Explanation:

The indefinite pronoun *several* is plural, so any pronoun, such as *their,* referring to this subject must also be plural. To find the true subject, cross out the intervening words.

EXERCISE

Fill in the correct pronoun in each of the following sentences.

1. The committee gave _____ approval to the new rule.

2. One of the boys is going to Africa for _____ summer vacation.

3. Many of the books are not in _____ correct places on the shelf.

4. Everybody must get _____ books before class starts.

5. The jury made _____ decision early this morning.

WRITING ASSIGNMENT

Imagine that someone has funded an expedition to explore some exotic land, and you have been chosen to head the project.

Step 1: Prewriting

Using the prewriting techniques listing and mapping, decide where you will go, what you will need, and what you expect or want to find there. For instance:

On which continent will this land be located?
What kind of climate and terrain will you encounter?
What equipment and supplies will you need to take with you?
Whom will you want to be in your expedition?

Step 2: Writing

Using the ideas you generated by the prewriting exercise, write a paragraph describing your expedition.

Step 3: Revising, Editing, and Proofreading

After completing the paragraph, circle all of the pronouns used in your paragraph. Also check your spelling.

5 Adjectives and Adverbs

Adjectives and adverbs are descriptive words that help readers visualize what you want to show them. They bring in the five senses of taste, sight, smell, hearing, and touch; they also convey emotion. Sentences and paragraphs without such descriptive words often fail to capture the reader's interest. However, these words must be used correctly. In this chapter, you will learn how to use adjectives and adverbs to add interest and originality to your writing.

Modifiers

Adjectives and adverbs are called **modifiers.** A *modifier* is a word, phrase, or clause that limits or describes another idea. In English, modifiers cannot stand alone but must be linked with a noun, a pronoun, a verb, or another modifier.

The following paragraph, written by Sheron LeGrant, was edited to remove most of the adjectives and adverbs. Notice how this paragraph simply states the bare facts without involving much of the reader's senses.

```
Elizabeth gazed at the table in the chamber. On

its top stood an array of bottles and a chest.

Elizabeth could not contain her curiosity. She ran

her hand over the top and front of the chest. She

opened the lid, revealing a mass of jewelry. Eliza-

beth gasped as she lifted up a necklace. The stones

glowed. She sighed, replaced the necklace, and

closed the lid. She picked up a bottle and pulled
```

out the stopper. The smell of perfume filled the

air.

The following paragraph is the original written by Sheron. Note that in this version, Sheron relies heavily on adjectives and adverbs to help you "see" the silver chest and its contents in your imagination:

Elizabeth gazed in wonder at the dressing table
in the queen's chamber. On its white marble top
stood an array of crystalline bottles and a large
silver chest. Elizabeth could not contain her
curiosity. Looking for a lock, she ran her hand
over the intricately embossed top and front of the
chest. She opened the lid, revealing a mass of
multicolored jewelry made of shiny, precious stones
of every description. Elizabeth gasped as she carefully lifted up an exquisite emerald and diamond
necklace. The stones, set in gold, glowed with what
seemed to be an inner light. She sighed, regretfully
replaced the necklace, and gently closed the lid.
She picked up a blue glass bottle and slowly pulled
out the stopper. The heady smell of oriental spices
filled the air.

EXERCISE

Think of a person you know well or admire, a place you like, or an interesting or attractive object you treasure. In the space provided below, write ten sentences containing enough adjectives and adverbs to allow your reader to visualize your subject. Possible topics include Michael Jackson dancing, the beach at sunset, or a beautiful rose.

1. _____

2. _____

3. _____

4. _____

5. _____

6. _____

7. _____

8. _____

9. _____

10. _____

Adjectives

Adjectives modify nouns, pronouns, and other adjectives. They answer the questions What kind? Which one(s)? How many? How much?

Examples:

We have a *Burmese* cat.   (What kind of cat? Burmese)

That car is mine.   (Which one of the cars is mine? That car)

We visited *ten* states in two weeks.   (How many states did you visit? Ten)

My suit is *smaller* than his.   (How much difference is there between your suits? Mine is smaller.)

The **positive form** of an adjective is the base word, such as *bright* or *mysterious*. Additional forms of adjectives include the comparative, superlative, and demonstrative.

COMPARATIVE AND SUPERLATIVE FORMS

Comparative and **superlative** adjectives are used to compare persons, places, and things. The positive, comparative, and superlative forms represent different degrees of a quality or characteristic: *hot, hotter, hottest.*

To compare two items, use the comparative form. To compare three or more items, use the superlative.

Points to Remember:
1. **One syllable adjectives form the comparative by adding *-er* and the superlative by adding *-est: bright, brighter, brightest.***
2. **Two-syllable adjectives that end in *-y* also follow this basic rule,**

but a minor spelling change is required: *pretty, prettier, prettiest* (see next section).

3. Other adjectives of two syllables or longer must use *more* in the comparative form and *most* in the superlative form: *mysterious, more mysterious, most mysterious.*

Adjective Forms		
Positive	*Comparative*	*Superlative*
large	larger	largest
hard	harder	hardest
great	greater	greatest
light	lighter	lightest
useful	more useful	most useful

Examples:

Rigel is a *bright* star, but Antares is *brighter.*   (Comparative—Only two stars are being compared.)

Rigel is a *bright* star, Antares is *brighter,* but Sirius is the *brightest* of all.   (Superlative—Three stars are being compared.)

Black holes are *more* mysterious than pulsars.   (Comparative—Only two cosmic phenomena are being compared.)

Black holes are the *most* mysterious phenomena that scientists have discovered in our galaxy.   (Superlative—Of all the phenomena in the galaxy, the black hole is the most mysterious.)

Irregular Forms and Adjectives Ending in -y

As mentioned earlier, most comparative and superlative forms are created by adding *-er* or *-est* or by using the words *more* or *most.* In some instances, however, the forms are **irregular.** The following list contains the most common irregular adjectives.

Positive	*Comparative*	*Superlative*
bad	worse	worst
good	better	best
ill	worse	worst
little (quantity)	less	least
many	more	most
much	more	most
well	better	best

An easy way to remember the use of the comparative and superlative forms of *good* is by memorizing the following rhyme:

Good, better, best,
Never let it rest
Until your good is better,
And your better is best.

To form the comparative of adjectives ending in *-y,* change the final *-y* to *i* and add *-er* or *-est.*

Positive	Comparative	Superlative
funny	funnier	funniest
crazy	crazier	craziest
easy	easier	easiest
happy	happier	happiest
silly	sillier	silliest
shiny	shinier	shiniest

Point to Remember:

Adjectives that end in *-y* are *never* used with *more* or *most* to form the comparative or the superlative.

EXERCISE

Write the comparative and superlative forms of each adjective below. If you are not sure of how to form the comparative and superlative of an adjective, look up the word in Webster's New World Dictionary. *The two forms will be listed as follows:*

large (larj) adj. larg'er, larg'est
unusual (un'usual) adj. more unusual, most unusual

	Comparative	Superlative
1. lazy		
2. merry		
3. beautiful		
4. heavy		
5. comfortable		

	Comparative	*Superlative*
6. lucky	_____	_____
7. shiny	_____	_____
8. pretty	_____	_____
9. transparent	_____	_____
10. well	_____	_____

Problems with Comparative and Superlative Forms

Two problems occur when using the comparative or superlative forms: **double comparatives** or **double superlatives** and **incomplete comparisons.**

Double comparatives and **double superlatives** occur when you use both *-er* or *-est* and *more* or *most.*

Incorrect Example:

The *most largest* of the buildings is on Kennedy Boulevard.

CORRECTED EXAMPLE:

The *largest* of the buildings is on Kennedy Boulevard.

Incomplete comparisons are sometimes used in conversation because the rest of the conversation makes the comparison clear. In writing, however, the context may not be as clear.

Incorrect Example:

This physics test is harder.   (Than what?)

CORRECTED EXAMPLE:

This physics test is harder *than the previous one.*

> ### EXERCISE

Correct the double comparisons, double superlatives, and incomplete comparisons in each of the sentences below.

1. Rico is one of the most handsomest students in the humanities class.

   _____

2. Sarah baked the beautifulest cake for the class party.

   _____

3. The humanities class enjoyed the Salvador Dali Museum more.

   _____

   _____

4. Dali's paintings are more unusualer than those of any other twentieth-century painter.

   _____

   _____

5. Kim had the most wonderfulest day seeing the ballet and visiting the St. Petersburg Museum and the Dali Museum.

   _____

   _____

6. Ilya speaks better Russian.

   _____

7. Ginger, Kristi, and Tiffani felt that the trip to the museum was the most best part of the humanities class.

   _____

   _____

8. Kristina had the mostest fun renaming all of Dali's paintings.

   _____

9. Amy and Gina had the most biggest laugh when Kristina renamed all of the paintings.

   _____

   _____

10. Visiting art museums is a more better way to explore the world of art than reading textbooks.

    _____

    _____

EXERCISE

For each of the following words, write a sentence using each form of the adjective: the positive form; the comparative form; and the superlative form.

1. *exotic*

_____

_____

_____

2. *shiny*

_____

_____

_____

3. *elaborate*

_____

_____

_____

4. *cloudy*

_____

_____

_____

5. *gentle*

_____

_____

_____

DEMONSTRATIVE ADJECTIVES

Demonstrative adjectives point out a particular person, place, or thing and can indicate its distance from the speaker. Demonstrative adjectives are never used alone; they are always linked with a noun or pronoun.

List of Demonstratives

this, these
that, those
which
what

Example:

Look at *this* rattlesnake over here and *that* rattlesnake by the car.

Explanation:

This points out a singular object close by, and *that* points out a singular object farther away.

Example:

Put *these* boxes on the truck and *those* boxes in the store room.

Explanation:

These points out plural objects close by, and *those* points out plural objects farther away.

Example:

Which bridge(s) fell into the river?

Explanation:

Which can refer to a singular or plural person, place, or thing.

Example:

I do not understand *what* test(s) you are discussing.

Explanation:

What can refer to a singular or plural person, place, or thing.

EXERCISE

*Choose the correct demonstrative (*this, that, these, those, what, *or* which*) to complete each of the following sentences.*

1. Look at _____ eagle flying above the mountains.

2. _____ ring on my left hand with the large emerald was given to me by my mother.

3. I cannot get _____ microscope in focus.

4. Come over here and look at _____ ants on your patio.

5. We will soon reach _____ mountains if we keep driving.

6. I can see _____ lake from here.

7. _____ group of people looks like a bunch of specks from up here.

8. Look at all of _____ baby ducks in the lake over there.

9. _____ trees over here seem to be growing better than _____ trees over there.

10. I am holding _____ kitten in one hand.

11. _____ schedule is used?

12. _____ speaker comes first?

Adverbs

Adverbs modify verbs, adjectives, and other adverbs. They answer the questions Where? When? How? and How much?

Examples:

We will go *outside.*   (*Where* should we go? Outside)

He *never* remembers my phone number.   (When does he remember? Never)

Hit the ball *softly* toward third base.   (How should he hit the ball? Softly)

She objected *very strongly* to the judge's statement.   (How much did she object? Very strongly)

FORMING ADVERBS

Many adverbs end in *-ly* and are created from the positive form of the adjective.

Adjectives	Adverbs
soft	softly
quiet	quietly
thunderous	thunderously
loud	loudly

Adjectives answer the question What kind?

The music was *soft*.
The *quiet* girl sat in the theater.
The *thunderous* waves broke on the shore.
A *loud* voice came through the speakers.

Adverbs answer the question How?

The music played *softly*.
The girl sat *quietly* in the theater.
The waves broke *thunderously* on the shore.
A voice came *loudly* through the speakers.

EXERCISE

For each adjective below, form an adverb and write a sentence using it.

1. *curious*

   _____

   _____

2. *placid*

   _____

   _____

3. *soft*

   _____

   _____

4. *clear*

   _____

   _____

5. *profuse*

   _____

   _____

What about adverbs that do not end in *-ly*? These adverbs are generally used to indicate time or frequency, place or direction, degree, and manner. The following panel shows many of these adverbs, including those that end in *-ly,* that look the same as nouns, prepositions, and adjectives.

Time/Frequency: *When?*	Place/Direction: *Where?*	Degree: *How much?*	Manner: *How?*
always	across	completely	beautifully
before	around	entirely	carefully
eventually	backwards	excessively	coldly
forever	here	however	earnestly
frequently	in	less	equally
days of the week	out	mildly	handily
never	over	most	hotly
now	sideways	much	nicely
occasionally	there	nearly	orderly
often	through	quite	quickly
once	under	somewhat	resentfully
seldom	upstairs	thoroughly	tirelessly

ADVERBS MODIFYING ADJECTIVES AND OTHER ADVERBS

An adverb can also describe an adjective or another adverb, usually telling us How often? How much? or To what degree?

Example:

Holly paints *very frequently.*

Explanation:

Very is an adverb describing the adverb *frequently. Very* tells us how *frequently* (How often?) Holly paints.

Example:

Salvador Dali was a *most extraordinary* artist and Holly's favorite painter.

Explanation:

Most is an adverb describing the adjective *extraordinary. Most* tells us how *extraordinary* (To what degree?) the artist Salvador Dali was.

EXERCISE

Underline the correct adjective or adverb in each of the following sentences.

1. Heidi has a (beautiful/beautifully) smile.

2. Angela's art portfolio was (excellent/excellently).

3. Kenna Jo and Tanya play golf (exceptional/exceptionally) well.

4. Whitney bought an (unusual/unusually) pen at Sea World.

5. Bobby led Gina (quick/quickly) into the museum room containing the crystal-embedded Excalibur.

6. Lisa walked (slow/slowly) into the art gallery, wearing a fake arrow through her head.

7. David plays basketball (extreme/extremely) well.

8. Sara is an (expert/expertly) swimming instructor.

9. Carl, Sarah, Rico, Bobby, and Whitney (swift/swiftly) walked to the pier.

10. From the top of the pier, Sarah and Carl viewed an (unusual/unusually) large yacht.

COMPARATIVE AND SUPERLATIVE FORMS

Like adjectives, the **positive** is the base form of an adverb: *hard, quietly.* Moreover, adverbs are used in comparative and superlative forms. The **comparative** is formed by adding *-er* or using the word *more—harder, more quietly—*while the **superlative** requires adding *-est* or using the word *most—hardest, most quietly.*

Examples:

A successful student tries *hard.*   (positive)

Of the two students, Ginger tries *harder.*   (comparative)

In English class, Ginger tries *hardest.*   (superlative)

Point to Remember:

In general, adverbs ending in *-ly* use only the words *more* and *most* to form the comparative and superlative: *more slowly,* not *slowlier; most slowly,* not *slowliest.* (The exceptions to this rule are the words *early* and *lowly: early, earlier, earliest; low, lowlier, lowliest.*)

Positive	Comparative	Superlative
deep	deeper	deepest
fast	faster	fastest
happily	more happily	most happily
long	longer	longest
early	earlier	earliest
low	lower	lowest
near	nearer	nearest
unfortunately	more unfortunately	most unfortunately

Example:

Ginny walks *more quickly* than Tom.

Explanation:

This sentence compares walking speeds between Ginny and Tom. Ginny is walking faster than Tom is walking.

There are only a few irregular comparative and superlative adverb forms.

Positive	Comparative	Superlative
much	more	most
well	better	best

EXERCISE

Circle the correct comparative or superlative form of the adverb in each sentence below.

1. When the humanities class was assigned to write a medieval legend, Stacy and Art wrote the (most cleverly/cleverliest) of anyone in the class.

2. Of all the prewriting techniques, mapping allows you to develop your topic the (most quickly/quickliest).

3. Of all the problems writers have, writer's block affects writers (most seriously/seriousliest).

4. The editor replied (most favorably/favorabliest) to our proposal for a new book.

5. Of all the people at the party, Rob arrived (most early/earliest).

6. The old steam engine moved (more slowly/slowlier) than the diesel engine.

7. The diesel picked up speed (more easy/easier) than the steam engine.

8. John would have (more gladly/gladlier) ridden in the Model T than in his father's truck.

9. Jim sat (more near/nearer) to me than his brother did.

10. We both watched the television program (more closely/closelier) since we knew our sister would appear as one of the actresses.

Adjective or Adverb?

In many instances, adjectives are incorrectly used in place of adverbs. The most prevalent problems occur with *good/well, bad/badly,* and *real/really.*

GOOD/WELL

Good is an adjective that can also be used after a linking verb as a predicate adjective.[1] Do not use *good* to modify a verb, another adjective, or an adverb. Unlike most adjectives, the adverb form of *good* is not created by adding *-ly;* instead, the adverb form is *well.*

Incorrect Example:
Van Gogh painted landscapes *good.*
CORRECTED EXAMPLE:
Van Gogh painted landscapes *well.*

Examples:
Holly is a *good* artist.   (adjective)

Holly paints *well.*   (adverb)

Point to Remember:
Note that an exception to this rule is using *well* as an adjective to mean "in good health."

Example:
After she recovered from pneumonia, Jane felt *well.*
Explanation:
Here *well* is used as an adjective to mean "in good health."

EXERCISE

Circle the correct adjective or adverb in each of the following sentences.

1. Although Vincent Van Gogh's psychological health had improved, just when many people thought he was getting (good/well), he committed suicide.

2. It is often hard for an artist to make a (good/well) living.

3. However, during the Renaissance, such painters as Michelangelo had art patrons who provided for them very (good/well).

[1]See Chapter 13, "Sentence Formats," for an explanation of predicate adjectives.

4. It is hard to judge whether a work of art is (good/well) because what one person may like, another may dislike.

5. Perhaps it is (good/well) that people have such diverse tastes in art since there are so many different art forms.

BAD/BADLY

The adjective *bad* is often mistaken for the adverb *badly. Bad* is used to describe a noun or pronoun; it is *never* used to modify a verb, an adverb, or another adjective. *Bad* refers to the degree of something or to the condition of the subject.

Examples:

That was a *bad* mistake.

I feel *bad* about missing your party.

The refreshments tasted *bad.*

Explanation:

In the first sentence, *bad* modifies *mistake,* describing what kind of mistake it is. In the second and third sentences, *bad* refers to the condition of the subjects *I* and *refreshments.*

Badly, an adverb, indicates that something is done poorly or ineptly. It is used to modify a verb, another adverb, or an adjective and often follows an action verb.

Example:

Rod played the piano *badly* last night.

Explanation:

In this sentence, *badly* describes how Rod played—poorly or ineptly.

EXERCISE

Circle the correct adjective or adverb in each of the following sentences.

1. There is nothing worse than sitting through a (bad/badly) ballet.

2. He wanted (bad/badly) to exchange his opera tickets for football tickets.

3. The refreshments served after the ballet tasted (bad/badly), especially the oysters.

4. It is too (bad/badly) Van Gogh (1853–1890) only sold a few paintings during his lifetime.

5. The soprano felt (bad/badly) about her performance in the opera.

REAL/REALLY

The adjective *real* is often used incorrectly as an adverb. When modifying a verb, adjective, or another adverb, always use *really.*

Incorrect Example:
We had a *real* good time at the art museum.
CORRECTED EXAMPLE:
We had a *really* good time at the art museum.
Explanation:
Remember, the adjective *real* means "true or factual."

EXERCISE

Circle the correct adjective or adverb in each of the following sentences.

1. Vincent Van Gogh was (real/really) troubled by auditory hallucinations as a result of his mental state.

2. Often, it was hard for Van Gogh to tell what was (real/really) in the world around him.

3. Van Gogh would be (real/really) surprised if he knew the value of his art today.

4. It is a (real/really) tragedy that a great artist such as Vincent Van Gogh should suffer so much during his lifetime and not be recognized until after his death.

5. Van Gogh was a (real/really) good artist.

WRITING ASSIGNMENT

What was your most memorable experience?

Step 1: Prewriting

Using the prewriting techniques freewriting and mapping, describe your most memorable experience.

What made you choose this particular event?

Where did it take place?

How long ago did it occur?

What made it so remarkable?

Step 2: Writing

Using the ideas you generated by the prewriting exercise, write a paragraph describing your experience. Be sure to use varying types of adjectives and adverbs to involve the reader's senses and emotions in your subject. Remember that using descriptive words adds vivid details to your writing.

Step 3: Revising, Editing, and Proofreading

After completing the paragraph, read it to see if you have used the adjectives and adverbs correctly. Did you use a variety of comparative and superlative adjectives and adverbs? Also check your spelling.

6 *Verbs*

The verb is the most complex and versatile part of speech in the English language. The more you learn about how to use verbs, the more vivid and energetic your writing will be. Verbs can be used to express action (The jet *roared* past the tower.), describe conditions (The paint looks *faded.*) or states of being (I *feel* sick.), and establish the time in which an action or state of being occurs (He *didn't come* yesterday, but he *is coming* today.). Verb forms also can be used as nouns, adjectives, or adverbs and to express active and passive voice.

As you can imagine, the correct verb form is crucial to the meaning of a sentence. Chapters 7 through 10 show how to use the six basic tenses and the progressive forms. Chapter 11 covers mood and fixed-form helping verbs. This chapter presents an overview, including:

> Person and number in verbs
> Four principal parts
> Overview of the six tenses
> Active and passive voice

Person and Number

As you learned in Chapter 3, English verbs are grouped into **action, linking, and helping verbs.**

Action   Lieutenant Bouchard *discovered* the Rosetta Stone.
Linking   Ancient Egyptian *is* now easier to translate.
Helping   I *have* translated several works myself.

Every verb—whether action, linking, or helping—has person and number. **Person** refers to the subject of the verb, which can be either a noun or pronoun.

First Person: The subject of the sentence is the speaker.

Examples:

I like ancient history.

We built a scale model of a Greek temple.

Second Person: The subject is someone to whom you are speaking.

Example:

You should spend more time relaxing.

Third Person: The subject is someone or something about which you are speaking.

Examples:

He sailed 3,000 miles across the open sea.

The *water* grew rough during the storm.

They were happy to reach port.

Number is the term used to indicate whether a verb is singular or plural. Remember, singular subjects require singular verbs; plural subjects require plural verbs. The following panel shows person and number for the verb *to walk*.

	Singular	Plural
First Person	I walk	We walk
Second Person	You walk	You walk
Third Person	He, she, it walks	They walk

Point to Remember:

Notice that only the third-person singular changes (*walks*). For regular verbs, simply add *-s* to the verb form. If the verb ends in *-ch, -o, -s, -sh, -x,* or *-z,* add *-es* to the end of the verb to form the third person singular in the present tense.

Look at the examples below:

cat*ch*	→	catch*es*	wi*sh*	→	wish*es*
d*o*	→	do*es*	fi*x*	→	fix*es*
pa*ss*	→	pass*es*	bu*zz*	→	buzz*es*

Four Principal Parts

Each verb has four basic parts from which all of the tenses can be created. The four principal parts of a verb are the **present** (also known as the **infinitive**), the **past,** the **past participle,** and the **present participle.**

Examples:

Present: I *walk* once a day.   (*walk*)

Past: I *walked* yesterday.   (*walked*)

Past participle: I *have walked* many times.   (*walked* + helping verb)

Present participle: I *am walking* home today.   (*walking* + helping verb)

Point to Remember:

Forms of the past participle and present participle are used with helping verbs, such as *am, is, are, has*, and *have.*

REGULAR VERBS

The majority of verbs in the English language are regular verbs. **Regular verbs** form the past participle by adding *-ed* or *-d* to the verb stem[1] and the present participle by adding *-ing*. Regular verbs that end in *-e* (*love, move,* etc.) drop the final *-e* and add *-ing*.

Examples:

Present: I often *talk* to my friends.

Past: I *talked* to my friends yesterday.   (*talk + ed*)

Past participle: I *have talked* with them many times.

Present participle: I *am talking* with her this evening.   (*talk + ing*)

Present: We often *move* from city to city.

Present Participle: We are *moving* to Seattle next month.   (*move − e + ing*)

IRREGULAR VERBS

English contains about 200 irregular verbs. In contrast to regular verbs, **irregular verbs** always form the past tense and past participle by changing their spelling. The present participle, however, is formed by adding *-ing,* as is the case with the regular verbs.

[1]Some regular verbs have an alternative spelling for the past participle: *burned* or *burnt.* Most regular verbs, however, follow the *-ed* rule.

Examples:

To swim

Present: I often *swim* in cold weather.

Past: Last winter, I *swam* in the lake.

Past participle: I *have swum* in winter for years.

Present participle: I *am swimming* again this year.

Examples:

To do

Present: I *do* my home work every night.

Past: I *did* four assignments yesterday.

Past participle: I *have done* four papers this week.

Present participle: I *am doing* a paper on Salvador Dali.

A complete list of the four basic parts of irregular verbs can be found in Appendix B (pages 435–439).

EXERCISE

In each of the following sentences, fill in the past tense form of the verb given in the parentheses.

1. (*to eat*)   The small bear cub _____ some berries.

2. (*to fly*)   The bat _____ right past our heads.

3. (*to swim*)   The shark _____ under the boat, and we never saw him again.

4. (*to get*)   I _____ an extra pump for my aquarium.

5. (*to drink*)   The camel at the zoo _____ 15 gallons of water.

6. (*to come*)   A water moccasin _____ out of the water where we were fishing, and I retreated rather quickly.

7. (*to buy*)   My friend _____ a tarantula and actually thinks that I should be thrilled about it.

8. (*to build*)   My professor _____ an ant farm for his ants, and they were quite interesting to watch.

9. (*to freeze*) My professor _____ a flower in liquid nitrogen and smashed it on the table, breaking the frozen flower into pieces.

10. (*to teach*) My friend _____ his parakeet to say insulting words to his guests.

EXERCISE

In each of the following sentences, fill in the correct form of the verb to be *in the past tense (*was *or* were*).*

1. Albert Einstein _____ a great physicist.

2. Thomas Edison and Alexander Graham Bell _____ both successful inventors.

3. Leonhard Euler (1707–1783) _____ the most prolific mathematician of his generation.

4. Charlemagne _____ Emperor of the Holy Roman Empire.

5. Sonya Kovaleski (1850–1891) and Amalie Noether (1882–1935) _____ outstanding women mathematicians.

6. Archimedes and Pythagoras _____ ancient Greek mathematicians.

7. Marie Curie _____ Polish.

8. Roulette _____ first a popular game in France in the seventeenth century.

9. Anders Celsius and Carl von Linné _____ both involved with giving us the modem Celsius scale.

10. In 1958, Seymour Cray _____ the world's first "supercomputer" inventor; a supercomputer can handle at least 10 million instructions per second!

Overview of the Six Verb Tenses

English contains six basic verb tenses to help describe time. These six tenses are divided into **simple tenses** (present, past, future) and **perfect tenses** (present perfect, past perfect, future perfect). Each verb also has a **progressive form** to express ongoing action in the past, present, or future. Conjugations of irregular verbs can be found in Appendix C (pages 439–444).

SIMPLE TENSES

Present tense expresses an action or state of being that takes place in the present time. Present tense is also used to express habitual actions and general truths.

Examples:

Present action: These pictures *look* interesting.

Habitual action: She *sits* next to me every Wednesday in biology class.

General truth: Mammals *are* animals.

Literary present: The author *states* his viewpoint clearly.

Past tense expresses an action or state of being that was completed at a definite time in the past.

Example:

I *passed* my exam yesterday.

Future tense expresses an action or state of being that will take place in the future.

Example:

I *will call* you in the morning.

(Chapter 7 explores the simple tenses more fully.)

PERFECT TENSES

Present perfect tense expresses an action or state of being begun in the past that continues in an unbroken manner up to the present moment.

Example:

I *have been* with the company for two years.

Past perfect tense expresses an action or state of being that took place before some other event in the past.

Example:

I *had* just *fallen* asleep when the telephone rang.

Future perfect tense expresses an action or state of being that will be completed in the future.

Example:

I *will have finished* the chapter by then.

(Chapter 8 examines the perfect tenses more fully.)

PROGRESSIVE FORMS

The progressive forms describe actions or states of being that are presently occurring or that began sometime before and are continuing in the present, past, or future.

Present progressive form expresses a present, ongoing action or state of being.

Example:

We *are composing* a song.

Past progressive form expresses an ongoing action or state of being that began some time in the past.

Example:

He *was laughing* at the comedian.

Future progressive form expresses an ongoing action or state of being that will occur in the future.

Example:

I *will be calling* you in the morning.

Present perfect progressive form expresses an action or state of being that began in the past and is continuing in the present. Note that all the progressive forms of the perfect tenses show continuing action.

Example:

She *has been seeing* him for a long time.

Past perfect progressive form expresses an ongoing action or state of being completed before another past time.

Example:

Until this week, the drivers *had been working* 40 hours per week.

Future perfect progressive form expresses an ongoing action or state of being regarded as having begun before a later time.

Example:

By 9:00 tonight, I *will have been studying* for 12 hours.

(Chapter 9 describes the progressive forms in more detail and provides exercises for practice.)

> Verb tenses are classified as present, past, and future. Each tense has a simple, perfect, and progressive form.

Active and Passive Voice

In English, verbs can be in either the active or passive voice. If the subject of a sentence performs an action, the verb is in the **active voice.** If the subject receives the action, the verb is in the **passive voice.** The passive voice is formed by combining the helping verbs *to be* or *to have* with the past participle.

Examples:

Diane *washed* the clothes.   (active voice)

The clothes *were washed* by Diane.   (passive voice)

The clothes *have been washed.*   (passive voice)

Explanation:

In the first sentence, the subject *Diane* performs the action: *washed the clothes.* In the second and third sentences, however, the subject *clothes* receives the action. Therefore, the verbs are in the passive voice.

Point to Remember:

Notice that in the passive voice, the actor who performs the action can disappear altogether: The clothes have been washed—By whom or what? Thus, the passive voice tends to be rather static and dull; avoid it in your own writing.

For further illustration, compare the two passages below.

Passive Voice

Last night, a forest fire *was started* by a

lightning bolt and *was spotted* by an alert forest

ranger. In less than an hour, three fire-fighting

stations *were notified* and *were rushing* to the

scene. Water *was pumped* from nearby lakes to douse

the flames. Earthen dikes *were built* to try to keep

the fire from spreading. Nevertheless, by early the

next day, nearly 20 homes *had been burned,* and

three people *were reported* missing.

Who or what alerted the fire stations, pumped water, built dikes, and reported people missing? With the passive voice, not only do these questions remain unanswered, but what could have been an exciting story is reduced to a flat, dull paragraph.

Active Voice

Last night, a stray lightning bolt *started* a

forest fire in Alameda County. An alert forest

ranger *spotted* the blaze and *notified* three fire-

fighting stations, whose trucks *rushed* to the

scene. Firefighters *pumped* water from nearby lakes

and *built* earthen dikes, trying to keep the fire

from spreading. Nevertheless, by early the next

day, the fire *had burned* 20 homes, and the county

sheriff's office *had reported* three people missing.

Use of the active voice brings the actors back into the scene and creates a more lively paragraph. As a general rule of thumb, use the active voice in your writing.

EXERCISE

Revise the following paragraph, changing the passive voice to the active voice.

The Rosetta Stone was discovered by accident by

Lieutenant Bouchard of Napoleon's army in 1799.

During this time, Egypt was occupied by the French Napoleonic forces. In 1801, Egypt was surrendered by the French troops to the English government. The Rosetta Stone was brought to England and was placed in a museum. It was examined by scholars and was reported to be an astonishing key to unlocking the secrets of ancient languages. For the first time, scholars had been given a way to break the "code" of Egyptian hieroglyphics. Even today, the Rosetta Stone is regarded with awe by scholars who study Middle Eastern cultures.

_____

_____

_____

_____

_____

_____

_____

_____

_____

_____

_____

_____

_____

_____

(Consult Chapters 7 through 10 for more information on how to use various verb tenses in your writing and how to avoid some of the common mistakes beginning writers make in forming and using verb tenses.)

WRITING ASSIGNMENT

Imagine that archaeologists from the year A.D. 3300 have discovered our civilization. What conclusions do you think they will make about our culture based on the articles they have uncovered?

Step 1: Prewriting

Using the prewriting techniques listing and mapping, decide what the archaeologists will find.

What do you think these articles might convey about our civilization?
What conclusion might they make about our culture?

Step 2: Writing

Using the ideas you generated by the prewriting exercise, write a paragraph describing what the archaeologists will conclude about our culture.

Step 3: Revising, Editing, and Proofreading

In your paragraph, underline the subject and verb of each sentence and circle the prepositional phrases or clauses. Also check your spelling.

7 *The Simple Tenses*

Have you ever wanted to travel in time? The English language allows you to do so by using the verb tenses. Simply by changing the verb tense, you may travel to the future, then to the past, and back again.

Examples:

I *will travel.*   (future tense)

I *travelled.*   (past tense)

I *travel.*   (present tense)

You may add modifying words, such as *today* or *yesterday,* to these sentences, but the additional words are not necessary to change the time setting. In English, the verb tense does all of the work, unlike a language such as Chinese in which the verb never changes form.

Your personal "time machine" is the three simple verb tenses: the present, the past, and the future. We will discuss each in turn.

Present Tense

As you learned in Chapter 6, the **present tense** expresses an action or state of being occurring in the present time. It is also used to express habitual action and general truths and to describe literary works.

Examples:

He *rides* his bicycle.   (present action)

She *calls* her mother every day.   (habitual action)

Children *like* cartoons.   (general truth)

Huckleberry Finn *escapes* down the Mississippi River with his friend Jim.   (literary present)

A verb in the present tense can be singular or plural.

	Singular	Plural
First Person	I move	We move
Second Person	You move	You move
Third Person	He, she, it moves	They move

EXERCISE

Rewrite each of the following sentences, changing the subject from singular *to* plural *and changing the verb form and any other words necessary to agree with it.*

Example:
The koala is not a bear.
Revision:
Koalas are not bears.

1. This chimpanzee eats a lot.

_____

2. The koala prefers leaves of certain eucalyptus trees.

_____

3. The tree kangaroo sleeps in trees.

_____

4. The tree kangaroo spends a lot of time on the ground.

_____

5. The wallaby is much smaller than the kangaroo.

_____

6. The wallaroo ranges in size between that of a wallaby and a kangaroo.

_____

7. The tree kangaroo climbs trees to find a place to sleep.

_____

EXERCISE

Rewrite each of the following sentences by changing the subject from plural *to* singular *and changing the verb form to agree with it. Add necessary articles.*

Example:
   Insectivores eat insects.
Revision:
   The insectivore eats insects.

1. Hedgehogs are mammals.

   _____

2. Shrews are nocturnal.

   _____

3. Shrews eat crop-destroying insects.

   _____

4. Bats fly in a zig-zag pattern in contrast to the smooth pattern of birds.

   _____

5. Bats locate objects by sonar, but many bats actually have good vision.

   _____

6. Fish-eating bats live in Mexico.

   _____

7. Armadillos always bear four young of the same sex.

   _____

EXERCISE

Circle the correct verb forms in each of the following sentences.

1. About one million species of animals (inhabit/inhabits) the earth.

2. About 4,500 species (is/are) mammals.

3. Some shrews (weigh/weighs) about as much as a dime.

4. Some blue whales (weigh/weighs) over 170 tons.

5. Wild yaks (inhabit/inhabits) the steppes of northern Tibet at altitudes of over 16,000 feet.

6. The spiny anteater (eat/eats) ants.

7. Spiny anteaters (live/lives) in open, wooded, and grassy areas.

8. The anteater (digs/dig) with its sharp claws in order to open ant hills.

MOST OFTEN USED VERBS

The verb *to be* indicates existence, the verb *to have* indicates possession, and the verb *to do* indicates performing an action. These verbs are the most commonly used verbs in the English language.

To Be

Of all the verbs in the English language, the verb *to be* is used most frequently. It is possible to write entire paragraphs with just the various forms of *to be*. In fact, overuse of *to be* is so easy to become accustomed to that your instructors will ask you to avoid doing so and instead introduce more descriptive action verbs into your writing. You should learn to use the forms of *to be* correctly, but avoid overusing them.

To be is the most important linking verb.

	Singular	*Plural*
First Person	I am	We are
Second Person	You are	You are
Third Person	He, she, it is	They are

Examples:

I *am* a scuba diver.

The treasure *is* here.

Forms of *to be* are also used before the progressive forms of verbs ending in *-ing*.[1]

EXERCISE

For each of the following sentences, circle the correct verb form corresponding to the person and number indicated.

---

[1]See Chapter 9, "The Progressive Forms," for a complete explanation of the progressive forms.

1. (first-person plural)   We (am/is/are) excited about the trip to Florida.

2. (third-person plural)   The suitcases (is/are) full of clothing.

3. (third-person singular)   Thomas Edison's winter home (am/is/are) in Fort Myers, Florida.

4. (third-person plural)   Many of his inventions (am/is/are) on display in his home.

5. (third-person singular)   Edison's home (am/is/are) now a museum.

6. (first-person singular)   I (am/are) curious about his life and creativity.

7. (second-person plural)   You (is/are) certain to find the museum interesting.

To Have

Since it shows possession, *to have* is another of the most commonly used verbs. In addition, later, you will use the forms of *to have* as helping verbs.

The present tense of *to have* is easier to create than the present tense of *to be* because there are only two forms: *has* and *have*.

	Singular	Plural
First Person	I have	We have
Second Person	You have	You have
Third Person	He, she, it has	They have

EXERCISE

For each of the following sentences, circle the correct verb form corresponding to the person and number indicated.

1. (first-person singular)   I (have/has) a book about the lost mysteries of the world.

2. (third-person singular)   The book (have/has) many beautiful photographs of mysterious objects and places.

3. (first-person plural)   We (have/has) unanswered questions about the lost city of Atlantis and mysterious Stonehenge.

4. (third-person singular)   The ancient city of Jericho (has/have) walls that are 9,000 years old, three times as old as Rome.

5. (third-person plural)   The foothills of Iran, Iraq, Israel, Jordan, and Syria (have/has) traces of the earliest settlements in the world.

6. (third-person singular)   The Bible (have/has) many stories of ancient civilizations, such as those of Egypt and Sumeria.

7. (third-person singular)   An archaeologist (have/has) the desire to find the lost mysteries of the world.

8. (second-person singular)   (Has/Have) you an interest in ancient and mysterious civilizations?

9. (third-person singular)   Easter Island (have/has) the nickname "navel of the world."

10. (third-person singular)   Easter Island (have/has) huge statues of stone men.

To Do

To do is another frequently used verb because it indicates performing an action.

Example:

I *do* the laundry.

	Singular	Plural
First Person	I do	We do
Second Person	You do	You do
Third Person	He, she, it does	They do

The forms of *to do* are also used as helping verbs in negative statements in the present tense and in the emphatic form.

Examples:

They *do not* swim well.   (negative)

She *does* swim well.   (emphatic)

She *does not* swim well.   (emphatic and negative)

Point to Remember:

> The third-person singular, present tense (*he, she, it,* or any singular noun) requires a verb that ends in *-s*. The third-person singular of *to do* is *does*.

Incorrect Example:

> He *do* not like ice cream.

CORRECTED EXAMPLE:

> He *does* not like ice cream.

EXERCISE

For each of the following sentences, circle the correct verb form corresponding to the person and number indicated.

1. (third-person plural)   Archaeologists (do/does) an incredible job of piecing together the past from broken pottery and old bones.

2. (third-person plural)   (Do/Does) they know everything about ancient history?

3. (third-person plural)   Many people (does not/do not) realize the importance of the rain forests to the world's ecology.

4. (third-person singular)   The uninformed citizen (do not/does not) care about the earth's ecology.

5. (first-person singular)   I (does not/do not) like to think of this beautiful planet being destroyed by pollution.

6. (second-person singular)   (Does/Do) you know about the earth's ecosystem?

EXERCISE

Write five sentences about your present activities. Be sure to use the present tense.

1. _____

2. _____

3. _____

4. _____

5. _____

Past Tense

The simple **past tense** expresses an action or state of being that was completed at a definite time in the past.

REGULAR VERBS

Normally, it is easy to form the past tense of regular verbs: Simply add *-ed* or *-d* to the present form of the verb. For some regular verbs, however, the final letter *y* is changed to *i* and then *-ed* is added. Some regular verbs have a vowel before the final consonant, such as *trim*. In this case you double the final consonant before the *-ed* is added: *trimmed.*[2]

Following are the past tense forms of the regular verb *to jump*.

	Singular	Plural
First Person	I jumped	We jumped
Second Person	You jumped	You jumped
Third Person	He, she, it jumped	They jumped

Point to Remember:

Regular verbs in the past tense do not change form in the third-person singular.

EXERCISE

The sentences below are in the present tense. Rewrite each sentence and change the verb form to the past tense.

1. The child dusts the sand off the seashell.

_____

2. The ocean looks calm today.

_____

3. In February, some people wade in the cold ocean water.

_____

[2]For further help with spelling, consult Chapter 28, "Spelling."

4. Emily walks down the beach to the open-air restaurant.

   _____

5. The smell of salt saturates the balmy air.

   _____

6. The beaches wash away because of the sea walls in front of the hotels.

   _____

   _____

7. The beach umbrellas protect tender skin from the hot sun.

   _____

   _____

8. Seaweed floats onto the beach with the incoming tide.

   _____

9. The sea gulls hover over the beach, waiting for handouts.

   _____

10. The bright sunshine glints off the water.

    _____

IRREGULAR VERBS

Verbs that do not add *-ed* or *-d* to form the past tense are called *irregular verbs.* For a list of irregular verbs, see Appendix B (pages 435–439), or look up the verb in a dictionary. If the verb is irregular, its four principal parts will be listed.

EXERCISE

Look up the following verbs in a dictionary and write down the principal parts.

Verb	Present	Past	Past Participle	Present Participle
to grow	_____	_____	_____	_____
to shake	_____	_____	_____	_____
to drink	_____	_____	_____	_____

When you look up *to grow, to drink,* and *to shake,* you will find that the dictionary lists the principal parts for these irregular verbs. For example, the dictionary entry for the verb *to swim* has the following information:

swim vi. swam, swum, swimming

The *second* item in the list of principal parts will always give you the *past-tense form* of the irregular verb.

EXERCISE

Look up each of the following irregular verbs in the dictionary. Use the principal parts to determine the past-tense form of the irregular verb in each of the following sentences.

1. (to take)   Nicolo and Maffeo Polo _____ the 17-year-old Marco with them to China.

2. (to send)   Kublai Khan _____ Marco on an mission to a country six months' journey away.

3. (to spend)   Marco, Nicolo, and Maffeo _____ 17 years in the service of Kublai Khan.

4. (to grow)   The Venetians _____ rich during their stay in China.

5. (to come)   Marco always _____ back to China with interesting stories for the Khan.

6. (to have)   His father and uncle _____ other great adventures prior to this trip to China.

7. (to become)   They _____ rich on another venture to the court of Barka Khan, son of Genghis Khan.

8. (to sell)   The men _____ a stock of jewels to Barka Khan for a large profit.

9. (to be)   Marco Polo _____ the favorite ambassador of Kublai Khan.

10. (to do)   The three men _____ not return to Venice for 24 years.

EXERCISE

Write five sentences about an event in the past, using the past tense.

1. _____

2. _____

3. _____

4. _____

5. _____

Future Tense

The **future tense** expresses an action or state of being that will occur at a later time. The future tense is formed by adding *shall* or *will* to the present form of the verb.

Examples:

I *shall go* to the museum tomorrow.

You *will be* home later.

She *will take* the test on Saturday.

The distinction between *shall* and *will* is now rarely observed, even by educated writers and speakers. Today, *will* is commonly used for all persons (*I, you, he, she, it*) except in the first person or in questions (*Shall I leave?*) and in formal contexts (*We shall consider your formal demands.*). In questions, using *will* changes the meaning (*Will I leave?*).

	Singular	Plural
First Person	I will (shall) give	We will (shall) give
Second Person	You will give	You will give
Third Person	He, she, it will give	They will give

EXERCISE

In each of the following sentences, change the present-tense verb in parentheses to the future tense and write it in the blank.

1. (return)   According to ancient legend, King Arthur of Britain _____ someday.

2. (hold)   The future _____ many technological advances that will enhance our lives.

3. (become)   Someday, Princess Diana _____ the Queen of England.

4. (appear)   What new fad _____ on the fashion scene next?

5. (learn)   When _____ we _____ to protect our fragile environment?

6. (find)   Perhaps in the future, archaeologists _____ buried treasures as valuable as those in King Tutankhamen's tomb.

7. (go)   _____ he _____ to the library to find some books on the mystery of Stonehenge?

8. (locate)   _____ anyone ever _____ the Holy Grail?

9. (see)   The visitors to Walt Disney's EPCOT _____ what life may be like in the future.

10. (be)   Robotics _____ the industry of the future.

WRITING ASSIGNMENTS

1: PAST TENSE

Using the theme of exploration and discovery, write a paragraph about something you discovered or explored when you were a child, such as a secret hideaway or old house.

Step 1: Prewriting

Using the prewriting techniques listing and mapping, think about which adventure you want to use as your topic.

Step 2: Writing

Using the ideas you generated by the prewriting exercise, write a paragraph *in the past tense* about your adventure.

Example:

Ralph and I *ran* down to the river bank to see if the black box still *was hidden* under the rocks.

Step 3: Revising, Editing, and Proofreading

After completing your paragraph, reread it to make sure all verbs are in the past tense. Also check your spelling.

2: PRESENT TENSE

Using the theme of exploration and discovery, write a paragraph about packing for a long voyage of exploration.

Step 1: Prewriting

Using the prewriting techniques listing and mapping, think about what you want to take with you. Where are you going—the tropics, the Antarctic, the Sahara Desert, a South Sea island, another planet?

Step 2: Writing

Using the ideas you generated by the prewriting exercise, write a paragraph in the present tense about packing for your adventure.

Example:

I *take* down the suitcase and *dust* it off. I *need* my boots because the mountain trails *are* rugged.

Step 3: Revising, Editing, and Proofreading

After completing your paragraph, reread it to make sure all verbs are in the present tense. Also check your spelling.

3: FUTURE TENSE

Using the theme of exploration and discovery, write a paragraph about an adventure, exploration, or discovery that you would like to make in the future.

Step 1: Prewriting

Using the prewriting techniques listing and mapping, think about what you want to discover or explore.

Step 2: Writing

Using the ideas you generated by the prewriting exercise, write a paragraph in the future tense about your adventure.

Example:

> I *will explore* the great canyon of Mars and *will be* the first to walk along the mile-deep canyon floor.

Step 3: Revising, Editing, and Proofreading

After completing your paragraph, reread it to make sure all verbs are in the future tense. Also check your spelling.

8 *The Perfect Tenses*

"Time travelling" in your writing assignments can be more complex than the simple tenses can convey. When you need to explain more subtle or detailed time sequences, the perfect tenses are there to help you.

The perfect tenses relate actions in one time to actions in another, providing a logical sequence for the reader: *I had just stepped into the shower when the telephone rang.* More complex time relationships are indicated by the perfect and progressive[1] forms of the present, past, and future tenses. In this chapter, we will address the present perfect, past perfect, and future perfect tenses.

Overview

A verb in one of the **perfect tenses** expresses what was or will be completed at the time of another action. The perfect tenses are created by using a form of the verb *have* with the past participle of a verb:

has/have/had/ or *will have* + past participle.[2]

Point to Remember:
> **An important aspect of the perfect tenses is that time is indicated by the form of the helping verb *have*.**

In the **present perfect tense,** the helping verb is in the present tense form of *to have: have* or *has.*

Examples:
I *have talked* to my mother this morning.

You *have chosen* the right answer.

[1]See Chapter 9, "The Progressive Forms."
[2]See Appendix C (pages 439–444) for a complete conjugation of the irregular verb *to have.*

She *has ridden* a horse several times.

In the **past perfect tense,** the helping verb is in the past tense form of the verb *to have: had.*

Example:

I *had talked* to the professor before I began my assignment.

In the **future perfect tense,** the helping verb is in the future tense form of the verb *to have: will have.*

Example:

He *will have mowed* the lawn by noon.

Present Perfect Tense

The **present perfect tense** describes an action or state of being begun in the past that proceeds continuously up to the present. The present perfect tense is constructed by combining the present tense of *to have* (*has* or *have*) with the past participle of the verb.

Examples:

John *studied* for the test.   (past tense)

John *has studied* for the test for two days.   (present perfect tense)

In the first example, the past-tense verb *studied* shows that the action started and ended in the past. In the second example, the verb phrase *has studied* means that John began studying two days ago and is still studying at present.

Examples:

Anthony Quinn *is* a great actor.   (present)

Anthony Quinn *has been* a great actor for many years.   (present perfect)

Explanation:

The present perfect differs from the simple present because the present perfect implies that an action begun in the past may not continue past the present into the future.

Consider the relationship between the present and present perfect tenses on the following continuum showing time, past to future:

Past	Present perfect	Present	Future

Words that indicate use of the present perfect tense include *for, since, just, already, yet,* and *recently.* The present perfect tense can also show that an action has just happened or occurred very recently. The words *for* or *since* are used with the present perfect to indicate that an action began in the past and has continued to the present. The words *recently, already,* and *just* are used with the present perfect to show that an action has occurred very recently.

Example:

The scientists *have just decided* to launch another telescope into space.

EXERCISE

In each of the following sentences, underline the correct verb tense. You will use the past tense or the present perfect tense depending on the meaning of the sentence.

1. In 1924, American astronomer Edwin Hubble (demonstrated, has demonstrated) that ours was not the only galaxy in the universe.

2. For the last 20 years, Professor Steven W. Hawking, widely regarded as the most brilliant theoretical physicist since Einstein, (spent, has spent) his life in a wheelchair because of Lou Gehrig's disease.

3. In 1988, Professor Hawking (wrote, has written) *A Brief History of Time,* a popular work explaining nature and the universe.

4. For decades, Professor Hawking (explored, has explored) many theories of astronomy and astrophysics, from the "big-bang" theory to black holes in space.

5. Both Aristotle and Newton (believed, have believed) in absolute time.

EXERCISE

Write three sentences in the present perfect tense using the person and number given.

1. (*to learn:* first-person singular) _____

_____

2. (*to start:* third-person plural) _____

3. (*to feel:* second-person singular) _____

_____

Past Perfect Tense

The **past perfect tense** relates two events in time with one event occurring before the other. The first action was finished or completed before the second one took place.

Examples:

Bill and Ted *worked* on the time machine yesterday.   (past)

Bill and Ted *had worked* on the antenna before they fixed the time machine.   (past perfect)

Explanation:

In the simple past, the time of the action, working on the time machine, is not identified other than our being told it happened sometime yesterday. With the past perfect, the two events took place in sequence: Bill and Ted worked on the antenna *before* they fixed the time machine.

The past perfect tense is used for an action already completed by the time of another past action, as illustrated below:

Past	Past perfect	Past	Present	Future
	had worked on the antenna	fixed the time machine		

EXERCISE

In each of the following sentences, underline the correct verb tense. You will use the past tense or the past perfect tense depending on the meaning of the sentence.

1. In the third century B.C., the ancient Greek astronomer Aristarchus (developed, had developed) the theory that the earth moved around the sun before Copernicus developed the same theory 18 centuries later.

2. Many earlier astronomers (believed, had believed) that planets were hard, polished spheres made of a jewel-like substance, perfect and unchanging,

until Copernicus' followers reasoned that the planets, like earth, may also be made of rocks, water, and mud.

3. The ancient astronomers (observed, had observed) the motion of the planets without the aid of the telescope.

4. A remarkable astronomer and mathematician, Johannes Kepler, (analyzed, had analyzed) the motions of the planets and from his observations derived three general laws of planetary motion.

5. Sir Isaac Newton (used, had used) the results of Johannes Kepler's observations to formulate his theories on the nature of gravity.

EXERCISE

Write three sentences in the past perfect tense using the person and number given.

1. (*to splash:* first-person singular) _____

   _____

2. (*to topple:* third-person plural) _____

   _____

3. (*to grow:* second-person singular) _____

   _____

Future Perfect Tense

The **future perfect tense** indicates that an action begun in the past will be completed some time in the future.

The simple future tense implies when an action will take place.

Example:

The time machine *will be* ready tomorrow morning.

In contrast, the perfect tense tells when a future action will already have been completed.

Example:

By tomorrow, Bill and Ted *will have fixed* both the antenna and the time machine.

EXERCISE

In each of the following sentences, fill in the blank with the future perfect tense of the simple verb form within the parentheses.

1. By the year A.D. 2000, the United States _____ (send) many shuttle flights into orbit.

2. The space shuttles _____ (fly) many millions of miles by the time the space station will be built.

3. Hopefully, by the turn of the century, we _____ (land) on the moon again.

4. By the middle of the twenty-second century, space exploration _____ (exist) for nearly a hundred years.

5. By the time the space station is completed, scientists _____ (develop) food-processing procedures that will provide nutritious, tasty meals that can be stored and used in outer space.

6. When we are ready to explore the solar system, scientists _____ (devise) many electronic inventions to make the long trips easier and more diverting.

7. Space workers _____ (build) a moon base by the time we are ready to visit Mars.

8. The rockets used to transport people into space _____ (be) perfected by the time we are ready to explore the rest of our solar system.

9. Emergency rescue procedures for space flights _____ (plan) before the space station is put into operation.

10. Space travellers _____ (prepare) for the effects of weightlessness prior to leaving for a trip to the moon base.

EXERCISE

In each of the following sentences, fill in the present perfect, past perfect, or future perfect form of the verb indicated.

1. (*develop:* past perfect)

   The Egyptians _____ a solar-year calendar before other nations developed their own calendars.

2. (*use:* present perfect)

   Since 1582, most of the Western world _____ the calendar of Pope Gregory XIII.

3. (*adopt:* past perfect)

   Julius Caesar _____ the Egyptian calendar before he developed his Julian calendar.

4. (*live:* past perfect)

   Previously, the Romans _____ by an eight-day week, but by the early third century A.D., they changed to a seven-day week.

5. (*complete:* future perfect)

   By June 2000, the census takers _____ collecting the population data.

6. (*create:* past perfect)

   The Egyptians _____ crude sundials, but later the Greeks, who were adept at geometry, succeeded in making many advances in sundial design.

7. (*survive:* present perfect)

   A Greek sundial in the Tower of Winds in Athens _____ for centuries.

8. (*perfect:* past perfect)

   The Greeks, who _____ the sundial to measure daylight, later developed the water clock to measure night time.

9. (*become:* past perfect)

The water clock _____ a symbol of status in ancient Roman house-

holds before the sand-filled hourglass was invented.

10. (*reach:* future perfect)

By 1992, the "Baby-Boom" children _____ school age.

WRITING ASSIGNMENTS

1: PRESENT PERFECT

What has happened to you recently and is still continuing?

Step 1: Prewriting

Using the prewriting techniques listing and mapping, think about what has happened to you during this college quarter or semester that is still continuing.

Step 2: Writing

Using the ideas you generated by the prewriting exercise, write a paragraph in the present perfect tense about the ongoing event.

Example:

I *have been* in this class for three weeks.

Step 3: Revising, Editing, and Proofreading

After you finish the paragraph, reread it to make sure all verbs are in the present perfect tense. Also check your spelling.

2: PAST PERFECT

What had you accomplished by the time you were ten years old?

Step 1: Prewriting

Using the prewriting techniques listing and mapping, think about what you accomplished in your early childhood.

Step 2: Writing

Using the ideas you generated by the prewriting exercise, write a paragraph in the past perfect tense about your childhood accomplishment.

Example:

By the time I was ten, I *had attended* school from the first to the fifth grade.

Step 3: Revising, Editing, and Proofreading

After completing your paragraph, reread it to make sure all verbs are in the past perfect tense. Also check your spelling.

3: FUTURE PERFECT

What will you have accomplished by the year 2000?

Step 1: Prewriting

Using the prewriting techniques listing and mapping, think about what you plan to accomplish by the year 2000.

Step 2: Writing

Using the ideas you generated by the prewriting exercise, write a paragraph in the future perfect tense about what you plan to accomplish.

Example:

By the year 2000, I *will have completed* my college education.

Step 3: Revising, Editing, and Proofreading

After completing your paragraph, reread it to make sure all verbs are in the future perfect tense. Also check your spelling.

9 *The Progressive Forms*

A television reporter faces the camera and narrates the scene behind him: "The presidential jet *arrived* here moments ago at the Orly Airport in Paris, France. The president *is descending* from the plane to greet the welcoming committee. He *has been trying* for some time to arrange a meeting with the French prime minister."

In addition to the simple past, *arrived,* the reporter is also using the progressive forms to describe ongoing action: *is descending, has been trying.* As you learned in Chapter 6, the progressive forms allow you to talk about actions or states of being that are currently happening, that were begun in the past and are still going on, and that will be taking place in the future. In this chapter, you will learn how to use the simple and perfect progressive forms.

Present Progressive Form

The **present progressive form** expresses an action or state of being still in progress. Use the present tense of the verb *to be* (*am, is, are*), plus the present participle (verb + *ing*) to form the present progressive. The helping verb must agree with the subject in person and number. Regular and irregular verbs form the progressive in the same way.

Examples:

I *walk.*   (simple present tense)

I *am walking.*   (present progressive)

We *are having* a party.   (present progressive)

He *is doing* his work.   (present progressive)

The present progressive form shows action still in progress. The conjugation of the present progressive is as follows.

	Singular	Plural
First Person	I am walking	We are walking
Second Person	You are walking	You are walking
Third Person	He, she, it is walking	They are walking

EXERCISE

Each of the following exercises presents two sentences. The first sentence is in the present tense. For the second sentence, change the verb to the present progressive form and fill in the blank.

Example:

I plan to go to the Monterey Aquarium.

Revision:

I am planning to go to the Monterey Aquarium.

1. I visit the Monterey Aquarium in Monterey, California.

   I _____ the Monterey Aquarium in Monterey, California.

2. The sting rays glide through the water.

   The sting rays _____ through the water.

3. A shark swims slowly at the bottom.

   A shark _____ slowly at the bottom.

4. The sea creatures in the kelp forest expect to be fed twice a day.

   The sea creatures in the kelp forest _____ to be fed twice a day.

5. The visitors watch through large observation windows.

   The visitors _____ through large observation windows.

6. The attendant feeds the sea otters four times a day.

   The attendant _____ the sea otters four times a day.

7. Dolphins communicate with each other through eerie-sounding squeals.

   Dolphins _____ with each other through eerie-sounding squeals.

EXERCISE

For each of the following, write a sentence using each of the verbs indicated in the present progressive form.

1. (to help: third-person plural) _____

_____

_____

2. (to begin: first-person singular) _____

_____

_____

3. (to help: second-person singular) _____

_____

_____

Past Progressive Form

The **past progressive form** expresses a continuous action or state of being that was begun at some time in the past.

Examples:

I *walked.*   (past tense)

I *was walking.*   (past progressive)

The past progressive form in the second example shows an action or state of being that was in progress in the past. The past progressive is formed by using the past tense of the verb *to be* (*was* or *were*), plus the *-ing* form of the verb (the present participle).

	Singular	Plural
First Person	I was walking	We were walking
Second Person	You were walking	You were walking
Third Person	He, she, it was walking	They were walking

The past progressive form can also express a continuing action or state of being tied to a specific point in time by using the words *as, when,* or *while.*

Example:

Mary *was sleeping while* the storm *raged* outside.

Explanation:

The past progressive ties the action (Mary's sleeping) to a specific time (the time *while the storm raged*). Notice that the second verb in the sentence (*raged*) is in the simple past tense.

EXERCISE

Each of the following exercises presents two sentences. The first sentence is in the past tense. Fill in the blank to change the verb in the second sentence to the past progressive form.

Example:

We went to Sea World on my birthday.

Revision:

We were going to Sea World on my birthday, but it rained all day.

1. We viewed the dolphin show at Sea World from the balcony.

   We _____ the dolphin show at Sea World from the balcony when the sun came out.

2. My friend touched the killer whale.

   My friend _____ the killer whale while the trainer made the killer whale stick out its tongue.

3. The killer whale jumped out of the water.

   The killer whale _____ out of the water while the trainer balanced himself on the whale's nose.

4. The dolphins swam on top of the water.

   The dolphins _____ on top of the water while the trainer balanced on their backs.

5. The dolphins jumped out of the water.

   The dolphins _____ out of the water while the trainer swam beneath them.

6. The killer whale splashed water on the audience.

The killer whale _____ water on the audience while they watched the show.

EXERCISE

For each of the following, write a sentence using each of the verbs indicated in the past progressive form.

1. (to study: third-person plural)

   _____

   _____

   _____

2. (to work: first-person singular)

   _____

   _____

   _____

3. (to laugh: second-person singular)

   _____

   _____

   _____

Dolphins explore their world and communicate with one another using their own language.

Future Progressive Form

The **future progressive form** expresses a continuous action or state of being that will take place in the future.

Examples:

I *will write* tomorrow.   (future tense)

I *will be writing* tomorrow.   (future progressive form)

The **simple future** means that at a specific time in the future, an action will begin. The **future progressive** means that at some time in the future, a continuing action will be in progress. The future progressive is formed by using the verb *to be* in the future tense (*will be*), plus the *-ing* form of the verb (the present participle).

	Singular	Plural
First Person	I will be walking	We will be walking
Second Person	You will be walking	You will be walking
Third Person	He, she, it will be walking	They will be walking

Point to Remember:

Sometimes the present or present progressive is used to express future action.

Examples:

I *start* my class next Tuesday.   (present tense)

I *am starting* my art class next Tuesday.   (present progressive)

EXERCISE

Each of the following exercises presents two sentences. The first sentence is in the present progressive tense. Fill in the blank to change the verb in the second sentence to the future progressive.

Example:
The San Diego Zoo is opening a new exhibition.
Revision:
The San Diego Zoo will be opening a new exhibition.

1. I am going to the San Diego Zoo tomorrow.

I _____ to the San Diego Zoo tomorrow.

2. The elephants are eating peanuts.

   The elephants _____ peanuts later.

3. The veterinarian is vaccinating the tiger cubs.

   The veterinarian _____ the tiger cubs next week.

4. The zookeeper is feeding the lions.

   The zookeeper _____ the lions in the afternoon.

5. The children are watching the pandas.

   The children _____ the pandas next.

6. The giraffes are walking across their compound.

   The giraffes _____ across their compound when feeding time

   arrives.

7. The camels are drinking 15 gallons of water.

   The camels _____ 15 gallons of water when they get thirsty.

8. A three-ton rhinoceros is watching us.

   A three-ton rhinoceros _____ us when we walk past his

   compound.

9. A child is feeding a deer some whole-wheat crackers.

   A child _____ a deer some whole-wheat crackers.

10. We are watching the spider monkeys swing from tree to tree.

    We _____ the spider monkeys swing from tree to tree after we

    look at the chimpanzees.

Progressive Forms of the Perfect Tense

The progressive forms of the three perfect tenses—present perfect, past perfect, and future perfect—are created by adding the helping verbs in a fixed order to the present participle of the main verb: first, the perfect tense helping verb *have* in some form and then the progressive form helping verb *to be* in its past participle form, *been*. The equation is as follows:

have/has/had or *will have* + *been* + present participle.

Point to Remember:

The perfect progressive forms combine the rules of the perfect tense (in telling when an action occurred) and the progressive form of the verb (an action in progress).

Examples:

I *have been working.*   (present perfect progressive)

I *had been working.*   (past perfect progressive)

I *will have been working.*   (future perfect progressive)

PRESENT PERFECT PROGRESSIVE FORM

The **present perfect progressive form** expresses an action or state of being that began in the past and continues to the present. Since it is the progressive form, it stresses continuing action.

Examples:

I *have walked.*   (present perfect tense)

I *have been walking.*   (present perfect progressive)

The present perfect progressive form in the second example shows an action or state of being that began in the past but is still in progress at present. The present perfect progressive is formed by using the present perfect tense of the verb *to be* (*have been* or *has been*), plus the *-ing* form of the verb (the present participle).

	Singular	Plural
First Person	I have been walking	We have been walking
Second Person	You have been walking	You have been walking
Third Person	He, she, it has been walking	They have been walking

Example:

The senior class *has been rehearsing* for *The Sound of Music* for six weeks.

Explanation:

In the sentence above, the class began rehearsing six weeks ago and has continued to rehearse up to the present moment.

Example:

> Stacy, Melynda, and Shelly *have been practicing* their roles as the Baroness, Liesl, and Frau Schmidt until midnight every night for the last two weeks.

Explanation:

> In the sentence above, Stacy, Melynda, and Shelly began practicing their roles two weeks ago and have continued to practice up to the present moment.

Point to Remember:

> The third-person singular of the verb *to have* in the present tense is *has.*

Incorrect Example:

> Turpin *have been working* hard for the last two weeks of rehearsals because he has two roles.

CORRECTED EXAMPLE:

> Turpin *has been working* hard for the last two weeks of rehearsals because he has two roles.

Incorrect Example:

> Melynda and Art *has been practicing* Liesl and Rolf's duet since rehearsals began six weeks ago.

CORRECTED EXAMPLE:

> Melynda and Art *have been practicing* Liesl and Rolf's duet since rehearsals began six weeks ago.

EXERCISE

Each of the following exercises presents two sentences. The first sentence is in the present perfect tense. Fill in the blank to change the verb in the second sentence to the present perfect progressive form.

Example:

John has jogged every morning this week.

Revision:

John has been jogging every morning this week.

1. I have visited EPCOT for the past three years.

   I _____ EPCOT for the past three years.

2. The fireworks have gone off.

   The fireworks _____ off for 30 minutes.

3. The sharks have attracted interest.

    The sharks _____ attracting interest since the Living Seas exhi-

    bition at EPCOT first opened.

4. The three-dimensional movie starring Michael Jackson has fascinated people

    since it opened.

    The three-dimensional movie starring Michael Jackson _____

    people since it opened.

5. The various countries in the World Showcase at EPCOT have also delighted

    many tourists since they opened.

    The various countries in the World Showcase at EPCOT _____

    tourists since they opened.

PAST PERFECT PROGRESSIVE

The **past perfect progressive form** expresses an action or state of being
that was in progress and was completed in the past. This progressive action and its
completion took place before another event in the past.

Examples:

I *had walked* for hours before I reached my destination.

I *had been walking* for hours before I reached my destination.

Explanation:

The past perfect progressive form in the second example shows an action or
state of being in progress for some period of time that was completed in the
past before another past action. The past perfect progressive is formed by
using the past perfect tense of the verb *to be* (*had been*), plus the *-ing* form of
the verb (present participle).

	Singular	*Plural*
First Person	I had been walking	We had been walking
Second Person	You had been walking	You had been walking
Third Person	He, she, it had been walking	They had been walking

Example:

    I *had been practicing* my guitar for two hours when my neighbor told me to stop.

Explanation:

    The action of *practicing my guitar* was in progress for two hours. The action was then completed in the past when another action occurred in the past tense (*my neighbor told me to stop*).

EXERCISE

Each of the following exercises presents two sentences. The first sentence is in the simple past tense. Fill in the blank to change the verb in the second sentence to the past perfect progressive form.

Example:

    I waited in line to enter EPCOT.

Revision:

    I had been waiting in line to enter EPCOT for 15 minutes before the gates opened.

1. I enjoyed EPCOT.

   I _____ EPCOT when my friend told me it was time to go.

2. We watched *Captain E-O*.

   We _____ *Captain E-O* when the three-dimensional movie starring Michael Jackson ended all too quickly.

3. My friends fed the flamingos near the Mexican Pavilion.

   My friends _____ the flamingos until the birds flew away.

4. We watched the "Illuminations" laser light show at EPCOT.

   We _____ the "Illuminations" show at EPCOT until it was over.

5. We watched the manatees at the Living Seas.

   We _____ the manatees at the Living Seas until we decided to visit the *Spaceship Earth* exhibition.

FUTURE PERFECT PROGRESSIVE

The **future perfect progressive form** expresses an action or state of being that will continue into the future and will be completed before another future action. Since it is a progressive form, it stresses continuing action.

Examples:

> I *will have walked* three hours by the time I will reach the campground.   (future perfect)

> I *will have been walking* for three hours by the time I will reach the campground. (future perfect progressive)

The future perfect progressive form in the second example shows an action or state of being that will be in progress at some time in the future and will be completed before some future action. The future perfect progressive is formed by using the future perfect tense of the verb *to be* (*will have been*), plus the *-ing* form of the verb (present participle).

	Singular	Plural
First Person	I will have been walking	We will have been walking
Second Person	You will have been walking	You will have been walking
Third Person	He, she, it will have been walking	They will have been walking

Example:

> We *will have been practicing* our songs for three months before the concert takes place on the twelfth.

Explanation:

> The action of *practicing our songs* will be in progress for three months. The action will then be completed when another future event occurs (*the concert takes place*).

EXERCISE

Each of the following exercises presents two sentences. The first sentence is in the simple future tense. Fill in the blank to change the verb in the second sentence to the future perfect progressive form.

Example:

> The guide will take you through "The Land" exhibit.

Revision:

> The guide will have been taking you through "The Land" exhibit for 20 minutes before you will see the motion picture about humans' relationship with the land.

1. We will eat lunch at the German Pavilion at EPCOT.

We _____ lunch at the German Pavilion at EPCOT for two hours before we see the dinosaurs at the World of Energy exhibition.

2. I will watch the German musicians at EPCOT.

I _____ the German musicians for 30 minutes by the time you arrive.

3. We will shop at the Chinese gift shop.

We _____ at the Chinese gift shop for quite some time before the movie about China starts.

4. In the American Adventure exhibition, an Audio-animatronic robot of Benjamin Franklin will speak to the audience.

In the American Adventure exhibition, an Audio-animatronic robot of Benjamin Franklin _____ to the audience for a short time before the robot of Mark Twain will begin talking.

5. The *Spaceship Earth,* an 18-story geosphere, will take the tourists on a time machine ride back to the dawn of civilization.

The *Spaceship Earth,* an 18-story geosphere, _____ the tourists on a time machine ride back to the dawn of civilization before the tourists will be launched into outer space to see the earth from an astronaut's point of view.

WRITING ASSIGNMENT

Imagine that you are a reporter narrating a dramatic event as it occurs, such as the arrival of the president, the opening of King Tutankhamen's tomb, or some current event such as a forest fire.

Step 1: Prewriting

Using the prewriting techniques listing and focused freewriting, write down the sequence of events that you are observing.

Step 2: Writing

Using the ideas you generated by the prewriting exercise, write a paragraph about the event in the present progressive form, using the past and future progressive whenever you can.

Example:

> I *am standing* at the bottom of the steps of the United Nations building. The delegates *are coming* toward me. They *have been debating* the current Gulf crisis for six hours now. By the end of this week, they *will have been discussing* this issue for over four months. No one *is promising* any quick solution.

Step 3: Revising, Editing, and Proofreading

After completing your paragraph, reread it to make sure that your verbs are in the present progressive form and the past and future progressive forms when necessary. The present progressive form will allow your reader to picture the events as they are happening. Also check your spelling.

10 | *Verb Tenses*

In English, verb tenses are not easy to master. The most common errors occur when writers incorrectly change tense in the middle of a sentence or paragraph without a logical reason: The king *took* the sword and *strikes* the stone. These errors confuse the reader because the timeframe jumps back and forth from one to another. It is as if your "time machine" were bouncing from the present to the future while trying to focus on the same event.

This chapter will give you some guidelines for avoiding common mistakes and for changing tense correctly.

Incorrect Tense Shifts

The most common verb tense mistake occurs when you forget the tense you started using at the beginning of a sentence or paragraph and shift to another tense.

Point to Remember:
> **Avoid shifting tenses when you are writing about events that occur in only one timeframe, whether past, present, or future.**

Incorrect Example:
> The sailboat *had* one mast with a boom that *is* nearly the length of the craft.

CORRECTED EXAMPLES:
> The sailboat *has* one mast with a boom that *is* nearly the length of the craft.
> (present tense)

> The sailboat *had* one mast with a boom that *was* nearly the length of the craft.
> (past tense)

The tense is determined by the time in which the action occurred. If the action is presently occurring, *all* of the verbs in the sentence should be in the present tense. If the action occurred in the past, *all* of the verbs in the sentence should be in the past tense.

EXERCISE

In each of the following sentences, one verb must be corrected so that all of the verbs are in the past tense. Underline the incorrect verb and write the correct verb form in the blank.

1. (past tense) _____ He rose before dawn to prepare for his trip, and his wife and children are still asleep.

2. (past tense) _____ He moved quietly around the small house while he dresses and prepared a small breakfast.

3. (past tense) _____ He heard the sound of chickens as the first rays of sunlight begin to appear.

4. (past tense) _____ His wife got out of bed and comes to the door.

5. (past tense) _____ He turned from the table and smiles at her.

EXERCISE

In each of the following sentences, one verb must be corrected so that all the verbs are in the present tense. Underline the incorrect verb, and write the correct verb form in the blank.

1. (present tense) _____ She moves gracefully toward the table, and he watched as she prepares his lunch.

2. (present tense) _____ She turned to her husband and hands him his lunch.

3. (present tense) _____ She walks outside with her husband and stood by the door as he walks down the path.

4. (present tense) _____ As he walks along the path through their small garden, he heard small animals moving through the bushes.

5. (present tense) _____ He reached the dock of rough-hewn

lumber where the boat dips and sways to the eternal motion of the tides.

Correct Tense Shifts
for Logical Sequence

Some tense shifts are correct and are used to show a particular sequence of events in which one action occurred before another.

Example:

My doctor *told* me that I ***had injured*** my back.

Explanation:

Told is in the past tense and ***had injured*** is in the past perfect to show that the *injuring* occurred before the *telling*.

Example:

Since I *signed* up for my humanities class, I ***have learned*** about the most interesting ancient civilizations.

Explanation:

Signed is a past tense verb because the writer signed up in the past at a definite time. ***Have learned*** is in the present perfect because the *learning* started in the past and is continuing.

The two paragraphs in the following exercise are taken from a story based on the painting *The Gulf Stream* by the American painter Winslow Homer.

The Gulf Stream by Winslow Homer

EXERCISE

In each of the following paragraphs, correct the verbs so that they are in the past or past perfect tense. Cross out the incorrect verb, and write the correct form above it.

A. The boat glided over the water and picks up speed as Jacques neared the center of the bay. The boat cuts through the dark water, and he narrowed his eyes against the glare of the sun. As he sailed out to sea, he waves to the other villagers who waved back to him. They shout their good wishes and return to their village. Jacques' plans were to fish off the tip of an island, so he turns to face the open sea. He reached his fishing spot in a short time, furls his sail, and settles in for a day of fishing. His luck was good, and he concentrates so hard that he does not notice the storm until the sky grew dark and the wind cold. He puts his catch in the storage boxes and prepared to wait out the storm. Jacques watches in horror as the water spout bore down on him. He wraps ropes around his wrists and prayed.

B. The water spout passed. His catch of fish washes overboard and was feeding the swarming sharks. He clung to the ropes, and the sun beats down unmercifully on him. It seems years ago that he left his dock and started out on a day of fishing. The boat rode the deep swells of the sea. The sharks

are frenzied, attacking one another as the blood

scent flooded their senses. Jacques looks around.

He saw the water spout making its way out to sea.

He squints his eyes; he barely makes out a vague

shape that seemed to be a ship trying to outrun the

storm. He felt a jolt as one of the larger sharks

bumps the bottom of his boat. Jacques was lying in

a state of exhaustion, and the bump jolts him out

of his stupor.

WRITING ASSIGNMENT

In the picture on page 129, you can see Jacques at the point where the two exercise paragraphs end. Now it is your turn to narrate the story.

Step 1: Prewriting

Using the prewriting techniques brainstorming (with classmates) and mapping, decide Jacques' fate.

What will happen to Jacques?
Will he perish at sea or be rescued in some miraculous way?

The decision is yours. You are the narrator.

Step 2: Writing

Using the ideas you generated by the prewriting exercise, write a story about Jacques, narrating events in the past tense.

Step 3: Revising, Editing, and Proofreading

After completing your narrative, review it to make sure that all of the verbs are in the past tense and that you have used the correct verb forms. Also check your spelling.

11

Mood and Fixed-Form Helping Verbs

Your writing will become more complex as you learn more about how the English language is structured. Verbs not only express intricate changes in time but also show subtle shadings of meaning through the use of different *moods*. Choosing verbs that express different moods will add variety to your sentences as well as allow you to express more subtle relationships.

This chapter introduces mood and explains how fixed-form helping verbs can enable you to express yourself more clearly.

Mood

Many people think that *mood* means soft music, candlelight, and roses, but this setting is not the mood we are talking about. In terms of language, mood describes how a verb expresses an idea.

Mood reflects how a verb is stated: as a fact (indicative mood); as a desire (subjunctive mood); as a command (imperative mood); or as a possibility (conditional mood).

INDICATIVE MOOD

The **indicative mood** is used to state a fact. Most sentences in the English language are in the indicative mood.

Examples:

The *Voyager* flights are the two most successful projects of the American space program.

Dr. Carl Sagan, Professor of Astronomy and Space Sciences at Cornell University, has played a leading role in the *Mariner, Viking,* and *Voyager* expeditions to the planets.

EXERCISE

Write five sentences in the indicative mood.

1. _____

   _____

2. _____

   _____

3. _____

   _____

4. _____

   _____

5. _____

   _____

IMPERATIVE MOOD

In the **imperative mood,** a sentence gives a command or makes a request. Imperative sentences have an "understood you" as the subject.

Examples:

Stop.

Go away.

EXERCISE

Write five sentences in the imperative mood.

1. _____

   _____

2. _____

   _____

3. _____

   _____

4. _____

_____

5. _____

_____

SUBJUNCTIVE MOOD

The **subjunctive mood** is used to express a condition contrary to fact or a wish. The plural form of the past tense expresses the subjunctive.

Examples:

If I *were* braver, I would try sky diving.   (condition contrary to fact)

I wish I *were* braver.   (wish)

The subjunctive mood is also used in a *that* clause after a verb to convey a strong suggestion or recommendation. The subjunctive uses the base of the verb (*be, go, do, move,* etc.).

Examples:

Her father suggested *that* Stacey *go* to the University of Michigan.

The committee member moved *that* the meeting *be* adjourned.

Point to Remember:

Even for a third-person singular subject such as *Stacey* that would normally take the *-s* form of the verb, we use the base form *go* for the subjunctive mood.

Some verbs that commonly take *that* clauses in the subjunctive mood are *ask, command, demand, insist, move, order, propose, recommend, require,* and *suggest.*

EXERCISE

Complete each of the following sentences with clauses that are in the subjunctive mood.

1. We suggest that _____

_____

2. He demands that _____

_____

3. Jonathan asks that _____

_____

4. The contract requires that _____

_____

5. The school board recommends that _____

_____

The most common use of the subjunctive mood is to express a wish.

Incorrect Examples:

I wish I *was* healthy, wealthy, and wise.

I wish she *was* my mother.

CORRECTED EXAMPLES:

I wish I *were* healthy, wealthy, and wise.

I wish she *were* my mother.

To form the subjunctive mood to indicate a wish, change *was* to *were*.

EXERCISE

Complete each of the following sentences with clauses that are in the subjunctive mood.

1. We wish he _____

_____

2. I wish Michael _____

_____

3. He wishes she _____

_____

4. The teacher wishes the class _____

_____

5. I wish I _____

_____

The subjunctive mood also occurs in *if* clauses that express a condition contrary to fact. The clause following the *if* clause, which states the result, must contain a fixed-form conditional helping verb. (See the next section on the conditional mood.) Other introductory words that require the subjunctive mood are *as if* and *as though*.

Examples:

> If I *were* rich, I *could* really help the homeless.
>
> If I *were* at that university, I *would* study nuclear physics.

In clauses such as these, *were* is the correct form of the verb *to be,* no matter what the subject is.

Examples:

> If she *were* my teacher, I *would* learn more.
>
> If I *were* rich, I could *travel* around the world.

EXERCISE

Complete each of the following sentences in the space provided with a result clause containing a conditional fixed-form helping verb.

1. If I were wealthy, _____

   _____

2. If John were here, _____

   _____

3. If Stacey were working, _____

   _____

4. He seems as if _____

   _____

5. The actor appears as though _____

   _____

CONDITIONAL MOOD

As you have learned in previous chapters, **helping (auxiliary) verbs** are added to the main verb to form a verb phrase. A **verb phrase** is a main verb plus one or more helping verbs. Helping verbs can be in the **changeable form** (*to have* or *to be*) or **unchangeable (fixed) form.** Unlike the changeable helping verbs, the fixed-form helping verbs do not have to change to agree with the subject.

Examples:

Changeable

I *am* dancing.   (first-person singular, present progressive tense)

You *will have* danced for two hours before the class is over.   (second-person singular, future perfect tense)

He *has* danced.   (third-person singular, present perfect tense)

Examples:

Fixed-Form

I *can* dance.   (first-person singular subject)

You *can* dance.   (second-person singular/plural subject)

He *can* dance.   (third-person singular subject)

They *can* dance.   (third-person plural subject)

Fixed-Form Helping Verbs	
shall/should	can/could
must	will/would
	may/might

Fixed-form helping verbs affect the mood of the main verb. These fixed-form verbs convey the conditions of:

Possibility: I *could* work.
                  I *can* work.
Probability: I *might* work.
                  I *may* work.
Necessity: I *must* work.
Obligation: I *should* work.

The fixed-form helping verbs differ from the changeable helping verbs *to have* and *to be* in that they cannot be the main verb nor do they have the four parts: infinitive, past, past participle, and present participle.

The two forms of the fixed-form helping verbs, present and past, do not necessarily refer to time. The two forms indicate the degree of possibility, probability, necessity, or obligation of present or future events.

These fixed-form helping verbs allow us to express subtle differences in the meanings of our sentences.

Examples:

> *Could* you fix my car?
>
> *Can* you fix my car?
>
> *Would* you fix my car?
>
> *Will* you fix my car?

Explanation:

The difference between *can* and *could* is not tense. The sentence with the present tense form *can* expresses a question about whether you are able to fix my car. The sentence with the past tense form *could* expresses a feeling of hesitation about asking if there is a possibility that you will fix my car. The subtle difference between *will* and *would* is the degree of politeness being expressed. *Will* is more emphatic; *would* is more polite.

Examples:

> You *must* fix my car.
>
> You *may* fix my car.
>
> You *might* fix my car.
>
> You *should* fix my car.

Explanation:

The first sentence using the fixed-form helping verb *must* conveys that it is necessary that you fix my car. The second sentence, using the fixed-form helping verb *may,* indicates that you have my permission to fix my car or indicates the possibility that you will fix my car. The third sentence, using the fixed-form helping verb *might,* conveys a doubt that you will in fact fix my car. *Should* denotes that you have an obligation to fix my car.

Native speakers of English usually have little trouble selecting the proper fixed-form helping verb to convey the exact meaning they intend. For nonnative speakers, however, this subtle shading of meaning is a problem.

EXERCISE

Complete each of the following sentences with a proper fixed-form helping verb according to the condition stated in the parentheses.

1. I _____ consult the dictionary when I am not sure of the spelling

   of a word.   (obligation)

2. I _____ consult a dictionary or a thesaurus when I am not sure

   of the meaning of a word.   (necessity)

3. You _____ study vocabulary often so you will not forget what you have learned.   (obligation)

4. We _____ write the meaning of the vocabulary word as well as a sentence using that word.   (necessity)

5. You _____ want to put the vocabulary list in alphabetical order before looking up the words.   (probability)

6. There are two species of spiders in the United States that _____ give a fatal bite, but dying from one of these bites is rare.   (possibility)

7. Tarantulas _____ (possibility)   look scary, but they are actually quite timid and do not give a fatal bite, so when you see a person on television fearing for his or her life from a tarantula, you _____ want to laugh.   (probability)

8. Not all skunks have stripes; some _____ be spotted such as the spotted skunk.   (possibility)

9. The marine electric rays, although not as big as manta rays, _____ (possibility)   give an electric shock of about 80 volts, so you _____ want to avoid them.   (probability)

10. Electric eels _____ (possibility)   give an electric shock of about 350 volts, so you definitely _____ avoid them.   (necessity)

WRITING ASSIGNMENT

If you could correct any mistake you've made in your life, which would it be?

Step 1: Prewriting

Using any two of the prewriting techniques, explain why you chose this particular mistake in your life.

Why is undoing this mistake more important than undoing other mistakes in your life?

How do you think your life would be different now if this mistake had not
taken place?

Do you think you would be happier?

Step 2: Writing

Using the ideas you generated by the prewriting exercise, write a paragraph
about your mistake. Use some of the various moods and fixed-form helping verbs
that you learned about in this chapter.

Example:

The worst mistake I ever made was dropping out of high school. *Maybe* if I had
been smarter, I *would have stayed* in, but I didn't. I *must have been* crazy.
I did not think that a high school diploma was a big deal. It is, however, a
doorway to college. If I *could do* it all over again, I would finish high school.

Step 3: Revising, Editing, and Proofreading

After completing your paragraph, underline the fixed-form helping verbs and
circle any verbs that are in the subjunctive mood. Also check your spelling.

12 *Verbals*

The English language is incredibly flexible. The verb drives the sentence but can also be used as other parts of speech, thus adding a greater variety of nouns, adjectives, and adverbs to the language.

A **verbal** is a verb form that is used as another part of speech: a noun, an adjective, or an adverb. There are three kinds of verbals: gerunds, participles, and infinitives. We will discuss each in turn.

Gerunds

A **gerund** is a verb form ending in *-ing* (present participle) that is used as a noun.

Example:
Talking is enjoyable.
Explanation:
The noun of the sentence is *talking* and the verb is *is.*
A gerund can also be combined with other words to form a **gerund phrase.**

Examples:
Climbing mountains is my favorite sport.

David *enjoys going to the movies.*

Explanation:
In the first example, *climbing mountains* is the gerund phrase, and *is* is the verb. In the second sentence, *going to the movies* is the gerund phrase and *enjoys* is the verb.

Jacques-Yves Cousteau prepares for a dive.

EXERCISE

Underline the gerund or gerund phrase in each of the following sentences.

1. Jacques-Yves Cousteau likes exploring the underwater world of the earth's oceans.

2. Inventing the aqualung is one of Cousteau's most important accomplishments.

3. Sailing the ship *Calypso* around the world, Cousteau took his message about saving the earth's oceans to many different nations.

4. Writing *The Silent World* and *The Living Sea* helped Cousteau inform people about the fragile beauty and wonders of the ocean.

5. Jacques-Yves Cousteau is a hero to many people because of his attempting to save the oceans.

Participles

A **participle** is either a verb form ending in *-ing* (the present participle form) or the past participle of a verb. Participles are used as adjectives.

The word *participle* comes from a Middle English word that originated from

Latin, meaning "to take part." Past participles are used not only to form the perfect tenses and for the construction of the passive voice but also as adjectives.

Example:

The *daring* acrobat **attempted** a new stunt.

Explanation:

The word (participle) to describe the *acrobat* is *daring,* and the verb is **attempted.**

Example:

The *tired* youngster **fell** asleep in his father's arms.

Explanation:

The word (participle) to describe the *youngster* is *tired,* and the verb is **fell.**

Example:

The *stolen* car **was found** in the alley.

Explanation:

The word (participle) to describe the *car* is *stolen,* and the verb is **was found.**

PARTICIPIAL PHRASES

The present participle and the past participle can be combined with other words to form a **participial phrase.**

Example:

Growing rapidly, the weeds soon **covered** the yard.

Explanation:

The participial phrase *growing rapidly* describes the *weeds,* and the verb is **covered.**

Example:

The wide receiver, *running down the field,* **caught** the football.

Explanation:

The participial phrase *running down the field* describes the *wide receiver,* and the verb is **caught.**

Example:

The tennis ball, *hit by Chris Evert,* **sailed** over the net.

Explanation:

The participial phrase *hit by Chris Evert* describes the *tennis ball,* and the verb is **sailed.**

EXERCISE

Underline the participle(s) or participial phrase(s) that are used as adjectives in each of the following sentences.

1. The boy, hitting the target with the lance, is a *page* (young attendant) of a knight.

2. Made of dirt and wood, most medieval castles were homes for the poor nobles.

3. The larger castles, built of stone, are more familiar to us.

4. Dressed in heavy clothing, the serfs labored in the fields.

5. Blooming in the springtime, the flowers provided glorious colors to brighten up the *bailey* (courtyard) of the medieval castle.

6. Shining brightly, the sun soon dried the grain that the serfs had reaped.

7. Wearing heavy armor, the medieval knights rode huge war horses.

8. The students, listening intently to the professor, learned many interesting facts about the Middle Ages.

9. Wandering minstrels told the isolated noble families tales and legends.

10. Living in the *donjon* (a wooden tower), the families of the poor nobles were safe from attack.

EXERCISE

Write five sentences using participles as adjectives.

1. _____

_____

2. _____

_____

3. _____

_____

4. _____

_____

5. _____

_____

USING THE PAST PARTICIPLE AS AN ADJECTIVE

The past participle may be used by itself or with other words as an adjective modifying a noun or pronoun. When the past participle is combined with other modifying words, the group of words is called a **verbal phrase.** Without your realizing it, your everyday conversations are filled with past participles performing their various functions.

Point to Remember:

The past participle is used to form the perfect tenses: the present perfect, past perfect, and future perfect. Each of these tenses uses a form of the verb *to have* as the helping verb.

Examples:

The *frozen yogurt* at her shop is delicious.

I am *tired*.

Explanation:

The words (past participles) *frozen* and *tired* are used as adjectives.

Examples:

I was *disturbed by the storm*. I closed all the windows.

Disturbed by the storm, I closed all the windows.

Explanation:

The first sentence, *I was disturbed by the storm,* is in the passive voice because the subject is receiving the action. To eliminate the passive construction, combine the two short sentences as in the second example: *Disturbed by the storm, I closed all the windows.*

Examples:

The car was *stolen*. The police found the car in the alley.
The police found the *stolen* car in the alley.

The yogurt is *frozen*. The yogurt in her shop is delicious.
The *frozen* yogurt in her shop is delicious.

The radio is *broken*. John can fix it.
John can fix the *broken* radio.

Each of the following exercises presents two simple sentences. Join them into one sentence by using the past participle in the first sentence as an adjective in the second sentence. Underline the past participle in the first sentence.

Example:

Professor Jones was educated. Professor Jones taught classes in archaeology.

Revision:

The educated Professor Jones taught classes in archaeology.

1. Indiana Jones is a learned professor. Indiana Jones is a professor at the university, but he becomes a fearless hero when he sets out on archaeological quests for ancient treasures.

   _____

   _____

   _____

2. The screenplay was well written. Audiences worldwide enjoyed Indiana Jones in the screenplay *Raiders of the Lost Ark.*

   _____

   _____

3. The treasure was hidden. Indiana Jones used an old map to find the treasure of the Temple of Doom.

   _____

   _____

4. Indiana Jones' father was obsessed. He tried to find the Holy Grail all his life.

   _____

   _____

5. Indiana Jones' Stetson hat was battered. In each of the three motion pictures, Indiana Jones appears wearing his leather jacket and Stetson hat and carrying his whip.

   _____

   _____

   _____

EXERCISE

In each of the following sentences, form an adjective modifying the subject by writing the past participle of the verb (in parentheses) in each blank.

Example:

(*to favor*) <u>Favored</u> by the gods, Achilles was the greatest Greek warrior.

1. (*to write*) _____ in Greek by Homer, the *Iliad* and the *Odyssey* were two epic poems.

2. (*to invent*) _____ by the ancient poets, the epic is a long narrative poem that tells the history of a race or people.

3. (*to fill*) _____ with anger and pride, the great Greek warrior Achilles is the central character in the *Iliad*.

4. (*to disturb*) _____ with King Agamemnon for taking his woman Briseis away from him, Achilles refused to fight.

5. (*to lose*) _____ without their best warrior, the Greeks were at a great disadvantage.

6. (*to protect*) _____ by the gods, Achilles could not be killed in battle unless he was wounded in the heel.

7. (*to send*) _____ into battle by the Trojans, Hector killed Achilles' best friend Patroclus.

8. (*to shake*) _____ by the death of his best friend Patroclus, Achilles rejoined the fighting to kill Hector.

9. (*to build*) _____ by the Greeks, the Trojan horse was a trick to get the Greek warriors inside the walls of Troy.

10. (*to defeat*) The _____ Trojans gave Helen of Troy back to King Menelaus.

> **EXERCISE**
>
> *In each of the following sentences, form an adjective modifying a noun by writing the past participle of the verb (in parentheses) in each blank.*

1. (*to know*)   Odysseus, _____ for his cleverness, was favored by the goddess Athena.

2. (*to send*)   All of the ships except the one that Odysseus was aboard were destroyed by storms _____ by Poseidon.

3. (*to ride*)   The crew escaped from the Cyclops on sheep, _____ by clinging to their undersides.

4. (*to maroon*)   _____ on an island, Odysseus spent seven years with Calypso.

5. (*to mean*)   Poseidon, the god of the sea, hated Odysseus and sent storms _____ to destroy him.

6. (*to throw*)   Odysseus, _____ into the sea by the storms, swam many miles before he reached land.

7. (*to collapse*)   A princess and her ladies found Odysseus _____ on the beach.

8. (*to exhaust*)   The king and queen welcomed the _____ Odysseus and gave him clothes and food.

9. (*to relax*)   After the banquet, Odysseus _____ by the generous hospitality, recounted his adventures to the other guests.

10. (*to disguise*)   Odysseus, _____ as a poor traveller, returned to his home after ten years of war and ten years of adventure.

Infinitives

An **infinitive** is a verb form that consists of the word *to* plus the base form of the verb. An infinitive can be used as a noun, an adjective, or an adverb.

Example:

> *To swim **is** enjoyable.*   (noun)

Explanation:

> *To swim* is used as a noun, and the verb is ***is.***

Example:

> It is ***time*** *to go.*   (adjective)

Explanation:

> *To go* is used as a modifier to describe the noun ***time*** and thus acts as an adjective.

Example:

> She ***turned*** *to stare at the man clothed in white.*   (adverb)

Explanation:

> *To stare at the man clothed in white* is an infinitive phrase that modifies the verb ***turned*** and thus acts as an adverb.

INFINITIVE PHRASES

As with other verbals, infinitives can also be combined with other words to form **infinitive phrases.**

Examples:

> Many people like *to go to museums.*   (noun)
>
> Bill wants *to travel to Australia this summer.*   (noun)
>
> *To visit EPCOT* is my plan for an exciting vacation.   (noun)

EXERCISE

Underline the infinitive(s) or infinitive phrase(s) in each of the following sentences.

1. Batman was created by Bruce Wayne to fight crime in Gotham City.

2. Michael Keaton was chosen to play the role of Batman while Jack Nicholson played the Joker.

3. Batman's uncanny ability to appear out of the dark night frustrated and frightened the criminals.

4. To emphasize the dark, gothic mood of the movie, the director Tim Burton used animation and special effects.

5. To create an authentic set, Tim Burton had built a five-block replica of downtown Manhattan as it looked in the 1940s.

EXERCISE

Write five sentences using infinitive phrases as nouns, adjectives, or adverbs.

1. _____

   _____

2. _____

   _____

3. _____

   _____

4. _____

   _____

5. _____

   _____

SPLIT INFINITIVES

Consider these immortal words from *Star Trek:* "To boldly go where no man has gone before." We have heard these words so often that we fail to realize that the infinitive *to go* is split by the word *boldly.* Frankly, this mistake is made so frequently in the media and everyday use that some grammarians no longer consider it a serious error.

Point to Remember:

In edited American English, it is best not to split infinitives. You should certainly be able to identify this particular construction and avoid it when possible. Split infinitives may also appear on certain grammar tests, so learn to recognize them.

Example:

Jane wants *to, **if possible,** make* an appointment with the advisor on Monday.

Explanation:

The phrase ***if possible*** has been placed between the word *to* and the verb *make.* To revise the sentence, reunite the two parts of the infinitive.

CORRECTED EXAMPLE:

If possible, Jane wants *to make* an appointment with the advisor on Monday.

Example:

John told me *to **carefully** watch* the sky for the meteor shower.

Explanation:

The adverb ***carefully*** is placed between the word *to* and the verb *watch*. To correct the sentence, move the adverb ***carefully.***

CORRECTED EXAMPLE:

John told me *to watch* the sky **carefully** for the meteor shower.

EXERCISE

Revise each of the following sentences to eliminate the split infinitive.

1. Sherlock Holmes, the greatest detective in British literature, learned to quickly solve a crime from very few clues.

   _____

   _____

2. Sir Arthur Conan Doyle did not intend for people to truly believe his character was real; nevertheless, many readers did think Holmes was a real person.

   _____

   _____

   _____

3. Dr. Watson, the quiet assistant of Sherlock Holmes, continued to constantly be amazed every time his friend solved a crime.

   _____

   _____

4. As a literary hero, Sherlock Holmes is a character to really admire for his fearlessness, bravery, and intelligence.

   _____

   _____

5. From the time the first story, "A Study in Scarlet," was written in 1887, Doyle's character began to quickly be the prototype of the ultimate detective.

   _____

   _____

WRITING ASSIGNMENT

Achilles, Hector, and Odysseus are heroes of the Trojan War in Homer's epic the *Iliad.* Sherlock Holmes, a hero in British literature, has been well loved by readers for over one hundred years. In the past decade, the cinema heroes Batman and Indiana Jones have drawn huge audiences.

Who is your favorite hero in literature or film?

Step 1: Prewriting

Using the prewriting techniques brainstorming (with classmates) and mapping, decide which heroic character in literature or film is your favorite.

Why did you choose this particular character?
What noble qualities does this hero possess?
Why do you respect this hero?

Step 2: Writing

Using the ideas you generated by the prewriting exercise, write a paragraph about your hero.

Step 3: Revising, Editing, and Proofreading

After completing your paragraph, read it and circle the verbals that you used. Also check your spelling.

UNIT THREE

Writing: Exploring Sentences

From the beginning of recorded time, humans have ceaselessly sought to explore the world around them and to make what is new and unfamiliar their own.

We build our lives on the bits of information gathered from exploring the world around us. From the parts of speech, the writer creates a new structure: the sentence.

Sailing in their many-masted ships, early explorers sought answers to the world's mysteries. Columbus searched for India but found a new world. Today, modern explorers sail in their metal ships into the darkness of outer space searching for the answers to the mysteries of the universe.

Jean François Champollion used the Rosetta Stone to decipher the ancient written language of Egypt. Modern explorers use telemetry sent from space probes like *Voyager* to decipher the language of the stars.

Humans are the great tool makers: from stone axes to masted sailing ships to space probes. But without the greatest invention, language, exploration would be impossible.

Sentences are the tools by which we explore the inner space of our minds and chart the universe of ideas through words. The writer, awash in a sea of words, must be able to build those elusive words into a pattern that will express an idea in a clear, complete manner.

Unit Three will aid you in your quest to write clearly. You will learn how to construct sentences from the simplest to the most complex. This unit also includes explanations about subject-verb agreement, sentence fragments, modifier problems, and parallelism.

Once you have mastered this skill of constructing correct sentences, Unit Four will help you learn how to use those sentences to build different types of paragraphs.

Sentence Formats

At one time, the Old English period from A.D. 450 to 1100, English was very heavily *inflected.* With an inflected language, the listener can identify parts of speech by their special word endings, not by where they appear in a sentence. German is an example of an inflected language.

Today, however, Modern English is largely uninflected. For example, no special word endings designate whether a noun is being used as a subject, direct object, or indirect object. Instead, our modern language functions by the specific placement of the words in a sentence.

Be glad that we no longer have to memorize inflected word endings. However, keep in mind that you need to place words in their proper positions in sentences or you will be misunderstood. Learning the basic sentence formats will help you correctly position words to convey the clearest possible meaning.

Syntax

Syntax is the orderly arrangement of words in a sentence. Words are not placed in a random, jumbled order but in patterns that are characteristic of the language. If words are not used in the order in which we expect to see or hear them, it is difficult to understand each other.

For instance, it is assumed that normally the subject of a sentence comes first, followed by the verb. The direct object follows the verb.

Examples:

The *dog **bit*** me.   (*dog* is the subject)

I ***bit*** the *dog.*   (*dog* is the direct object)

Placing the word *dog* before the verb ***bit*** in the first sentence certainly gives us a different message than the one we read in the second sentence. However, the word *dog* is spelled the same way in each sentence and has no special word endings.

This lack of inflection is one of the most simple characteristics of the English language. Nonetheless, many people trying to learn English find other elements of its syntax very confusing. If you have ever studied a foreign language, you can probably relate to the difficulty of learning and using another syntax. Correct syntax is crucial, however, to effective communication.

Sentence Types and Purposes

All English sentences fit into one of these four classes, which are characterized by purpose: making a statement, asking a question, giving a command, or expressing strong emotion. Learning the four purposes of sentences will help you punctuate them correctly.

Points to Remember:

1. **The declarative sentence makes a statement. The majority of sentences we write are declarative. The declarative sentence is punctuated with a period.**

   Examples:

   Dr. Carl Sagan is a noted writer and scientist.

   Isaac Asimov taught biochemistry at Boston University.

2. **The interrogative sentence asks a question. The helping verb and sometimes the main verb precede the subject. The sentence is punctuated with a question mark.**

   Examples:

   Have you seen Woody Allen's *Crimes and Misdemeanors*?   (The subject is *you*, and the verb is *have seen*.)

   Did you know that Alfred Wallace and Charles Darwin both arrived independently at the same concept of natural selection?   (The subject is *you*, and the verb is *did know*.)

3. **The imperative sentence expresses a command or request. The subject *you* is generally not stated but implied and is called a "you understood" subject. The imperative sentence is usually punctuated with a period unless an exclamation point is appropriate for added emphasis.**

   Examples:

   Open your books.   (subject: you)

   Sit down.

   Call the police.

Call the police!   (for added emphasis)

4. **The exclamatory sentence expresses surprise or extreme emotion. It always ends with an exclamation mark.**

Examples:

The car battery is dead!

I just won the lottery!

Your engagement ring is beautiful!

EXERCISE

Read each of the following sentences, and identify its purpose. If the sentence is declarative, write D. *If it is a question, write* Q. *If it is imperative, write* I. *If it is exclamatory, write* E.

1. ____   Be quiet.

2. ____   Michelangelo sculptured the *David* out of a piece of marble no one else wanted.

3. ____   Where was Michelangelo born?

4. ____   Michelangelo was born in Caprese, Italy.

5. ____   I just won two tickets to Italy!

6. ____   Carve that marble.

7. ____   Michelangelo was a Renaissance artist who was one of the greatest sculptors of all time.

8. ____   When was Michelangelo born?

9. ____   He was born in 1475.

10. ____   I would love to visit Italy!

Sentence Formats

English syntax has five basic sentence formats to help writers understand and use word order to express their ideas. These formats can be particularly helpful for students who speak English as a second language and who may be confused about how to arrange their sentences in the proper word order. The five basic formats are as follows:

1. Subject/verb
2. Subject/verb/direct object
3. Subject/verb/indirect object/direct object
4. Subject/linking verb/predicate adjective
5. Subject/linking verb/predicate nominative

1: SUBJECT/VERB
(S-V)

This sentence format, the simplest in the English language, is composed of a subject and a verb. It is the foundation for the other four sentence formats. The subject answers the questions Who? or What? does or is something.

Examples:

```
        S    V
The canary sang.
```

Explanation:

The subject is *canary*. The verb is *sang*.

EXERCISE

Underline the subject and circle the verb in each of the following sentences.

1. Fish swim.

2. Birds fly.

3. Mothers-in-law complain.

4. Rabbits hop.

5. Bees sting.

EXERCISE

In each of the following sentences, fill in the blank with a subject.

1. _____ run.

2. _____ cry.

3. The _____ broke.

4. The _____ meows.

5. _____ growl.

EXERCISE

In each of the following sentences, fill in the blank with a verb.

1. Children _____.

2. Boats _____.

3. Dogs _____.

4. Cars _____.

5. Radios _____.

EXERCISE

Make up five of your own sentences using the format (S-V).

1. _____

2. _____

3. _____

4. _____

5. _____

2: SUBJECT/VERB/DIRECT OBJECT (S-V-DO)

This format is more complex than format 1. It is composed of a subject and a verb plus a direct object. The **direct object** receives the action of the verb.

Example:

```
      S    V      DO
The pilot flew the airplane.
```

Explanation:

The subject is *pilot*. The verb is *flew*. The direct object is *airplane*. The direct object answers the questions Who? or What? The *pilot flew* what? The *airplane*.

EXERCISE

Underline the direct object in each of the following sentences.

1. Carl Sagan gave a speech.

2. Albert Einstein played the violin.

3. Japan owns Rockefeller Center.

4. The scientist blew up the lab.

5. Chernobyl spewed radiation into the earth's atmosphere.

6. The doctor vaccinates the child.

7. The virus attacks the cell.

EXERCISE

In each of the following sentences, fill in the blank with a subject, a verb, or a direct object.

1. The _____ saw the filmstrip on the Renaissance.

2. The scientist discovered _____.

3. The restaurant _____ at nine.

4. My _____ broke the window.

5. Jonathan _____ his paragraph today.

6. Marilyn _____ Chinese food.

7. Columbus _____ the Atlantic.

8. He discovered _____.

9. _____ liked the movie *Presumed Innocent*.

10. Thomas Edison invented the _____.

EXERCISE

Make up five of your own sentences using the format (S-V-DO).

1. _____

2. _____

3. _____

4. _____

5. _____

3: SUBJECT/VERB/INDIRECT OBJECT/DIRECT OBJECT (S-V-IO-DO)

This format is yet more complex and is composed of sentence format 2 plus an indirect object. The **indirect object** tells who or what receives the direct object. The indirect object always comes before the direct object.

Example:

```
    S    V   IO   DO
  Tom gave Mary a rose.
```

Explanation:

The subject is *Tom*. The verb is *gave*. The direct object is *rose*. The indirect object is *Mary*. The indirect object tells who or what receives the direct object: Tom gave a rose to whom? Mary.

EXERCISE

Underline the indirect object in each of the following sentences.

1. Benjamin Franklin handed his friend the bifocals.

2. Walt Disney gave Mickey Mouse a charming personality.

3. My brother fed his tarantula a mouse.

4. Kristi bought her mother an iguana.

5. The ancient Egyptians gave King Tutankhamen an elaborate funeral.

6. Jonas Salk gave the world a polio vaccine.

EXERCISE

In each of the following sentences, underline the direct object and double underline the indirect object.

1. In 1935, Dr. Gerhard Domagk gave his dying daughter Prontosil to cure a bacterial infection.

2. This German scientist gave the world the cure for a deadly bacteria.

3. The committee awarded Dr. Gerhard Domagk the Nobel Prize for Medicine in 1939.

Make up five of your own sentences using the format (S-V-IO-DO).

1. _____

2. _____

3. _____

4. _____

5. _____

4: SUBJECT/LINKING VERB/PREDICATE ADJECTIVE (S-LV-PA)

Any form of the verb *to be* is a **linking verb,** including such verbs as *seem, feel, look, appear,* and *become.* Linking verbs connect the word that follows them to the subject. The **predicate adjective** describes or modifies the noun that is the subject of the linking verb.

Example:

```
 S  LV  PA
Cindy is beautiful.
```

Explanation:

The subject is *Cindy.* The linking verb, which shows a state of existence, is *is.* The predicate adjective, which modifies or describes the subject, is *beautiful.*

EXERCISE

Underline the predicate adjective in each of the following sentences.

1. Tarantulas appear vicious.

2. The dolphin's skin feels soft.

3. Jellyfish look harmless.

4. The ocean looks infinitely large.

EXERCISE

In each of the following sentences, underline the predicate adjective and double underline the linking verb.

1. Michael Jordan is popular.

2. Not all octopuses become large.

3. Under a light microscope, bacteria look enormous.

4. My checking account is empty.

EXERCISE

Make up five of your own sentences using the format (S-LV-PA).

1. _____

2. _____

3. _____

4. _____

5. _____

5: SUBJECT/LINKING VERB/PREDICATE NOMINATIVE (S-LV-PN)

A noun following a linking verb is called a **predicate nominative.** The predicate nominative can identify the noun, define it, or rename it.

Example:

    S LV   PN
    Don is a soldier.

Explanation:

The subject is *Don.* The linking verb is *is.* The predicate nominative—which renames, identifies, or defines the subject, *Don*—is *soldier.*

EXERCISE

Underline the predicate nominative in each of the following sentences.

1. Insects are animals.

2. Caterpillars become butterflies.

3. Sharks are cartilaginous fish.

4. Rosetta Stone is not the name of a woman.

5. EPCOT is now a theme park created by Walt Disney before he died.

EXERCISE

Make up five of your own sentences using the format (S-LV-PN).

1. _____

2. _____

3. _____

4. _____

5. _____

WRITING ASSIGNMENT

When Dr. Domagk's daughter was dying from a streptococcal infection that resulted from a pin prick, he decided to give her an oral dose of a dye called Prontosil, which had inhibited the growth of streptococci in mice. Dr. Domagk not only saved his daughter's life but initiated a new and productive phase in modern medicine.

Which disease are you concerned about the most?
Why do you want to find a cure for it?

Step 1: Prewriting

Using one of the prewriting techniques, explain why you would find a cure for a particular disease.

Why did you choose this particular disease?
What results will come from the cure?
How will it affect our society and the lives of those with the disease?

Step 2: Writing

Using the ideas you generated by the prewriting exercise, write a paragraph about curing the disease that you chose.

Step 3: Revising, Editing, and Proofreading

After completing your paragraph, go back and label the subjects, verbs, linking verbs, direct objects, and indirect objects. Identify the types of sentence formats you have used. Make sure that you use a variety of them. Also check your spelling.

14 Subjects and Verbs

Language is perhaps humanity's greatest invention. In all the thousands of languages that have been created since the beginning of communication, the subject-verb structure is the fundamental unit of thought.

This chapter explores more complex subject-verb arrangements, helping you to identify action, linking, and helping verbs and to find the real subject of a sentence. The more you understand how to use these subject-verb arrangements, the more varied and interesting your writing can be. This chapter covers simple subjects and verbs and compound subjects and verbs, as well as how to find the real subject.

Simple Subjects and Verbs

The **simple subject** is the main word or group of words that comprise the subject. It can be singular or plural. Even one-word commands have an understood simple subject, *you*. The subject answers the questions Who? or What? does or is something.

Every sentence contains both a subject and a verb, even the simplest one-word commands:

Examples:

Stop.

Jump!

Look.

Each contains an action verb and the understood subject, *you*.

Examples:

(You) Stop.

(You) Jump!

(You) Look.

After one-word commands, the next shortest sentences in the English language contain two words, a subject that is clearly stated and a verb:

Examples:

John stops.
They stop.

He jumps.
Children jump.

Mary looks.
They look.

EXERCISE

Underline the simple subject and circle the verb in each of the sentences below.

1. The dolphin jumped 20 feet out of the water.

2. We found a tiny kitten on our front porch.

3. Black holes in the universe mystify astronomers.

4. American Indians hunted buffalo for food and clothing.

5. Coral snakes are extremely poisonous.

EXERCISE

Write five short sentences using a simple subject and verb.

1. _____

2. _____

3. _____

4. _____

5. _____

Point to Remember:

Adjectives and other modifiers are not included in the simple subject unless they are part of a proper noun. *The Washington Bridge gleams in the light.* In this sentence, *Washington Bridge* is the simple subject, not just *Bridge.*

Simple verbs can be action or linking verbs. Helping verbs are added to action and linking words to create various verb tenses and forms. Each of these verbs can be used for different effects in your writing and can help you to identify the real subject of a sentence.

ACTION VERBS

As you learned in Chapter 3, **action verbs** tell what the subject is doing. When you find the action verb in a sentence, you will be able to identify the subject performing the action by asking Who? or What? *does* something. These verbs are lively, energetic words that add power to your sentences.

Example:
> The fire *raged* out of control.

Explanation:
> The verb is *raged.* What raged? The *fire. Fire* is the simple subject.

Example:
> The trees *toppled* with a deafening crash.

Explanation:
> The verb is *toppled.* What toppled? The *trees. Trees* is the simple subject.

Some Action Verbs				
break	call	draw	drive	explode
explore	fall	hit	jump	laugh
leap	ride	shout	think	throw

EXERCISE

Complete each of the sentences below by filling in the blank with an action verb.

1. Curt _____.

2. Dogs _____.

3. Superman _____.

4. Cats _____.

5. Paul McCartney _____.

EXERCISE

Write seven sentences that describe your daily activities using action verbs. When you finish, underline the action verbs.

1. _____

2. _____

3. _____

4. _____

5. _____

6. _____

7. _____

LINKING VERBS

Some verbs in English describe or identify the subject. When you find the **linking verb,** you can locate the subject by asking Who? or What? *is* something. These verbs are called *linking verbs* because they link or connect the subject to a predicate adjective or predicate nominative.

Examples:

```
        S    V    PN
Kangaroos are mammals.
```

```
   S    V    PA
Tigers look majestic.
```

```
        S    V      PN
Paul McCartney is a rock musician.
```

```
             S    V    PA
The scuba gear feels comfortable.
```

Explanation:

Find each verb and ask Who? or What? *is* or *are, looks* or *feels.* The answer will be the subject of the sentence.

The most common linking verb is the verb *to be* (*am, is, are, was, were*).

Other Linking Verbs

act*	appear*	become
feel*	get*	look*
remain*	seem	smell*
sound*	stay*	taste*

*These verbs can be action verbs, too.

Point to Remember:

It is not difficult to determine whether a verb such as *act* or *smell* is an action or linking verb if you look carefully at the words that follow. If those words describe or identify the subject before the verb, the verb is a linking verb.

Examples:

The shark *looks* scary.   (linking verb)
The shark *looks* at his prey.   (action verb)

The scuba gear *feels* comfortable.   (linking verb)
I *feel* the wet suit clinging to my body   (action verb)

The pizza *tastes* good.   (linking verb)
I *taste* the pizza.   (action verb)

The perfume *smells* exotic.   (linking verb)
I *smell* the perfume.   (action verb)

EXERCISE

The linking verb in each of the following sentences has been double underlined. Underline the subject in each sentence.

1. Walt Disney became world famous for creating Mickey Mouse.

2. Gold is a precious metal.

3. Spaghetti tastes delicious.

4. The audience remained calm.

5. Calculus seems difficult.

EXERCISE

Underline the linking verb in each of the following sentences.

1. Confucius became one of the most important Chinese philosophers.

2. The construction of the Great Pyramid at Giza remains a mystery.

3. Queen Elizabeth I was the greatest ruler of the Renaissance.

4. The Renaissance became a time of great learning and exploration.

5. Was Leif Ericson the first explorer to discover America?

6. Wolfgang Amadeus Mozart's harpsichord music sounds beautiful.

7. The rain forests of Brazil stay hot and humid all year.

EXERCISE

The verb in each of the sentences below has been underlined. In each space provided, put an A if the verb is an action verb and an L if the verb is a linking verb.

1. ____   Christopher Columbus accidentally discovered America while trying to find the East Indies.

2. ____   Florence Nightingale was the founder of modern nursing.

3. ____   Johann Gutenberg invented movable type and type metal in the fifteenth century.

4. ____   Hammurabi was a Babylonian king in 1792 B.C.

5. ____   Hammurabi became famous for creating the Code of Hammurabi, a list of Babylonian laws.

6. ____   King Nebuchadnezzar built the Hanging Gardens of Babylon for his wife in the sixth century B.C.

7. ____   The Hanging Gardens of Babylon was one of the seven wonders of the ancient world.

8. ____   Mary Shelley created the character of Frankenstein in her famous novel.

9. ____ A computer virus <u>replicates</u> itself in other computers.

10. ____ Silver <u>is</u> a precious metal and an excellent electrical conductor.

Write seven sentences describing a person you know. Use a linking verb from the list provided (see page 171) in each sentence. After you finish, underline the linking verb,

1. _____

2. _____

3. _____

4. _____

5. _____

6. _____

7. _____

HELPING VERBS

Both action and linking verbs can be used either by themselves or with one or more **helping verbs.** When a verb is used by itself as the main verb, it is either in the present or the past tense.

Examples:

Tourists *go* to Disney World for their summer vacation.   (present tense)

Many tourists *went* to Disney World last year.   (past tense)

All other forms of the verb are made by adding one or more helping verbs, which are also called **auxiliary verbs,** such as *will, has, have, is, am, do,* and *are.*

Examples:

Many tourists *are going* to Disney World this year.

Many tourists *will go* to Disney World next year.

Many tourists *have gone* to Disney World already.

Point to Remember:

When you are looking for the verb, remember to include the helping verb as well as the main verb in order to find the complete verb in any sentence.

The goslings follow their imprinted mother, Konrad Lorenz.

EXERCISE

Each of the following sentences contains only one verb. Underline it.

1. Konrad Lorenz was the father of ethology, the scientific study of animal behavior.

2. Konrad Lorenz discovered the concept of animal imprinting.

3. The baby duck views his first visual object as his mother.

4. In the experiment, the ducklings followed Lorenz's boots.

5. Konrad Lorenz won the Nobel Prize for Medicine in 1973.

EXERCISE

In each of the following sentences, one or more helping verbs is used before the main verb. The number of blanks before each sentence tells you the number of words that make up the complete verb. Write the complete verb in the blanks, and circle the main verb.

1. _____ _____ _____ Konrad Lorenz had been working with baby ducks for many years.

2. _____ _____ The ducklings had mistaken Lorenz's yellow boots for their mother.

3. _____ _____ A newly hatched duckling will follow any slowly moving

person or object.

4. _____ _____ Imprinting may have long-term consequences.

5. _____ _____ The scientist's concept of instinct has changed over the

years.

Compound Subjects and Compound Verbs

COMPOUND SUBJECTS

A sentence may have more than one subject, which is called a **compound subject.** Compound subjects are joined by a conjunction and take a plural verb. To find the compound subject, find the verb and ask Who? or What? *does* or *is* something.

Examples:

>   S   S   V
> *Fish* and *seals* swim.

>   S   S   V
> *Barracuda* and *sharks* look scary.

>   S   S   V
> *Pizza* and *spaghetti* taste good.

EXERCISE

Underline the compound subject in each of the following sentences.

1. Paul McCartney and Eric Clapton are rock musicians.

2. Gold and silver are precious metals.

3. Christopher Columbus and his crew accidentally discovered America.

4. Florence Nightingale and her staff of nurses helped the wounded in the Crimean War.

5. Disney World, EPCOT, and MGM Studios are three tourist attractions in Florida.

EXERCISE

Write five sentences about your favorite summertime activities using compound subjects.

1. _____

2. _____

3. _____

4. _____

5. _____

COMPOUND VERBS

It is possible for a sentence to have more than one main verb. Two or more verbs joined by a conjunction are called **a compound verb.**

Examples:

    S   V   V
John *stops* and *looks.*

    S   V   V
She *sneezed* and *coughed.*

    S   V   V
Carla *pouts* and *sulks.*

      S   V   V   V
Thomas Edison *perfected* the lightbulb, *invented* the phonograph, and *devised* a motion picture system.

EXERCISE

Underline the compound verb in each of the following sentences.

1. Albert Einstein was concerned about the misuse of nuclear power and warned the government about its danger.

2. Queen Elizabeth I reigned for many years and was the greatest ruler of the Renaissance.

3. The Renaissance became a great time of learning and produced many famous artists and inventors.

4. Hammurabi was a Babylonian King and became famous for his code of laws.

5. King Nebuchadnezzar built the Hanging Gardens of Babylon and gave it to his wife for a present.

EXERCISE

Write five sentences using compound verbs. Make sure the compound verbs are in the same tense, person, and number. (They all refer to the same subject.)

1. _____

2. _____

3. _____

4. _____

5. _____

BOTH COMPOUND SUBJECTS AND VERBS

A sentence may contain both a compound subject and a compound verb.

Examples:

    S   S   V   V
Pizza and *spaghetti smell* and *taste* good.

          S   S   V   V
Christopher Columbus and his *crew sailed* across the sea, *discovered* America,

          V
and *traded* with the Indians.

  S   S V   V
Gold and *silver are* precious metals and *conduct* electricity well.

      S   S   V   V
The *scuba gear* and *wet suit feel* comfortable and *are* easy to use.

EXERCISE

Each of the sentences below has both a compound subject and a compound verb. Underline the subject and circle the verb. Be sure to mark all subjects and verbs.

1. Florence Nightingale and her nurses treated the wounded and saved many lives in the Crimean War.

2. Hammurabi and his wife enjoyed the Hanging Gardens of Babylon and visited it often.

3. Albert Einstein and other scientists feared the atom bomb and warned the government of its dangers.

4. Baby ducks and goslings followed Konrad Lorenz and viewed him as their mother.

5. Konrad Lorenz, Karl von Frisch, and Niko Tinbergen studied animal imprinting and found instinct to be a powerful force.

6. Paul McCartney and Eric Clapton are great rock musicians and have sold millions of records.

7. Sharks and barracuda swim quickly and are aggressive carnivores.

Finding the Real Subject

How do you find the real subject of a sentence? The first simple step is to find the verb. Then ask Who? or What? Some sentences, however, are not so straightforward. Knowing how to find the subject will be very helpful in working through the next chapter, "Subject-Verb Agreement." Here are some guidelines to keep in mind.

Points to Remember:
1. **The subject of a sentence can *never* be the object of a preposition. Crossing out prepositional phrases can help you locate the real subject of the sentence.**

   Examples:
Preposition	*Object of the Preposition*
on	the beach
through	the dark woods
during	the late afternoon
on behalf of	my client
due to	unforeseen circumstances

   Avoid confusing the subject of a sentence with the object of a preposition. The preposition connects a noun or noun substitute (pronoun) to the rest of the sentence. Prepositions combined with nouns and

their modifiers, if any, form prepositional phrases. A prepositional phrase always has at least one noun or pronoun as the object of the preposition.

Example:

The girl *in the black evening gown* stood at the door.

Explanation:

The verb is *stood.* Ask *Who stood?* The *girl.* Therefore, *girl* is the subject. *Gown* is not the subject because it is in the phrase *in the black evening gown,* which modifies *girl.*

Example:

Neither *of the boys* complained about the cold.

Explanation:

The verb is *complained. Who complained? Neither.* Therefore, *neither* is the subject. *Boys* is in the prepositional phrase *of the boys* and cannot be the subject.

Single-Word Prepositions

aboard	about	above	across
after	against	along	among
around	as	at	before
behind	below	beneath	beside
between	beyond	but (= "except")	by
concerning	despite	down	during
except	for	from	in
inside	into	like	near
of	off	on	onto
out	over	past	regarding
since	through	throughout	till
to	toward	under	underneath
until	up	upon	with
within	without		

Compound Prepositions

along with	apart from	as for
as of	as to	aside from
because of	by means of	by way of
contrary to	due to	except for
for the sake of	in addition to	in behalf of
in case of	in favor of	in front of

in place of	in regard to	in spite of
in view of	next to	on account of
on behalf of	regardless of	with regard to
with respect to	with the exception of	

2. The subject is *never* found in a modifying clause. Crossing out the clause can help you find the real subject.

Example:
The hero *who helped Athens win countless battles* was named Pericles.
Explanation:
The verb is *was named. Who was named?* The *hero.* Other nouns such as *Athens* and *battles* are in the clause modifying *hero* and cannot be the subject of the sentence.

Example:
The tulips *that bloom in spring* are planted in the early fall.
Explanation:
The verb is *are planted. What are planted? Tulips* is the subject. *Spring* is in the clause modifying *tulips* and cannot be the subject.

EXERCISE

In each of the following sentences, draw a line through the prepositional phrase and circle the subject.

1. The aqualung was invented by Jacques-Yves Cousteau.

2. The discovery of King Tutankhamen's tomb was a great archaeological find.

3. Howard Carter discovered the tomb in 1922.

4. Dr. Carl Sagan is concerned about the ecology of our planet.

5. Marco Polo was a Venetian explorer famous for his journey to China in 1271.

EXERCISE

In each of the following sentences, draw a line through the prepositional phrase or clause and circle the subject.

1. Sir Edmund Hillary with his guide Tenzing Norkay reached the summit of

   Mount Everest, the world's highest mountain, in 1953.

2. Orville and Wilbur Wright on December 17, 1903, flew the first successful aircraft at Kitty Hawk, North Carolina.

3. Wernher Von Braun, in spite of the danger, came to America in 1945 and later helped put the first American satellite into orbit.

4. Von Braun, who was assisted by American scientists, also developed the Saturn rocket and pioneered the concept of the space shuttle.

5. Paul Cézanne, who is among the most influential painters of modern time, was French.

6. Geoffrey Chaucer, because of his composition of the *Canterbury Tales,* became one of the first great poets and established English as a literary language.

7. Buddha, at the age of 29, experienced human misery for the first time and searched for the path to peace and serenity.

8. George deMestral, of Swiss engineering fame, invented Velcro in 1948.

9. The black scientist, George Washington Carver, due to his many experiments with the peanut, discovered many uses for it and introduced the practice of crop rotation to farmers.

10. Dr. Carl Sagan along with Richard Turco and other scientists discovered the threat of nuclear winter.

3. **To find the subject in a question turn the question into a statement.**

Example:
Where did you put my purple gloves?   (question)

You did put my purple gloves where.   (statement)

Explanation:
The verb is *did put. Who did put? You.* Therefore, *you* is the subject of the sentence, not *gloves* or *where.*

4. *Here* and *there* are generally not the subjects of verbs. They are adverbs or expletives used to start a sentence. Watch out for these impostors when you are looking for the real subject.

Example:
Here are the Great Smoky Mountains.
Explanation:
The verb is *are. What are? Great Smoky Mountains.* In this sentence, *here* is an adverb telling where the mountains are.

Example:
There is some truth to what you say.
Explanation:
The verb is *is. What is? Truth. Truth* is the subject while *there* is an expletive used to start the sentence and *to what you say* is a prepositional phrase.

EXERCISE

In each exercise below, the sentence begins with the expletive here *or* there. *Underline the subject in each sentence.*

1. There are many excellent Indian actors in the movie *Dances with Wolves.*

2. Here is a picture of Kevin Costner, who plays Lieutenant John Dunbar in the film.

3. There is an Omaha Indian, Rodney Grant, who plays the warrior Wind in His Hair, the spirit and backbone of the Indian community Dunbar encounters.

4. Here is a copy of the official pictorial book *Dances with Wolves* that explains how the film was created.

5. There is a buffalo hunt in the screenplay that is one of the most exciting scenes of the movie.

6. There are 24 Indians riding bareback with Kevin Costner as they race with 3,000 buffalo.

7. Here is an epic movie that portrays the beauty of the lost frontier and the grandeur of the American Indian.

Avoiding Sentence Fragments

As you have learned in this chapter, every sentence must have a subject and verb to express a complete thought. However, many beginning writers mistakenly leave out the subject or the verb or both in their rush to put ideas down on paper. The result is known as a **sentence fragment.**

Examples:

Took the stone to the temple.

Explanation:

You cannot answer the question Who? or What? took the stone because this group of words lacks a subject. To correct the fragment, add a noun or pronoun that completes the meaning of the sentence.

CORRECTED EXAMPLES:

Indiana Jones took the stone to the temple.

He took the stone to the temple.

Example:

The rope bridge over the gorge.

Explanation:

This fragment contains a Who? or What? word (*bridge*) and a prepositional phrase (*over the gorge*). However, there is no verb to complete the thought. To correct the fragment, add an action or linking verb.

CORRECTED EXAMPLE:

The rope bridge *swayed* over the gorge.   (action verb)

The rope bridge over the gorge *seemed* strong.   (linking verb)

Chapter 19, "Sentence Fragments," offers a more detailed look at how to detect and correct fragments in your writing.

EXERCISE

Correct the fragments in the paragraph below by adding subjects or verbs as needed.

```
    Of all the famous Revolutionary War people, I

would choose to talk with Benjamin Franklin.

Because a writer, politician, and inventor. Impor-

tant in the early history of our country. Franklin
```

```
was born in Boston in 1706. And died 1790. Meeting

this interesting man. He a printer. Also made money

so he could experiment in science and participate

in politics. Ask what gave him the idea for his

Franklin stove and bifocals and how felt when

lightning struck his kite. Also, I interested in

his writing Poor Richard's Almanac, a parody of

weather predictions and folk wisdom. My conver-

sation with Benjamin Franklin fascinating.
```

WRITING ASSIGNMENT

You have been chosen to hold a conversation with any famous person in history. To whom do you want to talk?

Step 1: Prewriting

Using two of the prewriting techniques explained in Chapter 1, freewriting and mapping, decide on a historical person.

Why did you choose this particular historical figure for your conversation?
How do you feel about meeting this famous person?
What are you going to discuss during the conversation?

Step 2: Writing

Using the ideas you generated by the prewriting exercise, write a paragraph describing what you will talk about or ask.

Step 3: Revising, Editing, and Proofreading

After completing your paragraph, label the subjects and verbs. Then identify whether each verb is an action verb or a linking verb. Also check your spelling.

15 *Subject-Verb Agreement*

Many students feel bewildered by the rules for subject-verb agreement. Granted, they are not always clear. Yet once you understand the basic guidelines, you will be able to determine the real subject and the correct verb for any sentence regardless of tense or form. This skill will help you revise your writing and make sure your meaning is clear.

This chapter covers basic subject-verb agreement, singular subjects, plural subjects, and exceptions in singular and plural subjects.

Basic Subject-Verb Agreement

When the subject and verb agree, they both have the same **person** (first, second, or third) and the same **number** (singular or plural). In most situations, this rule is simple to follow.

First-person singular	I *am* fascinated by the history of the American Indian tribes.
Second-person singular	You *like* American Indian folklore.
Third-person singular	Each Indian tribe *believes* that its territory is donated to it by the Great Spirit.
First-person plural	We *need* to learn more about Indian traditions and customs.
Second-person plural	*Are* you aware that the Indians believe that nature is infused with spirit life?
Third-person plural	In *Dances with Wolves,* the Indian actors *wear* their own eagle feathers because it is only legal for Indians to possess them.

While subject-verb agreement seems at first to be a minor problem, sometimes even the simplest sentences can be confusing. The confusion comes about because most common nouns and verbs form their plurals in directly opposite ways: All regular nouns form their plurals by adding -*s* or -*es*; however, most verbs add an -*s* only in the third-person singular.

EXERCISE

Underline the correct verb in each of the following sentences.

1. Archaeology (is/are) the study of historic or prehistoric peoples and their culture.

2. Artifacts (is/are) any objects made by people in ancient cultures.

3. Archaeologists (use/uses) many scientific techniques.

4. Excavation (is/are) a painstaking procedure.

5. Archaeologists (discover/discovers) artifacts all over the world.

EXERCISE

Underline the correct singular or plural subject in each of the following sentences.

1. The (pyramid/pyramids) are burial tombs for Egyptian pharaohs.

2. The (pharaoh/pharaohs) were the kings of ancient Egypt.

3. Huge (statue/statues) line the Temple of Rameses II.

4. In 1968, the (temple/temples) was moved to higher ground because the Egyptians built the Aswan Dam.

5. The (reconstruction/reconstructions) was an amazing feat accomplished by modern technology.

Singular Subjects

Some subjects seem to require plural verbs when in fact they are singular and require singular verbs.

> ## Overview: Singular Subjects
>
> Singular subjects require singular verbs:
>
> 1. Compound subjects introduced by *many a, such a, no, every, each*
> 2. Collective nouns when considered as a unit
> 3. The name of a book, quotation, clause, title, or group of words expressing a single idea
> 4. Some nouns joined by *and* but considered to be a unit
> 5. Mathematical problems or plural nouns of quantity when considered as one unit
> 6. Plural-form nouns, such as *politics, mathematics*
> 7. Certain indefinite pronouns, such as *no one, everyone*
> 8. The pronouns *either, neither*
> 9. The introductory word *i t*

We will discuss each of these singular subjects in turn.

Points to Remember:

1. **When a compound subject is introduced by *many a, such a, no, every,* or *each*, the verb is singular.**

Examples:

           S   S   V
Many a *field* and *stream* ***is*** being polluted today.

           S   S   V
Such a *sight* and *spectacle* ***is*** not unusual.

       S   S   S   V
No *man, woman,* and *child* ***wants*** to be ignored.

          S   S   V
Every *museum* and *library* ***is*** interesting.

         S   S   V
Each *book* and *magazine* ***is*** a source of information.

EXERCISE

Underline the correct verb in each of the following sentences.

1. Many a child and mother (is/are) smiling.

2. Such a prize and possession (is/are) rare.

3. No flower and plant (grow/grows) on the moon.

4. Every boy and girl (love/loves) presents.

5. Each towel and washcloth (has/have) my initials on it.

2. **Collective nouns—such as *army, band, jury, navy,* and *team*—are considered singular and require a singular verb when all of the members of the group are considered as one unit.**

   Examples:

          V
   The *team **is*** ready for the game.

          V
   The *jury **was*** late in returning to the courtroom.

   Examples of Collective Nouns

audience	company	government
choir	crew	group
clan	crowd	school
class	family	society
college	flock	tribe
committee	herd	

   ## EXERCISE

   Circle the correct verb for the collective noun in each of the sentences below.

   1. Each society (have/has) special customs.

   2. The school (is/are) for marine biologists.

   3. The tribe (is/are) bilingual.

   4. The choir (sing/sings) in the key of E minor.

   5. The committee (has/have) an important decision to make about the environ-ment.

3. **When a subject is a title, a clause, a quotation, or some other group of words expressing a single idea, the verb is singular.**

Examples:

      S   V

*Crimes and Misdemeanors **is** Woody Allen's best movie.*

      S   V

*"To be or not to be" **is** the most famous line in William Shakespeare's tragedy*
Hamlet, Prince of Denmark.

         S   V

*Butch Cassidy and the Sundance Kid **stars** Robert Redford and Paul Newman.*

EXERCISE

Circle the correct verb in each of the following sentences.

1. The movie *Bonnie and Clyde* (was/were) Faye Dunaway's first hit.

2. "Walk softly and carry a big stick" (are/is) a famous quotation by Teddy Roosevelt.

3. Leo Tolstoy's *War and Peace* (is/are) a Russian novel about Napoleon's defeat in Moscow.

4. "In God we trust" (are/is) printed on the dollar bill.

5. "This note is legal tender for all debts, public and private" (are/is) also printed on the dollar bill next to George Washington's portrait.

4. Some nouns that are joined by *and* but thought of as a unit are singular.

Examples:

       V

*Ham and eggs **is** a favorite breakfast dish in America.*

            V

*The Stars and Stripes **flies** over every government building in America.*

         V

*Tuna and mayonnaise **is** my favorite sandwich spread.*

EXERCISE

Circle the correct verb in each of the following sentences.

1. Spaghetti and meatballs (are/is) my favorite Italian dish.

2. Oil and vinegar (is/are) a good salad dressing.

3. Baseball and football (are/is) my favorite sports.

4. Bagels and lox (is/are) a traditional Jewish favorite.

5. A horse and buggy (are/is) still used by the Amish in Pennsylvania.

6. Chicken and yellow rice (is/are) a traditional Spanish dish.

7. Gold and platinum (is/are) precious metals.

5. **Plural nouns of quantity (when considered as one unit) and mathematical problems take singular verbs.**

Examples:

        V
*Ten miles **is** a long distance to jog on a hot day.*

           V
*Sixty pounds **is** a lot of weight to lose.*

         V
*Five dollars **is** the price for an evening movie.*

            V
*Two times two **is** four.*

     V
*Forty **is** a sacred number in the Old Testament.*

             V
*Eleven plus eleven **is** twenty-two.*

Circle the correct verb in each of the following sentences.

1. Five pounds (seem/seems) to be all he can lose.

2. Ten times six (is/are) sixty.

3. Fifty dollars (are/is) a lot to spend for designer jeans.

4. Twenty-six miles (is/are) the length of the Boston Marathon.

5. Four fluid ounces (are/is) half a cup.

6. **Some nouns that are plural in form require singular verbs. The following nouns, although they end in *-s*, always take a singular verb:**

civics   economics   mathematics
measles   molasses   mumps
news   physics   politics

Examples:

V
*The news **is** on television at midnight.*

V
*Politics **is** a touchy subject for some people.*

EXERCISE

Circle the correct verb in each of the following sentences.

1. Measles (are/is) a dangerous disease for adults.

2. Mathematics (is/are) the basis for all fields of science.

3. Algebra (is/are) my favorite class.

4. These pants (are/is) expensive.

5. Molasses (has/have) a bitter taste.

6. Physics (are/is) the science that deals with energy, matter, motion, and force.

7. Her new crystal glasses (are/is) from Austria.

7. These indefinite pronouns take a singular verb:

anybody   anyone   anything
each   everybody   everyone
everything   no one   nobody
nothing   one   somebody
someone   something

Examples:

V
*Everybody **needs** water.*

V
*Everything **has** energy if it has mass, according to Einstein's equation $E = mc^2$.*

V
*Something **is** amiss.*

EXERCISE

Underline the correct verb in each of the following sentences.

1. Everybody (does/do) his homework.

2. Both of the rides at the amusement park (is/are) scary.

3. No one (has/have) to hand in her homework today.

4. One (need/needs) a clean, well-lighted place.

5. Few of the explorers (want/wants) to miss the opportunity to visit Australia.

6. Something (smell/smells) good in your kitchen.

7. Everyone (calculate/calculates) numbers in physics class.

8. *Either* and *neither,* when used as pronouns, are singular and require a singular verb.

Note: Remember that the object of the preposition can never be the subject. Notice also that a prepositional phrase comes between the subject and verb in the first three examples.

Examples:

                V
Neither of the men **has** climbed Mount Rushmore.

                    V
Neither of the politicians **has** spoken at the meeting.

                V
Either of the models **is** currently available.

       V
Neither **is** here today.

EXERCISE

Underline the correct verb in each of the following sentences.

1. Neither of the explorers (has/have) found the Holy Grail.

2. Either of the books (explain/explains) the trigonometry problem.

3. Either of the paintings (is/are) beautiful, but neither (are/is) for sale.

4. Neither of the television programs (help/helps) promote education.

5. Neither (is/are) able to attend the stockholder's meeting.

9. **The introductory word *it* is always followed by a singular verb whether the noun that follows is singular or plural. *It* in this case is called an *expletive* because the word prepares the way for the subject that will follow the verb. Nevertheless, the word *it* controls the verb, and the verb is always singular.**

Try to avoid overusing *it is* or *it was* to begin sentences in college writing. But if you do use *it* to begin a sentence, make sure you use a singular form of the verb.

EXERCISE

Underline the correct verb in each of the following sentences.

1. It (was/were) the Greek playwrights who first developed the tragedy as an art form.

2. It (are/is) the children who will benefit from the conservation of the environment.

3. It (were/was) King Hammurabi who developed the first code of law.

Plural Subjects

Most common nouns in the English language can change form from singular to plural. The plural subject must take a plural verb.

Note: If the noun forms its plural by adding -s or -es, there will never be an -s on the end of the verb form.

EXERCISE

In each of the following sentences, underline the plural verb for the plural subject.

1. Rockets (is/are) necessary for space travel.

2. The whales (migrates/migrate).

3. Explorers (risk/risks) their lives searching for gold and other treasures.

4. Scientists (works/work) to find cures for diseases that affect people.

5. Writers (spend/spends) long hours developing ideas.

Again, most nouns are singular and can be changed to plural, but there are some exceptions.

Overview: Plural Subjects

Plural subjects require plural verbs:

1. Nouns with no singular form, such as *pants, scissors*
2. Compound subjects joined by *and*
3. Certain indefinite pronouns, such as *few, many*
4. Collective nouns when considered as individuals

We will discuss each of these plural subjects in turn.

Points to Remember:

1. **Some nouns have no singular form and are always plural. The following nouns have no singular form:**

gallows	scales	tongs
glasses (for eyes)	scissors	trousers
pants	suds	tweezers
pliers	thanks	

EXERCISE

Underline the correct verb in each of the following sentences.

1. The scissors (is/are) on the drawing table.

2. Suds (fill/fills) the kitchen sink.

3. My glasses (is/are) bifocals.

4. His trousers (fits/fit) well.

5. Thanks (is/are) in order for everyone who worked on the committee.

6. Her pants (matches/match) her blouse.

7. The doctor's scales (is/are) accurate.

8. Tweezers (are/is) helpful in removing splinters.

9. Pliers (assist/assists) in loosening tight bolts.

2. Compound subjects joined by *and* require plural verbs. If you have difficulty with compound subjects, consider the *and* as a plus sign, and add the subjects together.

Example:

S   S   V

Stanley and *Livingstone* ***are*** famous explorers of Africa.

Explanation:

Stanley + *Livingstone* = plural verb ***are.***

EXERCISE

Underline the correct verb in each of the following sentences.

1. Mark Twain and Kurt Vonnegut (is/are) two famous American writers of satire.

2. Sir Walter Raleigh and Sir Francis Drake (was/were) members of Queen Elizabeth's court.

3. Calvin and Hobbes (is/are) two delightful cartoon characters.

4. Spooks and ghouls (hide/hides) under Calvin's bed at night.

5. Sir Francis Drake and his crew (is/are) famous for sailing around the world.

6. Scissors and thread (is/are) necessary for sewing.

7. Lisa and Jeff (are/is) newlyweds.

3. The indefinite pronouns *few, many, both,* and *several* are plural.

Examples:

V

Few of the guests ***leave*** early.

V

Many of the rain forests ***are*** in danger of destruction.

V

Both of the sisters ***are*** intelligent.

V

Both ***are*** intelligent.

V

Several of the tropical fish ***are*** poisonous.

EXERCISE

Underline the correct verb in each of the following sentences.

1. Many of the microbiologists (conduct/conducts) research on deadly viruses.

2. Several of the experiments (has/have) exciting results.

3. Both of the scientists at the laboratory (work/works) with electron microscopes.

4. A few of the scientists (become/becomes) famous while most live in obscurity.

5. Few of us (appreciate/appreciates) the years of hard work needed to find a cure for a disease.

4. **Collective nouns require a singular verb when treated as a unit and a plural verb when considered as individuals.**

Examples:
Singular Verb

The *team is* ready for the game.
    (*Team* is treated as a single unit.)

The city *council is* interested in this issue.
    (The *council* is viewed as a single body.)

Plural Verb

The *team are* recovering from their injuries.
    (Individual members on the team were injured and cannot be regarded as a unit.)

The city *council are* divided on this issue.
    (Individual members disagree; the subject cannot be treated as a single unit.)

Exceptions: Special Singular and Plural Subjects

The most difficult situations in subject-verb agreement occur in the following cases, which are exceptions to regular rules. Because these cases are more difficult than the others you have learned, they often appear on tests and exams.

Overview: Exceptions

1. *Either-or, neither-nor* constructions
2. Indefinite pronouns that can be either singular or plural
3. The word *number*
4. An intervening phrase or clause
5. *Who, which, that* as intervening clauses
6. Sentences starting with the words *there, here*
7. *Who, which, that* as modifiers
8. In questions

Again, we will consider each exception in turn.

Points to Remember:

1. **When compound subjects are joined by *either-or* or *neither-nor*, the verb must agree with the subject closest to it.**

Example:

            S   S   V

Neither the *lioness* nor her *cubs* **were** hungry.

Explanation:

Since the subject, *cubs,* is closest to the verb, the verb must be plural: ***were.***

Example:

            S   S   V

Neither the *cubs* nor the *lioness* **was** hungry.

Explanation:

Since the subject, *lioness,* is closest to the verb, the verb must be singular: ***was.***

Example:

        S   S V

Either *you* or *I* **am** correct.

Explanation:

Since the subject *I* is closest to the verb, the verb must be singular: ***am.***

Always remember that with the *either-or, neither-nor* construction, the subject nearest the verb determines whether the verb is singular or plural.

EXERCISE

Underline the correct verb in each of the following sentences.

1. Neither Abraham Lincoln nor his parents (was/were) wealthy.

2. Neither his parents nor Abraham Lincoln (was/were) aware that one day he would become president.

3. Either Iceland or Greenland (is/are) a cold but beautiful country to visit.

4. Either the books or the magazine (contains/contain) good information.

5. Either the magazine or the books (contains/contain) good information.

6. Neither dolphins nor whales (is/are) fish.

2. ***All, none, most, some, half,*** **and fractions other than half are singular if they refer to quantity and plural if they refer to number.**

Example:

V
All of the *wine **is*** in the cellar.

Explanation:
In this sentence, *all* refers to quantity, not number; therefore, the subject is singular and requires a singular verb: ***is.***

Example:

V
All of the *pencils **are*** on the desk.

Explanation:
All refers to the number of *pencils;* therefore, the subject is plural and requires a plural verb: ***are.***

EXERCISE

Underline the correct verb in each of the following sentences.

1. None of the bread (contain/contains) cholesterol.

2. All of the pyramids (was/were) tombs for the Egyptian kings.

3. Some of the roses (is/are) from South America.

4. Three-fourths of a cup (is/are) six fluid ounces.

5. Half of a yard (is/are) 18 inches.

6. All of my house plants (are/is) doing well.

3. **The word *number* preceded by *a* requires a plural verb; the word *number* preceded by *the* takes a singular verb.**

Examples:

$\overset{\text{V}}{ }$

A *number* of students ***have*** signed up for the test.

$\overset{\text{V}}{ }$

The *number* of students ***is*** 120.

EXERCISE

Underline the correct verb in each of the following sentences.

1. The number of documents in my computer (is/are) large.

2. A number of these documents (is/are) important.

3. The number of people using personal computers (is/are) rising.

4. A number of people (has/have) problems with their computers.

5. The number of computers used in schools (is/are) increasing.

4. **An intervening phrase or clause does not influence whether the subject is singular or plural. Words that come between the subject and verb do not affect the subject-verb agreement.**

Example:

$\overset{\text{S}}{ }$ $\overset{\text{V}}{ }$

The *pyramids* ~~in Egypt~~ ***are*** thousands of years old.

Explanation:

The subject of the sentence, *pyramids,* is plural; therefore, the verb ***are*** is also plural. The words *in Egypt* are a prepositional phrase. These intervening words do not affect the subject-verb agreement in the sentence.

Note: Remember that the object of a preposition can never be the subject of a sentence

Example:

S   V

The *pyramids,* standing along the Nile River, **symbolize** the transition from prim-
itive tribal life to organized social living.

Explanation:

The subject of the sentence, *pyramids,* is plural; therefore, the verb **symbolize** is also plural. The intervening words *standing along the Nile River*
modify and describe the subject *pyramids* and do not affect the subject-verb
agreement.

EXERCISE

Underline the correct verb in each of the following sentences.

1. The massive pyramids outside the city of Cairo (is/are) the only one of the

   Seven Wonders of the Ancient World that still survives.

2. The Seven Wonders of the Ancient World (constitute/constitutes) the great-

   est examples of ancient architecture, art, and technology.

3. Greek and Roman authors of the ancient world (was/were) the compilers of

   the list of ancient Wonders.

4. The names on the list first (appears/appear) in the year 130 B.C.

5. Historians and scholars of the twentieth century (regret/ regrets) not being

   able to view the six lost Wonders of the Ancient World.

6. The Great Sphinx, towering 66 feet above the swirling desert sands, (has/

   have) fascinated people for centuries.

7. The Sphinx, built of stone from the quarry used for the Giza Pyramids, (was/

   were) once buried up to its neck in sand.

8. The Great Sphinx, sculptured by many masons, (has/have) the idealized face

   of Pharaoh Chephren.

9. Egypt's stone obelisks, raised in honor of the sun god, (is/are) granite pillars that weigh an average of 150 tons.

10. One of these obelisks, named Cleopatra's Needle, (was/were) moved from Egypt to London.

5. When *who, which,* and *that,* along with modifying words, come between the subject and the verb, they do not affect the subject-verb agreement.

Example:

S   V
The mighty *pharaoh,* who ruled thousands of ancient Egyptians, *was treated* as a living god.

Explanation:

The subject of the sentence, *pharaoh,* is singular; therefore, the verb *was treated* is singular also. The intervening words *who ruled thousands of ancient Egyptians* do not affect subject-verb agreement in this sentence.

EXERCISE

Underline the correct verb in each of the following sentences.

1. The Hanging Gardens of Babylon, which was built by King Nebuchadnezzar, (is/are) the second Wonder of the Ancient World.

2. The Temple of Artemis and the Statue of Zeus, which both once existed in Greece, (is/are) two more of the Seven Wonders of the Ancient World.

3. The Statue of Zeus that was built at Olympia (was/were) considered the most famous statue of the ancient world.

4. The statue, which was 40 feet high, (was/were) created by the famous Greek sculptor Phidias.

5. The statue, which had robes and garments of gold and flesh of ivory, (was/were) breathtaking.

6. **When you start a sentence with *there* or *here,* the subject comes after the verb. If the subject is singular, the verb is singular. If the subject is plural, the verb is plural.**

Note: The words *there* and *here* can never be the subject of a sentence.

Example:

<pre>
      V   S
</pre>
There *is* no *evidence* remaining of six of the Seven Wonders of the Ancient World.

Explanation:

The word *there* at the beginning of the sentence serves as an introduction to the subject that comes after the verb *is.* Since the subject, *evidence,* is singular, the verb *is* is also singular. The word *there* can never be the subject of a sentence.

Example:

<pre>
      V   S
</pre>
Here *are* the *Seven Wonders of the Ancient World:* the Pyramids of Egypt, the Hanging Gardens of Babylon, the Temple of Artemis at Ephesus, the Statue of Zeus, the Mausoleum at Halicarnassus, the Colossus of Rhodes, and the Lighthouse of Alexandria.

Explanation:

The word *here* serves as an introduction to the subject: the *Seven Wonders of the Ancient World.*

EXERCISE

Underline the correct verb in each of the following sentences.

1. Here (is/are) a small map of ancient Greece.

2. Here (is/are) maps of the ancient world.

3. There (was/were) many marvels of the ancient world that disappeared long ago.

4. There (is/are) a possibility that scientists will find the remains of the Hanging Gardens of Babylon.

5. There (is/are) no greater thrill than seeing the Great Pyramid and the Sphinx.

7. **The words *who, which,* and *that* require a singular verb if the noun or pronoun they modify is singular and a plural verb if the noun or pronoun they modify is plural.**

The Great Pyramid and the Sphinx rise above the desert sand as
perpetual mysteries to all who see them.

Example:

V

Zeus, who **was** the chief god of the Greeks, plays an important role in Greek
mythology.

Explanation:

The verb **was** is singular because it agrees with the pronoun *who. Who* is
singular because it refers to *Zeus,* a singular proper noun.

Example:

V

The *Greeks, who* **were** the first great philosophers of Western culture, are still
considered to be the greatest thinkers of all time.

Explanation:

The verb **were** is plural because it agrees with the pronoun *who. Who* is
plural because it refers to *Greeks,* a plural proper noun.

EXERCISE

Underline the correct verb in each of the following sentences.

1. Mausolus, who (was/were) a provincial leader in the Persian Empire, is famous for his large tomb.

2. The tomb, which (was/were) 135 feet high, was so famous that now all large modern tombs are called *mausoleums*.

3. The Lighthouse of Alexandria, which (was/were) 400 feet high, was visible for 30 miles at sea.

4. The lighthouses that (exist/exists) today are all based on the design of the ancient Egyptian lighthouse.

5. The ancient sailors, who (was/were) at sea, were delighted to see the first rays of light from this Egyptian lighthouse.

6. The Greeks and Romans, who (was/were) amazed at the size of the Egyptian pyramids, were unaware of their religious importance as tombs.

8. **The verb agrees with the subject even if the verb comes before the subject. In questions, the subject usually follows the verb.**

   Example:

      V   S

   Who ***was*** the *sculptor* who created the Statue of Zeus?

   Explanation:

   The subject of the sentence is *sculptor,* which is singular. Therefore, the verb must be singular: *was.*

EXERCISE

Circle the correct verb and underline the subject in each of the following sentences.

1. (Has/Have) you visited Greece?

2. Where (was/were) the ancient ruins of King Nebuchadnezzar's Hanging Gardens?

3. Why (was/were) the Egyptian pyramids built?

4. How (does/do) the modern archaeologist search for ancient treasures?

5. (Is/Are) you interested in ancient history?

6. When (was/were) the Great Sphinx built?

WRITING ASSIGNMENT

In this chapter, you have read about the Seven Wonders of the Ancient World. Make up an Eighth Wonder of the World, selecting from the art, architecture, or technology of the modern world.

Step 1: Prewriting

Using the prewriting techniques freewriting and listing, decide which modern Wonder of the world to choose.

What made you decide to choose this particular modern Wonder?
Where is it located?
What do you think makes it so important?

Step 2: Writing

Using the ideas you generated by the prewriting exercise, write a paragraph about your modern Wonder.

Step 3: Revising, Editing, and Proofreading

After completing your paragraph, identify the subjects and the verbs. Circle each subject and underline each verb, making sure that they agree. Also check your spelling.

16 *The Four Sentence Patterns*

Considering the thousands of words in the English language and the infinite number of sentences that can be constructed by combining them, it is remarkable that there are only four basic patterns underlying all English sentences. The four sentence patterns are:

1. the simple sentence
2. the compound sentence
3. the complex sentence
4. the compound-complex sentence

Learning how to use these four patterns correctly will enable you to improve your sentence variety, use language more vividly, and discover how flexible the English language is in conveying precise meaning to your audience.

Simple Sentences

A **simple sentence** is made up of a single independent clause. An **independent (main) clause** has both a subject and a complete verb, and it expresses a complete thought.

Examples:

My father is a biochemist.

A square has four equal sides.

The sun is a star.

Marco Polo travelled to China.

EXERCISE

Underline the subject and circle the verb in each of the following simple sentences.

1. Gregor Mendel was a monk.

2. He was born in Austria in 1822.

3. He was ordained as a monk at the age of 25.

4. He died in Czechoslovakia in 1884.

5. Gregor Mendel was also an Austrian botanist.

6. Gregor Mendel did his research with pea plants.

7. His work remained unknown until the 1900s.

EXERCISE

Fill in the missing subject or verb in each of the following simple sentences.

1. _____ took our ferret to the veterinarian.

2. I _____ my car yesterday.

3. _____ was president of the United States.

4. The diamond _____ no flaws.

5. Women _____ flowers.

6. The _____ tasted good.

EXERCISE

Place an F for fragment and an S for simple sentence in front of each of the following examples.

1. ____ Carefully looking into the microscope.

2. ____ I chose the path less travelled.

3. ____ Going to the mall this afternoon.

4. ____ Astronauts walked on the moon's surface.

5. ____ Colorado is a beautiful state.

6. ____ Swimming in the ocean at night.

7. ____ The astronomer at the planetarium.

8. ____ Looking over his shoulder.

Make up five of your own simple sentences.

1. _____

2. _____

3. _____

4. _____

5. _____

Compound Sentences

A **compound sentence** is composed of two or more simple sentences, that is, two or more independent (or main) clauses.

Examples:

My father is a brilliant biochemist, and my mother is a poet.

A triangle has three sides, a square has four sides, and a pentagon has five sides.

The sun is a star, and the earth is a planet.

Marco Polo travelled to China; he also spent time in prison.

I like deep sea fishing; however, I do not get to go very often.

Points to Remember:

As you can see from the examples above, the independent clauses that make up a compound sentence can be joined in several ways.

1. By a comma and a coordinating conjunction (see the first three sentences)
2. By a semicolon (see the fourth sentence)
3. By a semicolon and a conjunctive adverb followed by a comma (see the last sentence)[1]

[1]See Chapter 17, "Coordination," for more information about punctuating compound sentences.

Place a C *in front of each compound sentence and an* S *in front of each simple sentence.*

1. ____ Charles Darwin was born in 1809 and died in 1882.

2. ____ Darwin was an explorer, and he was a naturalist.

3. ____ Darwin was an explorer and a naturalist.

4. ____ Darwin formulated the theory of evolution by natural selection.

5. ____ Darwin sailed on a boat, and the name of the boat was the HMS *Beagle.*

6. ____ Darwin studied birds, turtles, and other animals.

7. ____ Alfred Russel Wallace came up with the same theories of evolution, but Darwin received more credit.

8. ____ Alfred Russel Wallace was born in 1823; he died in 1913.

Make up five of your own compound sentences.

1. _____

2. _____

3. _____

4. _____

5. _____

Complex Sentences

A **complex sentence** is composed of one independent clause and at least one dependent clause. In contrast to the independent (main) clause, the **dependent (subordinate) clause** has both a subject and a complete verb but does not express a complete thought. Therefore, it cannot stand alone.

Example:

After it rains, our yard is flooded.

In the example above, the dependent clause *After it rains* comes first in the sentence and is followed by the independent clause *our yard is flooded*. When the dependent clause begins the sentence, it is separated from the independent clause by a comma. Special words—called **subordinating conjunctions**[2]—are used to begin dependent clauses, including *after, if,* or *because*.

When the independent clause comes first in the sentence and is followed by the dependent clause, no comma is necessary.

Example:

Our yard is flooded *after it rains.*

EXERCISE

Underline the dependent clause in each of the following complex sentences.

1. After they left Tahiti with breadfruit tree seedlings, the crew of the HMS *Bounty* mutinied on April 28, 1789.

2. Because he was too cruel, the crew set Captain William Bligh and 18 loyal sailors adrift.

3. When the crew mutinied, Fletcher Christian, the first mate of the ship, was chosen to be the leader.

4. Although they were in an open boat, Captain Bligh and the sailors reached Timor in the East Indies after a remarkable journey of 4,000 miles.

5. Because 16 of the mutineers decided to stay in Tahiti, only Fletcher Christian, 8 mutineers, and 18 Tahitians sailed to Pitcairn Island.

6. The crew of the HMS *Bounty* mutinied on April 28, 1789, after they left Tahiti with breadfruit tree seedlings.

7. The crew set Captain Bligh and 18 loyal sailors adrift because he was too cruel.

8. Fletcher Christian, the first mate of the ship, was chosen to be the leader when the crew mutinied.

[2]See Chapter 18, "Subordination," for more information on punctuating complex sentences.

9. Captain Bligh and the sailors reached Timor in the East Indies after a remark-able journey of 4,000 miles although they were in an open boat.

10. Only Fletcher Christian, 8 mutineers, and 18 Tahitians sailed to Pitcairn Island since 16 of the mutineers decided to stay in Tahiti.

EXERCISE

Make up five of your own complex sentences.

1. _____

2. _____

3. _____

4. _____

5. _____

Compound-Complex Sentences

A **compound-complex sentence** contains at least two independent clauses with at least one dependent clause connected to one of the independent clauses. Because of the complexity of this sentence pattern, it is often the most difficult to punctuate. However, using it adds diversity and complexity of thought to your writing.

Examples:

> Before the dance was over, my friends and I left early; we went to a restaurant and talked for hours.

> As the fashion model walked down the runway, the audience applauded, and the designer was pleased.

Points to Remember:

1. **A semicolon often separates the final independent clause from the rest of the sentence.**
2. **The dependent clause will always begin with one of the subordinating conjunctions.[3] When you locate the subordinating conjunction, you have found the dependent clause.**

---

[3]See Chapter 18, "Subordination," for information on punctuating compound-complex sentences.

Subordinating Conjunctions

1. Contrasting or conditional relationship:
   although, even though, if, though, unless, whereas
2. *Where,* expressing a locational relationship:
   where, wherever
3. *When,* expressing a time relationship:
   after, as, as long as, as soon as, before, once,
   till, until, when, whenever, while
4. *Why,* expressing a cause-and-effect relationship:
   as if, as though, because, in order that, provided, since

EXERCISE

In each of the following compound-complex sentences, underline the dependent clause, and circle the subordinating conjunction.

1. After the mutineers reached Pitcairn Island, Fletcher Christian and his companions stripped the HMS *Bounty* of all usable material; on January 23, 1790, they burned the ship.

2. Although Fletcher Christian wanted an island paradise, the group had problems from the start; ten years later, only one man, 11 women, and 23 children had survived.

3. Because it was isolated from the outside world, the Pitcairn community learned to be self-supporting, and the inbreeding through marriages of cousins has had no ill effects on the modern descendants.

4. Since the story of the *Bounty* mutiny was first told in a trilogy of novels written by James Hall and Charles Nordhoff, three different movies about it have been produced, and three famous actors have portrayed Fletcher Christian.

5. Clark Gable played the central character, Fletcher Christian, in the first movie and was nominated for an Academy Award in 1935; Marlon Brando is famous for his interpretation of the Fletcher Christian character in the second version while Mel Gibson portrayed Christian as a romantic hero in the third version.

EXERCISE

Make up five of your own compound-complex sentences.

1. _____

2. _____

3. _____

4. _____

5. _____

Learning to use a variety of sentence patterns will make your writing more sophisticated and enjoyable to read. It will also free you from relying time after time on the same, monotonous sentence pattern.[4]

WRITING ASSIGNMENT

Against great odds, the small group of people who were marooned on Pitcairn Island survived, and their descendants live there to this day. Suppose you have been marooned on a deserted island. What items will you need to survive until you are rescued?

Step 1: Prewriting

Use the prewriting techniques listing and mapping to determine which items you will need to have with you.

Why did you choose these items?
How will you use them to survive?

Step 2: Writing

Using the ideas you generated by the prewriting exercise, write a paragraph using a variety of sentence patterns to describe your effort at survival.

Step 3: Revising, Editing, and Proofreading

After completing your paragraph, examine each sentence in it and identify the sentence pattern used. If you have relied too heavily on one or two types of sentence patterns, go back and revise your paragraph. Also check your spelling.

[4]See Chapter 25, "Sentence Variety."

17 *Coordination*

Chapter 16 reviewed the four basic sentence patterns that provide the models for all English sentences. In this chapter, you will take a close-up view of the second sentence pattern: the compound sentence. You will learn how to use coordinating conjunctions, conjunctive adverbs, and semicolons to coordinate two or more equal ideas into one smoothly flowing compound sentence. The compound sentence shows relationships between equal ideas. Using it will add variety to your writing.

Joining Independent Clauses

A single sentence may contain one or more ideas that may be equal or unequal in importance. When the ideas are equal, they are called **coordinate** ideas.

Examples:

Mr. Jones teaches virology.

Ms. Jones teaches bacteriology.

Explanation:
Both of these complete ideas are equal in importance.

These sentences can be combined to form a **compound sentence,** a sentence that has two or more independent clauses. When you combine the clauses in the new sentence, the clauses are called **coordinate clauses.** There are three ways to join coordinate clauses to form a sentence: using a coordinating conjunction, using a conjunctive adverb, or using a semicolon.

COORDINATING CONJUNCTIONS

To combine the two coordinate clauses, you can use a **coordinating conjunction.**

Coordinating Conjunctions	
1. *for*	because
2. *and*	plus, addition
3. *nor*	not one or the other
4. *but*	in contrast, except
5. *or*	represents alternatives
6. *yet*	same as *but*
7. *so*	subsequently, as a result

A way to remember the seven coordinating conjunctions is through the word *FANBOYS*. *FANBOYS* is a mnemonic device in which each letter stands for one of the coordinating conjunctions: *For, And, Nor, But, Or, Yet, So.*

Point to Remember:

Note that a comma always precedes the coordinating conjunction when it is used to join two coordinate clauses to form a compound sentence.

Example:

Mr. Jones teaches virology, *and* Ms. Jones teaches bacteriology.

Explanation:

The two coordinate clauses are properly joined with a coordinating conjunction (*and*) and a preceding comma. These are two complete and independent ideas joined to form a compound sentence.

Examples:

I did not go to the dance, *nor* did I want to.

Mary would like to freewrite, *so* she can feel uninhibited.

I always use my dictionary, *for* it is an important writing tool.

Amber likes to write at her own pace, *but* there is often a time limit.

I should do some reading tonight, *or* I will fall behind in my studies.

Mapping seems like an unusual prewriting technique, *yet* it works.

EXERCISE

*Use the correct coordinating conjunction (*for, and, nor, but, or, yet, so*) and the correct punctuation to complete each of the following sentences.*

1. The scientist has a full supply of glassware _____ he will not have to stop

   to clean up in the middle of an experiment.

2. Scientists are wrongly blamed for many of the earth's ecological problems _____ people still expect them to come up with the answers to diseases.

3. Charles Darwin did not intend to cause a problem with his theory of natural selection _____ he was unjustly accused.

4. All squares are rectangles _____ all rectangles are not squares.

5. Charles Darwin came up with the idea of natural selection _____ Alfred Wallace came up with the same idea independently.

6. I want to be a biologist _____ I want to be an archaeologist.

7. I would rather study physics next year _____ I have not had trigonometry.

8. William Shakespeare was Christopher Marlowe _____ Christopher Marlowe was William Shakespeare.

9. I do not believe the above statement _____ desperate graduate students still need something about which to write.

10. I would like to see what the Romantic era was like _____ I would not want to live in that time period because there were no modern conveniences.

EXERCISE

Complete each of the following sentences by adding another idea after the coordinating conjunction.

1. I will pay my registration fees today, *for* _____

2. You must pay for your books in cash, *or* _____

3. I would love to take an ecology class, *but* _____

4. She never leaves home without her calculator, *yet* _____

5. He likes to carry his book bag, *so* _____

_____

6. She is applying to work at Disneyland in the fall, *and* _____

_____

7. I will take Freshman English in the summer, *for*_____

_____

8. She used a dictionary and a thesaurus while she wrote, *but* _____

_____

9. Tracy and Chris are taking physiology, *but*_____

_____

10. Latin is a difficult language to learn, *so* _____

_____

CONJUNCTIVE ADVERBS

The second way to join two independent clauses is to use a **conjunctive adverb** (**adverbial conjunction**). A conjunctive adverb, preceded by a semicolon and followed by a comma, can be used instead of a comma and a coordinating conjunction to form a compound sentence. Furthermore, conjunctive adverbs show the relationship between the two independent clauses.

Examples:

Shangri-La may be a legend; *however,* it continues to excite the imagination.

The mystics of Tibet search for a spiritual peace on earth; *therefore,* it is appropriate that the Dalai Lama has been awarded the Nobel Prize for Peace.

Explanation:

The conjunctive adverb *however* in the first sentence is used to express a contrast. The conjunctive adverb *therefore* in the second sentence indicates a result. Each of these conjunctive adverbs show the relationship between the two independent clauses.

Incorrect Example:

Mr. Jones worked in his lab, *then* he worked in Ms. Jones' lab.

CORRECTED EXAMPLE:

Mr. Jones worked in his lab, **and** *then* he worked in Ms. Jones' lab.

Explanation:

The coordinating conjunction *and* is needed to join the two ideas.

Example:

Mr. Jones worked in his lab; *then,* he worked in Ms. Jones' lab.

Explanation:

There is no coordinating conjunction in this sentence. To combine the two sentences using *then,* a semicolon is needed before *then* and a comma after *then* because *then* is a conjunctive adverb. *Then* is not a coordinating conjunction.

Conjunctive adverbs can be grouped under the following relationships:

1. To show contrast: *even so, however, nevertheless, on the other hand, rather, still*
2. To show a time relationship: *currently, earlier, later, meanwhile, next, then*
3. To show addition: *additionally, also, furthermore, in addition to, likewise, moreover, similarly*
4. To show an alternative: *instead , otherwise*
5. To show a result: *consequently, hence, overall, primarily, therefore, thus*
6. To express emphasis: *in fact, indeed, to be sure*

EXERCISE

Use the correct conjunctive adverb and the correct punctuation to complete each of the following sentences.

1. There is nothing more thrilling than an ocean cruise to Alaska _____ you should plan your trip for the summer.

2. Alaska is a wonderful place to visit _____ it is one of the last wilderness areas of the world.

3. Sailing around the Greek Islands is relaxing _____ the scenery is breathtakingly beautiful.

4. There is nothing more exhilarating than seeing new places _____ every year millions of tourists travel to foreign countries.

5. First, you can visit France _____ you can tour the art centers in Italy.

6. You may not prefer to fly around the world _____ you may want to take a leisurely ocean cruise.

Complete each of the following sentences by adding another idea after the semi-colon, conjunctive adverb, and comma.

1. A trip across the United States is educational and entertaining; *therefore,* ____

   _____

2. A vacationer could first surf in the giant waves of the Hawaiian Islands; *then,*

   _____

3. Of course, travelling is expensive; *nevertheless,* _____

   _____

4. A traveller can ski or hike in Switzerland; *furthermore,* _____

   _____

5. Visiting Paris is the fantasy of many women; *moreover,* _____

   _____

6. Many people only visit the major cities in foreign countries; *on the other hand,*

   _____

7. England, France, and Spain are among the most popular countries to visit; *in fact,* _____

   _____

8. Many tourists join guided tours; *otherwise,* _____

   _____

9. Many travellers prefer to vacation in warm, sunny climates; *however,* _____

   _____

10. A vacation to Australia should be taken during the winter months in the United States; *later,* _____

   _____

SEMICOLONS

The third way to join two independent clauses is to use a **semicolon.** One of the primary purposes of punctuation is to provide a pause between elements of language. The semicolon does not have as long a pause as a period, but it has more of a pause than a comma. If you use a comma instead of a semicolon, it will be incorrect. This mistake is known as a *comma splice.*

Example:

> The ideal vacation would be both entertaining and educating; a trip across America is an ideal vacation.

Explanation:

The semicolon is used to join the two independent clauses. Notice that the two sentences are similar in thought and logically connected. If the semicolon is omitted, a serious error called a *run-on sentence* is created.

Common Conjunction Errors

The two most common errors are the run-on sentence and the comma splice. Many writers, even good ones, make these mistakes. Watch out for them. They make your writing confusing and hard to read.

RUN-ON SENTENCES

When two independent clauses are joined and no coordinating conjunction, conjunctive adverb, semicolon, or punctuation of any kind is used, the words literally run on. Thus, the mistake is called a **run-on sentence (fused sentence).**

Incorrect Example:

> The ideal vacation would be both entertaining and educating a trip across America is an ideal vacation.

CORRECTED EXAMPLE:

> The ideal vacation would be both entertaining and educating; a trip across America is an ideal vacation.

Explanation:

This run-on sentence is corrected by adding a semicolon between the two independent clauses.

EXERCISE

The following sentences are all run-on. Correct each by using one of the three options:

a. A comma + coordinating conjunction (for, and, nor, but, or, yet, so)
b. A semicolon + conjunctive adverb + comma
c. A semicolon

1. There are many churches and cathedrals in Paris the cathedral of Notre Dame de Paris is by far the largest.

   _____

   _____

2. The Louvre Museum in Paris was once a royal residence and treasury now it contains some of the most priceless art treasures in the world including the *Mona Lisa* by Leonardo da Vinci.

   _____

   _____

   _____

3. The excavations at Pompeii, Italy, have been in progress for more than two hundred years some two-fifths of the city is still buried under volcanic pumice and ash caused by the explosion of the volcano Vesuvius on August 24 in the year A.D. 79.

   _____

   _____

   _____

   _____

4. Ancient Rome held many architectural wonders many of these buildings were destroyed during the Renaissance in the 1400s by architects and builders who wanted to use the old stones to build new buildings.

   _____

   _____

   _____

5. The Roman Forum today lies in ruins they are fascinating to visit.

   _____

6. Over half of the Colosseum in Rome is still standing tourists are not allowed to enter all parts because of its fragile condition and the threat of its collapsing.

   _____

   _____

7. One ancient building in Rome built in A.D. 126 is the Pantheon the building is still in perfect condition and has a concrete dome with an opening called an *oculus* at the top 30 feet across to let in the light.

_____

_____

_____

8. In Istanbul, Turkey, stands the beautiful Hagia Sophia, or "Holy Wisdom," the building was once the principal church of Constantinople.

_____

_____

_____

9. In 1453, the Turks turned Hagia Sophia into a mosque the modern Turkish state has converted the mosque (a Moslem temple) into a museum for all visitors to see.

_____

_____

_____

10. Florence, Italy, was the birthplace of the Renaissance it contains today some of the greatest works of the Renaissance including Michelangelo's statue *David*.

_____

_____

_____

COMMA SPLICES

Another common error is the **comma splice** that is formed when a sentence contains two independent clauses that are joined with just a comma.

Incorrect Example:

The ideal vacation would be both entertaining and educating, a trip across America is an ideal vacation.

Points to Remember:

A comma splice can be corrected in the following ways:

1. Add a coordinating conjunction (*for, and, nor, but, or, yet, so*) after the comma.
2. Delete the comma, and add a semicolon.
3. Delete the comma, and add a semicolon + conjunctive adverb + comma.

CORRECTED EXAMPLES:

The ideal vacation is entertaining and educational, and a trip across America would be an ideal vacation.

The ideal vacation is entertaining and educational; a trip across America would be an ideal vacation.

The ideal vacation is entertaining and educational; therefore, a trip across America would be an ideal vacation.

Explanation:

The two independent clauses are now properly joined by one of the three methods. This helps the reader better understand the connection between the two ideas in the sentence.

EXERCISE

The following sentences are the same sentences you corrected in the exercise on run-on sentences. Now each sentence contains a comma splice. Correct each by using one of the three options.

1. There are many churches and cathedrals in Paris, the cathedral of Notre Dame de Paris is by far the largest.

   _____

   _____

2. The Louvre Museum in Paris was once a royal residence and treasury, now it contains some of the most priceless art treasures in the world including the *Mona Lisa* by Leonardo da Vinci.

   _____

   _____

   _____

3. The excavations at Pompeii, Italy, have been in progress for more than two hundred years, some two-fifths of the city is still buried under volcanic pumice and ash caused by the explosion of the volcano Vesuvius on August 24 in the year A.D. 79.

   _____

_____

_____

_____

4. Ancient Rome held many architectural wonders, many of these buildings were destroyed during the Renaissance in the 1400s by architects and builders who wanted to use the old stones to build new buildings.

_____

_____

_____

5. The Roman Forum today lies in ruins, they are fascinating to visit.

_____

6. Over half of the Colosseum in Rome is still standing, tourists are not allowed to enter all parts because of its fragile condition and the threat of its collapsing.

_____

_____

7. One ancient building in Rome built in A.D. 126 is the Pantheon, the building is still in perfect condition and has a concrete dome with an opening called an *oculus* at the top 30 feet across to let in the light.

_____

_____

_____

8. In Istanbul, Turkey, stands the beautiful Hagia Sophia, or "Holy Wisdom," the building was once the principal church of Constantinople.

_____

_____

_____

9. In 1453, the Turks turned Hagia Sophia into a mosque, the modern Turkish state has converted the mosque (a Moslem temple) into a museum for all visitors to see.

_____

_____

_____

10. Florence, Italy, was the birthplace of the Renaissance, it contains today some of the greatest works of the Renaissance including Michelangelo's statue *David*.

_____

_____

_____

EXERCISE

Each of the following exercises presents two sentences. Combine them to form a compound sentence.

1. Charles Franklin Kettering (1876–1958) was an American inventor. He invented the first electric cash register.

   _____

   _____

2. Johannes Kepler (1571–1630), a German astronomer, formulated Kepler's laws. These laws describe the motions of the planets in the solar system.

   _____

   _____

3. Francis Scott Key (1779–1843) was an American lawyer who wrote the words to "The Star-Spangled Banner." It became the national anthem of the United States in 1931.

   _____

   _____

4. Irene Joliot-Curie (1897–1956) was a French physicist and the daughter of Pierre and Marie Curie. She and her husband, Frederic Joliot (1900–1958), shared the 1935 Nobel Prize for Chemistry.

   _____

   _____

5. A British psychoanalyst, Ernest Jones (1879–1968), was a member of Sigmund Freud's inner circle. He wrote a three-volume biography of Freud (published 1953–1957).

EXERCISE

Read the following paragraph and rewrite it, using correct punctuation and any coordination devices to form compound sentences.

Charles Darwin was born in 1802. He died in 1882. He was an English naturalist. He formulated the theory of evolution by natural selection. Alfred Wallace formulated the same theory independently of Darwin. From 1831 to 1836, Darwin sailed around the world aboard the HMS *Beagle.* He received the experience he needed to be a naturalist. Darwin wrote *Origin of Species* in 1859. He spent the rest of his life in research to defend his theory. Darwin avoided debating his theories. He let others do the debating for him. Charles Darwin was from a wealthier family than Wallace's. Darwin is usually given the full credit for natural selection. Wallace came up with the same theory. Darwin actually wanted to let Wallace have the credit for the theory. Wallace wanted Darwin to take the credit. This theory has been causing controversy ever since it was formulated.

_____

_____

_____

_____

_____

_____

_____

_____

_____

_____

_____

_____

WRITING ASSIGNMENT

Charles Darwin visited many interesting places on his voyage around the world. On your trip around the world, which countries will you visit?

Step 1: Prewriting

Using the prewriting techniques brainstorming (with classmates) and mapping, decide which interesting places you will want to visit.

What will your mode of transportation be?
What special sights will you want to see?

Step 2: Writing

Using the ideas you generated by the prewriting exercise, write a paragraph about your voyage, as follows:

1. Write your paragraph using short, simple sentences.
2. Rewrite it using the different forms of coordination covered in this chapter.

Step 3: Revising, Editing, and Proofreading

After completing your paragraph, check it and correct any run-on sentences or comma splices. Also check your spelling and punctuation.

18 Subordination

Chapter 17, "Coordination," covered the second sentence pattern: the compound sentence. In this chapter, you will learn how to use subordinating conjunctions, relative pronouns, and restrictive and nonrestrictive clauses to create the complex sentence and the compound-complex sentence. Learning these last two patterns will greatly improve your sentence variety and allow you to express more complex thoughts than possible with only the simple and compound sentences.

Joining Subordinate Clauses

A single sentence may contain one or more ideas that may be equal or unequal to one another in importance. To review, when the ideas are equal, they are *coordinate* ideas. When they are unequal, the less important idea is ***subordinate*** to the other. Thus, the subordinate idea is *dependent* on the more important idea, which is ***independent.***

All clauses are either subordinate (dependent) or independent. A subordinate clause cannot stand alone, but an independent clause can. When a subordinate clause is joined to an independent clause, it forms a **complex sentence.** If a subordinate clause is joined to two or more independent clauses, a **compound-complex sentence** is formed.

When you subordinate, you make one idea (element) grammatically dependent on another, so that the subordinate idea becomes a **modifier:** either an adverb (using subordinating conjunctions) or an adjective (using relative pronouns).

SUBORDINATING CONJUNCTIONS

To join two clauses of unequal rank, a subordinating conjunction is placed in front of the subordinate clause and combined with the independent clause to form a complex sentence. Subordinating conjunctions provide many alternatives for expressing logical relationships between related ideas.

The conjunctions that are used as adverbs can be grouped under the following:

1. Contrasting or conditional relationship:
   although, even though, if, though, unless, whereas
2. *Where*, expressing a locational relationship:
   where, wherever
3. *When*, expressing a time relationship:
   after, as, as long as, as soon as, before, once, till, until, when, whenever, while
4. *Why*, expressing a cause and effect relationship:
   as if, as though, because, in order that, provided, since

Incorrect Example:

I refuse to use the electron microscope.

Because preparing the specimens is too difficult.

Explanation:

The two ideas are not equal. The subordinate clause cannot stand on its own but must be connected to the independent clause.

CORRECTED EXAMPLE:

I refuse to use the electron microscope *because* preparing the specimens is too difficult.

Point to Remember:

When the subordinate (dependent) clause comes after the independent clause, no comma is used. When the subordinate (dependent) clause comes at the beginning of a sentence, it is followed by a comma.

Example:

Because preparing the specimens is too difficult, I refuse to use the electron microscope.

Explanation:

Notice that the order of the clauses has been switched although the subordinate clause is still dependent on the second clause for its meaning.

EXERCISE

Add a subordinating conjunction to best express the idea in each of the following sentences.

1. _____ you are finished with your freewriting exercise, go back and correct any mistakes.

2. _____ you may want to correct the mistakes as you make them, you should keep on writing.

3. It is better to have a paragraph full of mistakes _____ writing no paragraph at all will defeat the purpose of the exercise.

4. You are to let your mind wander _____ doing the freewriting exercise.

5. Write what comes naturally to you _____ the time limit is up.

6. _____ you are writing, don't concern yourself with the importance of grammar.

7. This exercise should be enjoyable _____ you don't take it too seriously.

8. _____ you start to write, make sure you are comfortable.

9. This exercise will help you generate ideas _____ you won't need to think a long time about what you should write.

10. This method will help you get over writer's block _____ it stops you from worrying about the dreaded first few sentences.

EXERCISE

Complete each of the following sentences with an idea that contains a subject and a verb. The subordinating conjunction is underlined in each sentence.

1. After I am finished writing, _____

   _____

2. As long as _____, I will

   continue writing.

3. I will let my mind wander until _____

   _____

4. I get nervous whenever _____

    _____

5. If _____ , I will just

    let my mind wander about places I would like to visit.

6. While I am writing, _____

    _____

7. I write about things I see in my mind as if _____

    _____

8. After you are finished, _____

    _____

9. If you are totally confused about what to write, _____

    _____

10. Though _____ , I'm

    actually getting a lot done.

RELATIVE PRONOUNS

The relative pronouns *that, which,* and *who* begin dependent clauses that are used as adjectives. These adjective clauses relate two ideas and are called **relative clauses.**

Each of these pronouns is used in certain instances:

1. To describe people: *who, whom*
2. To describe things: *which, that*
3. Before a noun to show possession: *whose*

Examples:

The teacher ***who*** *taught the humanities class* will be teaching it again.

The teacher ***whom*** *the students liked so much* enjoys teaching.

The book ***that*** *was lying on the desk* is no longer there.

Restrictive and Nonrestrictive Clauses

When the relative clause is essential to the meaning of the sentence, it is called a **restrictive clause.** It adds information the reader must know in order to understand the sentence.

Example:

The student **who** *made the lowest score on the algebra test* will have to retake it.

Explanation:

The clause *who made the lowest score on the algebra test* is necessary to identify which student has to retake the test. Without this clause, the reader has no idea why the student must retake the test.

When a relative clause is not essential to the meaning of the sentence, it is called a **nonrestrictive clause.** Although it also adds information to a sentence, such details can be omitted without affecting the sentence's meaning.

Example:

His car, **which** *is a popular model,* is parked in a "no parking" zone.

Explanation:

The added information *which is a popular model* is incidental to the sentence; the main point is that the car is in a "no parking" zone. The nonrestrictive clause can be deleted without changing the meaning of the sentence.

Points to Remember:

Nonrestrictive clauses are always enclosed within two commas to show that they are not essential to the meaning of the sentence. Restrictive clauses, on the other hand, are never placed between two commas. The absence of commas indicates to the reader that the restrictive clause is necessary to the meaning of the sentence.

One simple way to keep these rules in mind is to use *that* to introduce restrictive clauses and *which* to introduce nonrestrictive clauses. In describing a person or persons with *who,* remember to add commas if the clause is nonrestrictive and to delete commas if the clause is restrictive.

EXERCISE

In each of the following sentences, put an R *if it contains a restrictive clause and an* NR *if it contains a nonrestrictive clause.*

1. ____ The male dolphin that is ten feet long is called Pete.

2. ____ My summer home, which sits at the side of the ocean, is called The Abbey.

3. ____ The pen that was on top of my book is missing.

5. ____ The professor who taught you Freshman English I is teaching Freshman English II this fall.

EXERCISE

The following exercises appeared at the end of the chapter on coordination. Before, you were instructed to turn the pair of sentences in each exercise into a compound sentence. Now, using what you have learned in this chapter on subordination, change each pair of sentences into a complex sentence.

1. Charles Franklin Kettering (1876–1958) was an American inventor. He invented the first electric cash register.

_____

_____

2. Johannes Kepler (1571–1630), a German astronomer, formulated Kepler's laws. Those laws describe the motions of the planets in the solar system.

_____

_____

3. Francis Scott Key (1779–1843) was an American lawyer who wrote the words to "The Star-Spangled Banner." It became the national anthem of the United States in 1931.

_____

_____

4. Irene Joliot-Curie (1897–1956) was a French physicist and daughter of Pierre and Marie Curie. She and her husband, Frederic Joliot (1900–1958), shared the 1935 Nobel Prize for Chemistry.

_____

_____

5. A British psychoanalyst, Ernest Jones (1879–1958), was a member of Sigmund Freud's inner circle. He wrote a three-volume biography of Freud (published 1953–1957).

_____

_____

WRITING ASSIGNMENT

You have joined the space program. Describe your flight to the moon with a group of United States astronauts.

Step 1: Prewriting

Using the prewriting techniques brainstorming (with classmates) and mapping, explain why you want a chance to travel with the astronauts to the moon.

What do you think it will feel like to lift off in a rocketship?

What do you think the sensation of weightlessness will be like during your travel, and how do you think it will feel to be one-sixth of your weight on the moon's surface?

What experiments will you perform and what observations will you make while on this voyage?

Looking back on the planet earth from the moon, how will your observations affect your views concerning environmental pollution of your home planet?

Step 2: Writing

Using the ideas you generated by the prewriting exercise, write a paragraph about your space voyage, as follows:

1. Write your paragraph using only short simple sentences.
2. Rewrite your paragraph using the different forms of subordination covered in this chapter.

Step 3: Revising, Editing, and Proofreading

After completing your paragraph, check it to see if you have used the subordinating elements correctly. If not, review this chapter and correct any errors. Also check your spelling and punctuation.

19 *Sentence Fragments*

When you write a sentence fragment, you are writing an incomplete thought. *You* may know what the fragment means since it was your thought, but to a reader, the incomplete meaning is both confusing and annoying. A sentence fragment is a serious problem that detracts from your reader's ability to understand your message.

In order for a group of words to be a sentence, it must have a subject and a verb and contain enough information to make a complete thought. A group of words cannot be a sentence if any one of these elements has been omitted. Learn to evaluate carefully what you write. A group of words is not necessarily a sentence just because it starts with a capital letter and ends with a period. In this chapter, you will learn to identify and correct the different types of sentence fragments.

Lack of Subject

Points to Remember:
1. **Some fragments are created by leaving out the *subject* of the sentence.**

Example:
Rides the camel.

Explanation:
The verb is *rides.* You cannot answer the questions Who? or What? *rides,* because there is no subject.

To correct this type of fragment, add a subject that is appropriate to the meaning of the sentence. Namely, answer the questions Who? or What?

CORRECTED EXAMPLE:
The explorer rides the camel.

EXERCISE

Each of the following exercises presents a sentence fragment. Add an appropriate subject before the verb that will answer the question Who? or What? and rewrite the fragment to change it into a complete sentence.

1. Hikes every weekend.

   _____

2. Goes to the movies four times a month.

   _____

3. Enjoy deep-sea fishing.

   _____

4. Learned a great deal from avoiding other people's mistakes.

   _____

5. Loves antique cars.

   _____

2. **Often, fragments are created when the writer mistakenly thinks the subject of the preceding sentence is also the subject of the next word group.**

   Example:
   The professor assigned the class a 20-page research paper on the *Odyssey* by Homer. But lectured only 30 minutes on the poem.

   Explanation:
   The second word group is a fragment because it contains no subject for the verb, *lectured.* The subject in the preceding sentence, *professor,* cannot function outside its own sentence as the subject of the second word group.

   There are two ways to correct this very common error. The first way is to add a subject to the fragment to make it a sentence.

   CORRECTED EXAMPLE:
   The professor assigned a 20-page research paper on the *Odyssey* by Homer. *He* lectured only 30 minutes on the poem.

EXERCISE

Each of the following exercises presents a sentence and a fragment. Add a subject to the fragment, making it a complete sentence.

1. Columbus sailed across the ocean to find India. But discovered a new continent instead.

   _____

2. Woody Allen is a gifted comedian. Also writes profound and clever movie screenplays.

   _____

3. Computers are wonderful inventions for the business world. Now are also used extensively for personal use.

   _____

4. The Statue of Liberty was recently renovated. Previously was in danger of structural collapse.

   _____

5. Zeus was the king of the Greek gods. Lived on Mount Olympus with the other gods and goddesses.

   _____

The second way to correct the error is to combine the fragment with the preceding sentence that contains the subject.

Example:
The professor assigned the class a 20-page research paper on the *Odyssey* by Homer. But lectured only 30 minutes on the poem.

CORRECTED EXAMPLE:
The professor assigned a 20-page research paper on the *Odyssey* by Homer but lectured only 30 minutes on the poem.

Explanation:
The fragment contains the verb, *lectured.* By joining the fragment to the sentence before it, you have created a complete sentence with the subject, *professor,* and the compound verb, *assigned and lectured.*

EXERCISE

Each of the following exercises presents a sentence and a fragment. Eliminate the fragment by joining it to the sentence that precedes it.

1. Columbus sailed across the ocean to find India. But discovered a new continent instead.

   _____

_____

2. Woody Allen is a great comedian. Also writes profound and clever movie screenplays.

_____

_____

3. Computers are wonderful inventions for the business world. Now are also used extensively for personal use.

_____

_____

4. The Statue of Liberty was in danger of structural collapse. But was recently renovated.

_____

_____

5. Zeus was the king of the Greek gods. Lived on Mount Olympus with the other gods and goddesses.

_____

_____

EXERCISE

Underline the sentence fragments in the following paragraph. Then rewrite the paragraph in the space provided, correcting all of the fragments.

Harry Houdini was the world's most famous magician and escape artist. Houdini was born on March 24, 1874. And died October 31, 1926. His real name was Ehrich Weiss. Was the son of a rabbi. Houdini was born in Budapest, Hungary. Was not born in the United States. In 1894, he married Wilhelmina Rahner. Assisted him in his magic acts. Houdini campaigned against mind readers, mediums, and

others who claimed they had supernatural powers.

Said they were all charlatans who produced their

effects through natural means and various tricks.

_____

_____

_____

_____

_____

_____

_____

_____

_____

_____

Lack of Verbs and Incomplete Verbs

Points to Remember:
1. **Some fragments are created by leaving out the *complete verb*. A group of words without a verb is not a sentence. The missing verb could be a verb that shows action or a linking verb that describes or identifies the subject.**

Example:
Michelangelo in his studio.

Explanation:
This fragment contains a Who? or What? word, *Michelangelo,* and a prepositional phrase, *in his studio.* However, there is no verb to complete the thought and tell you what Michelangelo is doing.

To correct the fragment, add an action or linking verb that will complete the thought.

CORRECTED EXAMPLES:

Michelangelo *carved* a beautiful statue in his studio.

Michelangelo *was* in his studio.

EXERCISE

Each of the following exercises presents a sentence and a fragment. Add a verb to the fragment, making it a complete sentence.

1. Rudyard Kipling won the Nobel Prize for Literature for *The Jungle Book* and *Captains Courageous.* He only 42 years old at that time.

   _____

2. William Butler Yeats, the Irish poet, won the Nobel Prize for Literature for *Collected Poems of W. B. Yeats.* William Butler Yeats happy to win the award.

   _____

3. George Bernard Shaw won the Nobel Prize for Literature for his plays *Androcles and the Lion* and *Pygmalion.* Shaw the award when he was 69 years old.

   _____

4. "The money is a lifebelt thrown to a swimmer who has already reached the shore!" George Bernard Shaw these words to the Nobel Prize judges.

   _____

   _____

5. Ernest Hemingway won the Nobel Prize for Literature for *The Old Man and the Sea* and *A Farewell to Arms.* Hemingway his award in 1954.

   _____

   _____

   _____

2. Some sentence fragments are caused by incomplete verbs. For instance, there are some tenses in which verbs cannot function without *helping verbs (auxiliary verbs).* Helping verbs show past, present, or future time. A helping verb is used with another verb that comes after it; the final verb is called the *main verb.* If the helping verb is left out of a sentence, you have an incomplete verb and, therefore, a sentence fragment.

Example:

Bill *looking* at the display of King Tutankhamen's golden treasures.

CORRECTED EXAMPLE:

Bill *is looking* at the display of King Tutankhamen's golden treasures.

Explanation:

The *-ing* form of the verb *look* requires a helping verb in order for the sentence to have a complete verb and make sense.

To correct this sentence, use a form of the verb *to be* as the helping verb. Some of the forms of the verb *to be* are as follows:

am	had been
are	has been
is	have been
was	
were	

Again, the helping verb will be combined with a main verb with an *-ing* ending to form a complete verb.

EXERCISE

Each of the following exercises presents a sentence fragment that has an incomplete verb. Complete each verb to change the fragment into a sentence.

1. Alfred Nobel invented dynamite, which is buffered nitroglycerin. He _____ been using pure liquid nitroglycerin, which was too dangerous.

2. In 1863, Nobel _____ setting up a factory to produce nitroglycerin in large quantities.

3. Alfred Nobel's father, Immanuel Nobel, was an inventor also. Immanuel _____ working for the Russian government on underwater explosives.

4. Many people _____ calling Nobel a "mad scientist" after his factory blew up in 1864.

5. Nobel _____ trying to find a way to handle nitroglycerin safely
and finally succeeded by creating dynamite.

Example:
The Rosetta Stone *hidden* for many years.
CORRECTED EXAMPLE:
The Rosetta Stone *had been hidden* for many years.
Explanation:
The past participle of the verb *to hide* is *hidden.* This form of the verb cannot
stand by itself. The past participle must have a helping verb.

To correct this sentence, use a helping verb, either a form of *to be* or *to have,*
to complete the thought.[1] Some of the helping verbs for the past participle are:

am	was
are	were
is	had been
had	has been
has	have been
have	

Again, the helping verb will be combined with the past participle form of the
main verb to form a complete verb.

EXERCISE

*Each of the following exercises contains a sentence fragment that has an incom-
plete verb. Complete each verb to change the fragment into a sentence.*

1. Alfred Nobel lived in Stockholm, Sweden. He _____ born in

   1833 and died in 1896.

2. Alfred Nobel _____ become a competent chemist by the time

   he was 16 years old.

3. Blasting gelatin, a more powerful form of dynamite, _____

   considered safe to use, and Nobel received a patent for it in 1876.

---

[1]See Appendix C for the conjugation of *to be* and *to have.*

4. Nobel _____ decided to leave his nine million dollar estate to create the Nobel Foundation two weeks before he died.

5. He _____ signed the will on a torn up piece of paper in front of four witnesses, but it was acceptable in court.

EXERCISE

Underline the fragments in the following paragraph. Then rewrite the paragraph in the space provided, correcting all of the fragments.

Alfred Bernhard Nobel was the inventor of dynamite and established the Nobel Prize awards. He one of the richest men in the world. Nobel wanted to ease his conscience about creating dynamite and did not believe in leaving his millions to relatives. Nobel his money to the Nobel Foundation in Stockholm, Sweden. The first Nobel Prize for Literature was to René F. A. Sully-Prudhomme for his *Stanzas and Poems*. He the award in 1901, but this first prize should have been awarded to Leo Tolstoy, the Russian writer. Thomas Edison, considered the most successful inventor of all time, received 1,300 United States and foreign patents. He never a Nobel Prize. Walt Disney, through his cartoon characters, made more people happier than perhaps any winner of the Nobel Prize for Peace ever did. Walt Disney never a Nobel Prize either.

_____

_____

_____

_____

_____

_____

_____

_____

_____

_____

Lack of Subject and Verb

Point to Remember:

Some sentence fragments are created by leaving out both the subject and the verb. Many of these fragments are simply prepositional phrases. Remember that the object of the preposition cannot be the subject of the sentence.

Example:

Under an apple tree.

Explanation:

This group of words does not answer the questions Who? or What? nor does it indicate an action or a state of being.

To correct this fragment, add a subject and a verb to complete the thought.

CORRECTED FRAGMENT:

S   V
Sir Isaac Newton sat under an apple tree.

EXERCISE

Add a subject and a verb to each of the following prepositional phrases to complete the thought and create a sentence.

1. Behind the closed door.

_____

2. After midnight.

_____

3. During the raging storm.

_____

4. Under the sea.

_____

5. In a medieval castle.

_____

Subordinating Conjunctions

Point to Remember:

Some sentence fragments are created by preceding a complete thought with a *subordinating conjunction*. Doing so transforms a sentence into a dependent (subordinate) clause.[2]

Complete Thought:

I am happy.   (sentence or independent clause)

Incomplete Thought:

When I am happy.   (dependent clause)

The following are subordinating conjunctions:

after	as though	since	when
although	because	though	whenever
as	before	unless	while
as if	if	until	

Many times, a dependent clause either precedes or follows a complete sentence. The writer does not realize that this dependent clause should be connected to a complete sentence. Standing alone, it is a fragment.

Example:

John gathered valuable information for the project. *Although he did not go to the library.*   (fragment)

[2]See Chapter 18, "Subordination."

CORRECTED EXAMPLES:

John gathered valuable information for the project *although he did not go to the library.*

Although he did not go to the library, John gathered valuable information for the project.

John gathered valuable information for the project. *He did not,* **however,** *go to the library.*

John gathered valuable information for the project, **but** *he did not go to the library.*

Points to Remember:

A dependent clause cannot stand alone. It must be corrected in one of three ways:

1. Join the dependent clause to the independent clause at the end or the beginning of the sentence (first two examples above).
2. Delete the subordinating conjunction, and change the dependent clause into a complete sentence (third example above).
3. Change the subordinating conjunction into a coordinating conjunction, and create a compound sentence (last example).[3]

EXERCISE

For each of the following exercises, write S *if it is a complete sentence and* F *if it is a fragment.*

1. ____ Although the first year Nobel Prizes were awarded was 1901.

2. ____ The five original awards for the Nobel Prize were in the fields of literature, physics, chemistry, medicine, and peace.

3. ____ Alexander Fleming won the Nobel Prize for Physiology and Medicine for the discovery of penicillin and its ability to cure certain diseases.

4. ____ When Fleming found that staphylococcal bacteria died near blue-green mold in 1928.

5. ____ Although Albert Einstein won the Nobel Prize in 1921.

6. ____ Albert Einstein won the Nobel Prize for Physics for general contributions to theoretical physics and the discovery of the law of photoelectric effect.

[3]See Chapter 17, "Coordination," and Chapter 18, "Subordination."

7. ____ While Marie Sklodowska Curie won the Nobel Prize for Chemistry for

discovering radium and polonium and for isolating radium.

8. ____ Marie Curie, Pierre Curie, and Antoine Becquerel won the Nobel Prize

for Physics for the study of the radiation phenomena, which were dis-

covered by Becquerel.

9. ____ Marie Curie won two Nobel Prizes.

10. ____ Because Marie Curie was also called Madame Curie.

EXERCISE

Each of the following exercises presents a set of sentences and fragments. In each, join the dependent clause to the independent clause to form a complete sentence.

1. When the Nobel Prizes were awarded in 1901. The five original awards were for the fields of literature, physics, chemistry, medicine, and peace.

_____

_____

_____

2. In 1928, Sir Alexander Fleming found that staphylococcal bacteria died near blue-green mold. Although he did not win the Nobel Prize for the discovery of penicillin and its ability to cure certain diseases until 1945.

_____

_____

_____

_____

3. Although Albert Einstein won the Nobel Prize for Physics in 1921. Einstein did not win the Nobel Prize for his general theory of relativity but for his discovery of the law of photoelectric effect.

_____

_____

_____

4. While Marie Curie, Pierre Curie, and Antoine Becquerel won a Nobel Prize for Physics in 1903. Marie Curie was awarded the Nobel Prize for Chemistry in 1911 for the discovery of radium and polonium.

_____

_____

_____

5. Marie Curie put in a modern bathroom and changed the wallpaper in her Paris home. After she won the Nobel Prize in 1903.

_____

_____

_____

WRITING ASSIGNMENT

The Nobel Prize is currently awarded in six fields: literature, physics, chemistry, medicine, peace, and economics. Create a new category for the Nobel Prize.

Step 1: Prewriting

Using the prewriting techniques listing and mapping, create a new category for the Nobel Prize.

Why do you think this field should be recognized with the honor of the Nobel Prize?
Whom do you want to receive the Nobel Prize for your new category?

Step 2: Writing

Using the ideas you generated by the prewriting exercise, write a paragraph about the Nobel Prize.

Step 3: Revising, Editing, and Proofreading

After completing your paragraph, read it carefully. Identify any fragments you find, and correct them by using one of the methods taught in this chapter. Also check your spelling.

20 *Modifiers*

We have already discussed prepositional phrases, gerunds, infinitives, and participles in other chapters. All of these words or phrases are used as adjectives and adverbs to enhance your writing, making it vivid and concrete. But to be effective, these modifiers must be correctly placed in a sentence. If not, they destroy the grammatical structure of the sentence, and the results will be illogical, confusing, and even absurd.

This chapter addresses how to use modifiers correctly, teaching you how to identify and correct two common problems: misplaced and dangling modifiers.

Identifying Modifiers

A phrase used as a **modifier** can begin with a preposition, a present participle, a past participle, or an infinitive.

Examples:

Small silver fish dart *through wavering river grass.*   (prepositional phrase)

Moss *hanging from the old oak trees* sways in the gusty summer breeze. (present participle phrase)

Sheltered by the trees and shrubs, the creek of cool, clear water dances over silver rocks.   (past participle phrase)

The alligator crawls onto the muddy bank *to bask in the warm sunlight.*   (infinitive phrase)

A clause that serves as an adjective can begin with *who, that, which, whom,* or *whose.* A clause that serves as an adverb can begin with *because, as, if, although, while, after, unless,* and so on.

Examples:

> Saw grass rustles in a sudden breeze *as ripples appear on the black swamp water.*   (adverbial clause)

> A tall stately pine *whose branches swayed in the soft summer breeze* reminded me of my childhood.   (relative clause used as an adjective)

Point to Remember:

> A *phrase* is a group of words that does not contain both a subject and a verb; however, a *clause* contains both a subject and a verb and may be either independent or dependent.

Misplaced Modifiers

One common problem with the use of modifiers is that they are misplaced in the sentence. To be clear, a modifier should be placed next to the word it modifies. If it is placed in another position, the meaning of the sentence becomes confused and often humorous.

A **misplaced modifier** can be corrected by changing the word order.

Example:

> The child played with the ball wearing sneakers.

Explanation:

> The *ball* is certainly not *wearing sneakers*. To correct this sentence, the participial phrase *wearing sneakers* must be moved next to the subject, *child*.

CORRECTED EXAMPLE:

> The **child** *wearing sneakers* played with the ball.

Example:

> Drinking from the birdbath, my grandmother saw a robin.

Explanation:

> The participial phrase *drinking from the birdbath,* used as an adjective, must be moved to the end of the sentence to modify *robin* (unless, of course, my grandmother has been drinking from the birdbath).

CORRECTED EXAMPLE:

> My grandmother saw a **robin** *drinking from the birdbath.*

Example:

> The cabin was located next to the waterfall made of wood.

Explanation:

> The *waterfall* is not *made of wood,* so the participial phrase must be moved next to the subject, *cabin.*

CORRECTED EXAMPLE:

> The **cabin** *made of wood* was located next to the waterfall.

Rewrite each of the following sentences to correct the misplaced modifier.

1. We saw a deer driving our car down the highway.

_____

2. Jumping from tree to tree, my father saw a squirrel.

_____

3. My friend spotted a bird playing football in our yard.

_____

4. Lying on top of my shelf, I found my baseball bat.

_____

5. I read about the baseball player who hit a home run in the newspaper.

_____

Dangling Modifiers

A **dangling modifier** is a participle or other modifier that does not logically describe the noun or pronoun closest to it in the sentence. For instance, if a participle comes at the beginning of the sentence but does not logically modify the subject, it is a dangling participle.

Point to Remember:
> You cannot get rid of a dangling modifier by just moving it around in the sentence; you must add the correct word that the phrase is modifying.

Example:
> Walking down the street, the curb tripped me.

Explanation:
> *Curbs* do not *walk down the street.* The sentence must be revised to include a noun that the participle *walking down the street* can modify.

CORRECTED EXAMPLE:
> *Walking down the street, I* tripped over the curb.

Example:
> To enroll in English class, the tuition must be paid.

Explanation:

The *tuition* does not *enroll in English class.* The sentence must be revised to include a noun that the infinitive phrase *to enroll in English class* can modify.

CORRECTED EXAMPLE:

To enroll in English class, the **student** must pay the tuition.

Example:

As a high school senior, the prom was an enjoyable event.

Explanation:

The phrase *as a high school senior* does not logically modify any word in the sentence. A person must be named—the high school senior.

CORRECTED EXAMPLE:

As a high school senior, **Joyce** enjoyed the prom.

EXERCISE

Rewrite each of the following sentences to correct the dangling modifier.

1. Watching the movie a second time, the plot became interesting.

   _____

2. Running down the street, the lawns were beautiful.

   _____

3. Walking in the mall, the shops were wonderful.

   _____

4. Painting all day, my room was finally completed.

   _____

5. Jumping in the lake, the water was cold.

   _____

EXERCISE

Rewrite each of the following sentences to correct the dangling or misplaced modifier.

1. Reaching our campsite, our lunches were already eaten.

   _____

2. After hanging the wallpaper, the glue had hardened.

_____

3. Climbing out of the bathtub, my towel fell on the floor.

_____

4. Sweating profusely, the table was moved into the kitchen.

_____

5. I kept calling her Miss Johnson after she got married by mistake.

_____

6. I saw a bird driving my motorcycle down the highway.

_____

7. I told him not to carry a rifle in his car that was loaded.

_____

8. We watched a hammerhead shark sitting on the pier in St. Petersburg.

_____

9. Breathing heavily, the chapter was finally finished by us at 2:00 A.M.

_____

10. Crawling under the refrigerator, my mother noticed the spider.

_____

WRITING ASSIGNMENT

You are given the power to solve one ecological problem in the environment. Your action will help to save the ecology of the earth.

Step 1: Prewriting

Using two of the prewriting techniques explained in Chapter 1, brainstorming (with the class) and listing, decide which problem you want to solve.

Why is this particular problem so dangerous to our environment?
What methods will you use to solve this problem?

How will eradication of this problem help humankind and the earth?

Step 2: Writing

Using the ideas you generated by the prewriting exercise, write a paragraph about solving an ecological problem.

Step 3: Revising, Editing, and Proofreading

After completing your paragraph, reread it. Look for any misplaced or dangling modifiers, and correct any you find. Also check your spelling and punctuation.

21 | *Parallelism*

Parallelism is a grammatical technique used by writers to improve their sentences. When your reader is making smooth progress through your sentence and comes across a sudden change in grammatical construction, it's like hitting a pothole. This chapter will show you how faulty parallelism can take your readers on a bumpy ride through what you have written. What's more, you will see how smooth the ride can be after you rewrite your sentence correctly.

Parallel Structure

Parallelism, (parallel structure) is a grammatical construction that adds smoothness and continuity to your writing. It means that similar items in the same sentence must be in the same part of speech. Parallel structure can be used for a series of single words, phrases, or clauses. Faulty parallel structure occurs when similar items are expressed in different grammatical constructions.

Incorrect Example:
> I like *to fish, to hunt,* and *boating.*

CORRECTED EXAMPLE:
> I like *fishing, hunting,* and *boating.*

Explanation:
> The word *boating* is a gerund (a verbal used as a noun), which is *not* the same part of speech as the two infinitives *to fish* and *to hunt.* In the corrected example, *fishing, hunting,* and *boating* are all gerunds, making it a parallel structure.

You can vary the structure of your sentences by the placement of articles (*a, an, the*) in the parallel structure. Items in a series that are in correct parallel structure may have an article placed only in front of the first item in the series or placed before each item in the series.

Examples:

> I am ***an*** *author, student,* and *guitarist.*   (article precedes first item only)
>
> I am ***an*** *author,* ***a*** *student,* and ***a*** *guitarist.*   (article precedes each item)

Similarly, dependent clauses with correct parallel structure, listed in a series, can have a relative pronoun as the subject of three different clauses or as the subject of one clause with a compound verb.

Examples:

> Bob is a person ***who*** *accepts responsibility,* ***who*** *works hard,* and ***who*** *accomplishes his goals.*   (relative pronouns as subjects of clauses)
>
> Bob is a person ***who*** *accepts* responsibility, *works* hard, and *accomplishes* his goals.   (relative pronoun as subject of clause with compound verb)

In both sets of example sentences, a reader can move smoothly through the sentences avoiding the jolts of faulty parallelism. Parallel structure also gives the writer an opportunity to make the sentences more interesting by using different constructions.

Point to Remember:

> In longer, more complicated sentences, it is more difficult to write with parallel structure. An important editing practice is to reread what you have written to check for parallelism.

EXERCISE

In each of the following lists of words, circle the one that is not parallel.

1. a. jump

    b. sing

    c. dancing

    d. play

2. a. seek

    b. find

    c. learned

    d. teach

3. a. running

   b. inventing

   c. pontificating

   d. confuse

4. a. type

   b. wrote

   c. read

   d. check

5. a. think

   b. explored

   c. discover

   d. find

EXERCISE

In each of the following lists of sentences, circle the one that is not parallel.

1. a. She owns a boat.

   b. He buys an airplane.

   c. She is working a computer.

   d. He washes his car.

2. a. The mathematician adds.

   b. The philosopher thought.

   c. The English professor writes.

   d. The astronomer finds.

3. a. The statistician is calculating.

   b. The biologist is discovering.

   c. The librarian is searching.

   d. The biochemist tests.

4. a. The romantic writer loved.

   b. The Neoclassical writer thought.

   c. The modern writer complains.

   d. The medieval writer pondered.

5. a. I am thinking.

   b. I am freewriting.

   c. I am correcting.

   d. I am finished.

EXERCISE

In each of the following lists of phrases, circle the one that is not parallel.

1. a. covered in jewelry

   b. clothed in silk

   c. under the rug

   d. wrapped in lace

2. a. two books

   b. three pencils

   c. using a pen

   d. several erasers

3. a. a brown table

   b. some large chairs

   c. carrying a table

   d. two small chairs

4. a. on the computer

   b. in the hard drive

   c. the disk drive

   d. under the printer

5. a. a brilliant histologist

    b. a great immunologist

    c. an intelligent grammarian

    d. a physicist calculates

EXERCISE

Rewrite each of the sentences to correct the faulty parallelism.

1. The anaconda climbs trees and swam well in water.

    _____

2. The camel drinks 15 gallons of water and ran in the desert for many days without water.

    _____

    _____

3. The astronomer discovers and exploring many interesting star systems through his telescope.

    _____

    _____

4. Matter can be in the form of a solid, a liquid, or gases.

    _____

5. About A.D. 1590, the Dutch spectacle maker Zacharias Janssen developed and uses the compound microscope.

    _____

    _____

6. A sugar maple tree produces 20 gallons of sap, which reduced upon processing to one-half gallon of pure maple syrup.

    _____

    _____

7. Mammals breathed and plants photosynthesize.

_____

_____

8. Friends, the Romans, and countrymen, lend me your ears.

_____

_____

9. Sigmund Freud (1856–1939) lectured and written a great deal to explain his ideas.

_____

_____

10. Sigmund Freud was well educated in literature, art, and anthropological.

_____

_____

WRITING ASSIGNMENT

Some people believe that cartoon characters are extensions of real personalities.

With what cartoon character can you draw a parallel?

Step 1: Prewriting

Use the prewriting techniques listing and mapping to determine why you identify with this particular cartoon character.

What characteristics does this cartoon character have that you think you have?

Which of these characteristics do you like or dislike?

Step 2: Writing

Using the ideas you generated by the prewriting exercise, write a paragraph comparing yourself with the cartoon character.

Step 3: Revising, Editing, and Proofreading

After completing your paragraph, reread it. Identify the parallel structures you have used, and correct any problems that you find. Also check your spelling.

UNIT FOUR

Writing:
Exploring Paragraphs

The Greeks called these marks *para graphos,*
which meant "mark beside."

Paragraphs had been used as essential blocks of writing long before the printing press was invented. Sections of documents were set off by marks such as this ¶ in the margin. The invention of movable type made placing these marks in the margin impossible, so printers began indenting the first line of the paragraph, a practice still used today. The Greek term continued to be applied to this new practice of indicating sections; thus, we still call these building blocks of writing para-graphs.

Unit Four will take you from the sentence skills learned in Unit Three through a technique of organizing your thoughts into a block of sentences called a *paragraph*. A paragraph is a unit of related sentences that expresses different aspects of the topic about which you are writing.

The structured technique taught in Chapter 22 on the expanded paragraph is just one way of learning how to write effective paragraphs. Once you have learned this technique, you will find it easier to write less structured paragraphs on a variety of topics.

After choosing a topic, your next decision will be to determine the audience you wish to address. In conversation, everyone tends to be more formal with persons in authority and more relaxed with peers or friends. Your writing will reflect this same attitude. For instance, a report written for a business associate or professor will include formal language and just the basic facts needed to express your purpose. However, a letter written to a friend will be much less formal; you will use colloquial language and fill it with those intimate details that only a friend would appreciate.

Thus, in considering your *audience,* you are also deciding what information to present and the language and manner in which to present it.

Another decision will be to determine the *purpose* of your writing: to describe, to narrate, to explain, to show cause-and-effect, to compare and contrast, to classify, to divide, to define, to persuade, or to solve a problem. Chapter 23 will present these various organizational strategies to help you decide on purpose.

22 *The Process of Writing a Paragraph*

In conversation, which is spontaneous, sentences are often disjointed and rambling and are sometimes even fragments. As you think of what to say and wait for your listener's response, your mind is racing ahead, half listening to what the other person is saying and half planning your response.

Writing is different from conversation. If you are outside with your friend and say, "It's a nice day," you don't need to prove your statement. Your friend can see for herself. In contrast, whenever you write, the reader cannot stop and ask questions or request further information. You must make sure that everything necessary to convey your message is written down with specific and concrete detail. You become your reader's eyes and ears. You become the creator of your reader's world. Your thoughts, ideas, opinions, images, and attitudes must be conveyed in a clear and coherent manner.

In Unit Three, you learned how to write a coherent and correct sentence. The next step, in Unit Four, is to group a number of related sentences together in a logical order to develop a main idea. Our topic is the paragraph.

The Paragraph

A **paragraph** is a unified group of related sentences that develops a main idea. It has a *beginning* (the topic sentence), a *middle* (support and detail sentences), and an *end* (a summary sentence). These segments are linked with transitional devices that help your reader move easily through the document.

THE TOPIC SENTENCE

The topic you have chosen to write about is stated in the most important sentence of the paragraph, the **topic sentence.** It has one purpose only: to state the main idea of the paragraph. The topic sentence lays a foundation for the other sentences in the paragraph since all of them relate to the topic sentence to prove and illustrate it.

The topic sentence consists of the **subject** (topic), and an **attitude** (statement of feeling) toward the topic. The topic sentence should be as clear and specific as possible, not vague or general. You must commit to a definite position.

Consider the function of the topic sentence as you review the following student paragraphs.

Danielle wrote the following paragraph on the subject *sailing*. Her attitude is that *she loves sailing*.

I love to go sailing; being out on the water and away from the fast pace of city life is relaxing and peaceful. (**Topic Sentence**) I set sail at early dawn and prepare for a voyage out on the ocean. I find it fascinating to watch the land grow smaller as I sail further out to sea. After sailing out approximately 20 miles, I drop anchor and lie back in my lounge chair for hours. It is so relaxing to listen to the splash of the waves against the hull and to feel the gentle rocking of the boat. Time passes quickly when I am on the ocean, and it is soon time to return to shore. Disappointment overwhelms me as we head toward land but fades as I watch a glorious sunset over the gray-blue water. As we dock, the city noises fill my ears, and I cannot wait for the next time to set sail and get away from it all.

Jessie Barrack wrote the following paragraph on *morning people*. His attitude is that *there are three humorous types*.

There are three types of morning people; some

people hate mornings, some sleep through them, and others like them. (**Topic Sentence**) The first type of morning person is affectionately called the "grouch." A grouch hates everything about mornings, especially waking up in them. The pleasure of waking a grouch is so great, it should only be performed by convicted criminals. Anyone who is not being punished should stay as far away from a morning grouch as possible. The second type of morning person is the "just-ten-minutes-more" person. This person usually sleeps through the morning. Although ten minutes seems short, she usually stretches it into 30 or 40 minutes with the help of a snooze alarm. This type of person would be late to her own funeral by at least ten minutes. The final type of morning person is the worst. This person actually *likes* mornings. Daybreak takes on a whole new meaning. Usually, for this type of person, alarm clocks are not necessary. He always gets up early and usually has chores done before anyone else is even awake. There may be many different kinds of people during the day, but in the morning, there are only three.

Debbie Owen wrote about the subject *white-water rafting* in her paragraph. Her attitude is that *Debbie enjoys white-water rafting.*

White-water rafting on the Chattooga River in

Georgia is the ultimate form of entertainment.

(**Topic Sentence**) During the seven-hour guided trip down the river, a rafter tackles many rapids with varying degrees of difficulty. Many of these rapids were in the well-known movie *Deliverance*, starring Burt Reynolds. The most wild and exhilarating rapids on the trip are the famed Bull Sluice Rapids with a three-foot drop and the feared Decapitation Rock at the bottom. The Chattooga River divides two national parks and is strictly regulated by the United States government. This government protection allows the river to be completely preserved in its natural state with no sign of human intrusion. River wildlife, such as turtles, snakes, and fish are abundant. The day on the river is broken up to allow a rafter to enjoy both the exciting rapids and silent beauty of the area. Lunch is the first break that consists of a deli-type sandwich followed by a short, chilly swim in the river. As the river and the day progress, the rapids are separated by long stretches of water that push the raft along leisurely while its occupants soak up the sun and relax. The challenge of the white-water rapids coupled with the beauty of nature truly make rafting the Chattooga River the ultimate form of entertainment.

EXERCISE

For each of the following exercises, choose the best topic sentence from the four given.

1. a. Disguised as a Muslim, Sir Richard Burton went into the bazaars in Sind to gather intelligence information for the commander of the English forces.
   b. Sir Richard Burton, one of the greatest scholar-explorers of the nineteenth century, sought out the world's few remaining mysteries.
   c. Sir Richard Burton's explorations were documented in the movie *Mountains of the Moon*.
   d. Disguised as an Afghanistan Muslim, Sir Richard Burton entered the sacred city of Mecca, where at great risk he sketched the mosque and the holy shrine, the Kábah.

2. a. Ludwig van Beethoven's drive for perfection is shown by his willingness to continue to work on counterpoint and fugue even after he had composed fine works.
   b. Ludwig van Beethoven used classical forms and techniques but gave them new power and intensity.
   c. The Romantic Age composers used Ludwig van Beethoven's innovative musical expressions to compose their own compositions.
   d. Ludwig van Beethoven opened new realms of musical innovation and profoundly influenced composers of the nineteenth century.

3. a. As a child, George Lucas loved science fiction and fantasy.
   b. George Lucas chose fairly unknown actors in casting the film.
   c. In an often stale, redundant entertainment industry, George Lucas brought out the child in each of us through *Star Wars*.
   d. Before translating ideas into film, George Lucas has artists sketch them into pictures.

4. a. The *Atocha's* official cargo included pieces of gold bullion, silver ingots, silver coins, copper planks, indigo, and tobacco.
   b. Mel Fisher spent sixteen years searching for the sunken treasure ship *Nuestra Señora de Atocha*.
   c. In 1971, Mel Fisher's crew found a huge anchor.
   d. Mel Fisher's son Derek found several bronze cannons from the *Atocha*.

5. a. On April 6, 1909, Robert Peary, five members of the exploration party, and 40 dogs reached the North Pole.
   b. On one of his expeditions, Robert Peary proved that Greenland is an island.
   c. Robert Peary's cravings for exploration and fame made him even more eager to discover new and unexplored places.
   d. President William McKinley granted Robert Peary a leave of absence from the navy in order to explore the Arctic.

EXERCISE

For each of the following exercises, take the broad topic given and create a topic sentence.

Example:

Broad Topic: *Transportation*

Topic Sentence: The main form of transportation in the United States is the auto-
mobile.

1. Broad Topic: *Sports*

   Topic Sentence: _____

   _____

2. Broad Topic: *Career choice*

   Topic Sentence: _____

   _____

3. Broad Topic: *Marriage*

   Topic Sentence: _____

   _____

4. Broad Topic: *Education*

   Topic Sentence: _____

   _____

5. Broad Topic: *Music*

   Topic Sentence: _____

   _____

SUPPORT SENTENCES

The middle of the paragraph consists of *main support sentences* that directly relate to the topic sentence. Main support sentences are further illustrated or explained by *detail support sentences* that relate to the main support sentence preceding them.

Main Support Sentences

Main support sentences are general statements that substantiate, clarify, or illustrate the topic sentence directly. Normally, they are *generalizations,* which are value judgments or abstractions.

Simple Paragraphs

A simple paragraph can be created with five sentences: a topic sentence, several main support sentences, and a summary sentence (see later in this chapter).

Topic Sentence
      Main Support Sentence 1
      Main Support Sentence 2
      Main Support Sentence 3
Summary Sentence

In the following paragraph on *tennis* by Sandra Morris, you have an illustration of the simple five-sentence paragraph:

```
I enjoy playing tennis. Tennis is a great way

to relieve stress. Tennis is also good exercise.

Tennis is a game of great challenge. I feel most

people would love the game of tennis once they try

it.
```

Sandra's paragraph can be diagrammed as follows:

Topic Sentence:	I enjoy playing tennis.
Main Support 1:	Tennis is a great way to relieve stress.
Main Support 2:	Tennis is also good exercise.
Main Support 3:	Tennis is a game of great challenge.
Summary Sentence:	I feel most people would love the game of tennis once they try it.

EXERCISE

Do two of the following exercises. For each topic sentence given, create three main support sentences (a, b, c).

1. My college education will change my life.

    a. _____

    b. _____

    c. _____

  2. Horror movies scare me to death!

    a. _____

    b. _____

    c. _____

  3. Travelling is exciting.

    a. _____

    b. _____

    c. _____

  4. My everyday activities cause me a lot of stress.

    a. _____

    b. _____

    c. _____

  5. Nothing is more wonderful than falling in love.

    a. _____

    b. _____

    c. _____

Detail Support Sentences

In Sandra's paragraph about tennis, her main support sentences directly prove the topic sentence; namely, they state the reasons she enjoys playing tennis. But note that each of these reasons is a personal opinion, or value judgment. Because these main support sentences are claims, they must be supported with concrete evidence that proves, clarifies, and illustrates them. These additional sentences are called **detail support sentences.**

Detail support sentences are not just more claims that must also be proven. Instead, they are specific statements of example, explanation, and fact. They are the actual proof behind the main support sentences.

A second type of paragraph, called the **expanded paragraph,** follows the basic structure of the simple paragraph but adds two detail support sentences for each main support sentence. The format of the expanded paragraph is as follows:

Expanded Paragraphs

An expanded paragraph contains a topic sentence, several main support sentences each followed by detail support sentences, and a summary sentence (see later in this chapter).

Topic Sentence
    Main Support Sentence 1
        Detail Support Sentence 1
        Detail Support Sentence 2
    Main Support Sentence 2
        Detail Support Sentence 1
        Detail Support Sentence 2
    Main Support Sentence 3
        Detail Support Sentence 1
        Detail Support Sentence 2
Summary Sentence

Sandra Morris wrote the following expanded paragraph on the same subject: *tennis.*

```
     I enjoy playing tennis. Tennis is a great way
to relieve stress. Hitting the ball with the tennis
racket relieves my tension. It also gets my mind
off my problems. Tennis is great exercise. I do a
lot of running when playing tennis, which is great
for my leg muscles. Also when playing, I strengthen
my arm muscles. Tennis is a game of great
challenge. The game is very competitive, especially
when I am playing against someone who is better
than I. Playing tennis makes me do my best and push
myself to my limits. I feel most people would love
the game of tennis once they try it.
```

Topic Sentence: I enjoy playing tennis.
    Main Support 1: Tennis is a great way to relieve stress.

Detail Support 1: Hitting the ball with the tennis racket relieves my tension.

Detail Support 2: It also gets my mind off my problems.

Main Support 2: Tennis is great exercise.

Detail Support 1: I do a lot of running when playing tennis, which is great for my leg muscles.

Detail Support 2: Also when playing, I strengthen my arm muscles.

Main Support 3: Tennis is a game of great challenge.

Detail Support l: The game is very competitive, especially when I am playing against someone who is better than I.

Detail Support 2: Playing tennis makes me do my best and push myself to my limits.

Summary Sentence: I feel most people would love the game of tennis once they try it.

In this expanded paragraph, the topic sentence states the main idea: *I enjoy playing tennis.* Sandra's subject is *tennis;* her attitude toward this topic is that *she enjoys it.*

Point to Remember:

Each topic sentence must contain a subject and attitude extensive enough to elaborate upon in one paragraph but small enough to cover in this limited space.

You may write one or more detail support sentences for each main support sentence. Detail support not only increases the volume of your content; it adds specific detail that makes your writing enjoyable and interesting to read. Consider the following paragraph:

```
The last time I had my in-laws over for dinner

was a disaster. (Topic Sentence) The yard looked

terrible. The house was a mess. My three children

were obnoxious. The dress I decided to wear looked

awful. My husband was in a bad mood. My mother-in-

law was rude. Dinner was mediocre. There wasn't

enough salad for everyone, and to top it off, the

cake was dry. After dinner, my husband and his

father got into an argument. His parents left

early. (Summary Sentence)
```

This paragraph is flat and dull. It lacks specific details, which would make it more interesting. If you will notice, the topic sentence is clear and specific. But all the support sentences are *main support sentences;* they present no details, only value judgments. Added detail support would give the reader a clear image of the scene described, not just a summary of it.

Use the same topic sentence and main support sentences, but add some details.

Topic Sentence: The last time I had my in-laws over for dinner was a disaster.

Main Support Sentences (Value Judgments)	*Detail Support Sentences* (Concrete Evidence)
1. The yard looked terrible.	a. The dog had dug holes all over the lawn.
2. The house was a mess.	a. Assorted toys were scattered over the wooden floor where the kids had left them.
3. My three children were obnoxious.	a. My daughter hit her younger brother, who had just broken her favorite doll.
	b. The youngest child clung to my skirt and whined all night.

EXERCISE

Continue to expand this paragraph. Add one detail support sentence to illustrate each of the following main support sentences.

1. The dress I decided to wear looked awful.

_____

2. My husband was in a bad mood.

_____

3. My mother-in-law was rude.

_____

4. Dinner was mediocre.

_____

5. There wasn't enough salad for everyone.

_____

6. The cake was dry.

_____

7. After dinner, my husband and his father got into an argument.

_____

Summary Sentence: His parents left early.

EXERCISE

In the following paragraph on entertainment *by Mandy Olivieri, write* MS *above each main support sentence and* DS *above each detail support sentence.*

I love to go windsurfing on the weekends.
(**Topic Sentence**) Being athletic, I consider
windsurfing to be a sport. One can play games, such
as jousting and racing while windsurfing and
perform acrobatic tricks. With enough practice, one
can turn a complete somersault with the board.
There is also beauty in windsurfing. In the morning
and at twilight, when the ocean is quietest, I
enjoy peering through the water to see the ocean
floor. Sometimes I see shells or rocks or even fish
but never any sharks. Windsurfing is also a great
muscle toner. Because I do not have a lot of arm
strength, I can use my back and stomach muscles to
help me when I am pulling the sail out of the
water. Instead of doing 50 sit-ups, I can go windsurfing for ten minutes and still get the same
workout plus more. For the sport, the beauty, and
the physical energy involved, windsurfing is my
favorite pastime. (**Summary Sentence**)

THE SUMMARY SENTENCE

The **summary sentence** restates the main idea of the paragraph, as expressed in the topic sentence, and concludes the paragraph.[1] This final sentence should be a logical conclusion of the topic discussed.

Student John Mitchell wrote the following paragraph about *knots.*

Knots are the only tool used by firemen that are manufactured on the spot for a specific purpose. The bowline is a good knot for making a loop that will not slip when pressure is applied. The bowline is easy to tie and untie. Its primary use is in rescue. The becket, or sheet bend, is a knot with only one use, yet it is essential. The becket is used to tie two ropes of equal or unequal size together and once tightened will not slip and is difficult to untie. The clove hitch knot is used to hoist equipment. It can be tied quickly and will tighten itself when pressure is applied. When pressure is released, the clove hitch will almost fall off. Chimney hitches are used to take up slack in a rope during an operation. Since the chimney hitch is easily tied and untied, it is the desired knot for roping off an area. The half hitch is the simplest of all knots to tie, but it is extremely important. While it is only a loop, this knot is used as a safety on all other knots. This simple knot ensures that the more complex knots will not

---

[1]Later on, when you learn how to write a complete essay, the summary sentence can also serve as a transition sentence between paragraphs, leading the reader on to the next concept. Transitions are discussed in the next section.

`slip or fall apart.` *Whether a fireman is rescuing a person, hoisting a tool, or roping off an area, the knot is an essential firefighting tool.* (**Summary Sentence**)

Each of the following exercises presents a paragraph written by Neil Fishner followed by three summary sentences. Choose the best summary sentence for each paragraph.

1. Tornadoes are violent storms. Twisters are generally funnel-shaped clouds extending downward from a connective cloud in a severe thunderstorm. In a tornado, air rises rapidly in the outer region of the funnel and descends in its core, which has very low pressure. High-velocity winds spiral in and around the core. Tornadoes have been known to move at 200 meters per second, causing total devastation and possible loss of life.
   a. Tornadoes are obviously dangerous and cause damage.
   b. Tornadoes are violent storms, causing destruction and death.
   c. Tornadoes can occur at any time in the United States and Australia.

2. Going to college for the first time is very challenging. Some students go away to another city or state, and some stay home and attend community colleges. Students must adjust to a more flexible class schedule. The first-time college student must also learn to balance time needed for studying, working, and having fun. For those students who leave home to attend distant colleges, an adjustment must be made to a life away from parents.
   a. Students who go away to college tend to party more.
   b. So whether at home or away, college is a very challenging step the first time around.
   c. Starting college requires a lot of time adjusting to flexible schedules and learning how to balance time among school, work, and play.

3. Speaking in front of a group of people for the very first time can be very nerve wracking. First, your body is shaking from stage fright, and you are sure that you are going to say the wrong thing. You quickly look down to see if your clothing is proper so that your audience will listen to you, not look at your attire. Nervously, you speak so fast that no one can understand what you are saying, and the fear arises that you may be putting your audience to sleep. You flip the last card, and finally, your speech is done.
   a. Men should always check their zippers before starting their speeches.
   b. Giving speeches can be a very scary and nerve-wracking event.
   c. Speeches are better the second time around.

TRANSITIONAL DEVICES

Transitions are words or phrases that bring unity and coherence to a paragraph by indicating the exact relationship between sentences. Transitions lead your reader logically through the paragraph; therefore, you must carefully choose the transitions that fit your meaning.

Transitional devices are like bridges from one idea to another. If the bridge is missing, the reader may not be able to cross to the next thought. Not every sentence has to contain a transitional device, but using transitions effectively will add coherence to your writing.

Commonly Used Transitional Devices

To indicate cause and effect: accordingly, as a result, because, consequently, for this purpose, hence, so, then, therefore, thereupon, thus, to this end

To indicate comparison: again, also, in the same way, likewise, once more, similarly

To indicate concession: although it is true that, granted that, I admit that, it may appear that, naturally, and of course

To indicate conclusion or summary: all in all, as a result, as has been noted, as indicated, in any event, in conclusion, in short, therefore, to conclude, to summarize, to sum up

To indicate contrast: although, but, despite, even though, however, in contrast, in spite of, instead, nevertheless, nonetheless, notwithstanding, on the contrary, on the other hand, regardless, still, though, yet

To indicate example: after all, even, for example, for instance, indeed, in fact, of course, specifically, such as, the following example, to illustrate

To indicate place: above, adjacent to, below, beyond, closer to, elsewhere, far, farther on, here, near, nearby, opposite to, there, to the left, to the right, straight ahead

To indicate sequence: again, also, and, and then, besides, finally, first, second, third, furthermore, last, moreover, next, still, too

To indicate time: after a bit, after a few days, after a while, afterward, as long as, as soon as, at last, at length, at that time, before, earlier, immediately, in the meantime, in the past, lately, later, meanwhile, now, presently, shortly, simultaneously, since, so far, soon, than, thereafter, until, when

---

The following paragraph by student Jeanette Cuervo has been edited to remove all transitional devices. The result is a choppy, abrupt flow of ideas that is hard to follow.

My name is Jeanette Cuervo, and I was born in Havana, Cuba, in 1969. I cannot remember all the names of important places in Cuba. I have a great love for all the friends, my first home, and some family members that I left behind. My parents and I moved to Spain for two years. Spain is a beautiful country with a lot of friendly people. I went to school, but classes over there are not so easy as compared to those here. One student in the eighth grade, who is taking a math class over there, will be more advanced than a student who is taking a math class here. A lot of teenagers never graduate from high school since the classes are so hard. Spain has a large percentage of people who are unemployed. Many teenagers start working at a young age and do not finish school. Having experienced two other countries with totally different governmental systems, I really believe the United States has the best one.

The following paragraph is the original written by Jeanette, in which she uses transitional devices to lead us through the narrative about her life:

My name is Jeanette Cuervo, and I was born in Havana, Cuba, in 1969. *Although* I cannot remember all the names of important places in Cuba, I have a great love for all the friends, my first home, and some family members that I left behind. *When I was eleven,* my parents and I moved to Spain for two years. *I must admit,* Spain is a beautiful country with a lot of friendly people. *During those two years,* I went to school, but classes over there are not so easy as compared to those here. *For example,* one student in the eighth grade, who is taking a math class over there, will be more advanced than a student who is taking a math class here. A lot of teenagers never graduate from high school since the classes are so hard. *Also,* Spain has a large percentage of people who are unemployed. *As a result,* many teenagers start working at a young age and do not finish school. *After* having experienced two other countries with totally different governmental systems, I really believe the United States has the best one.

EXERCISE

The following paragraph, written by Danielle, is missing transitional words. Fill in each blank with an appropriate transitional word. Refer to the list of commonly used transitions on page 279.

The sky projects a colorful character and several different personalities. A partly cloudy sky gives one the impression that it has many thoughts on its mind. _____, billowing white cotton candy clouds against a blue background create shapes of the sky's thoughts into marvelous

images that reveal its artistic imagination. _____
_____ playing hide and seek, the sun contributes by highlighting the unusual shapes, creating a picturesque work of art. _____,
the artistic personality of the sky surely can
radiate endearing beauty on the never ending canvas
it possesses. _____, the swift-moving,
darkening clouds reveal an emotional temperament.
The looming black and gray show the heaven's anger
with the roaring, cracking sounds of thunder;
_____, one should be wise enough to know
that there is no arguing back. _____,
the sky flares with brilliant anger, spitting bolts
of lightning, _____ indicating that
nature's creatures better stay out of its way.
_____, another side of the sky's person-
ality is a clear night, showing how serene and
friendly it can be. _____, the sky's
eyes twinkle with happy thoughts through the shining stars, _____ with the depth of clear
nights, the sky's mysterious thoughts stay well
hidden. _____ there is a glorious
sunrise or sunset, the sky displays a lovely color
of innocent blush. _____, the sky's
character and personality are interesting, and one
might wonder what this heavenly body will do next.

Putting It All Together

Once you've learned the structure of an expanded paragraph, do not feel that you must use it rigidly. Rather, use it as a simple but effective strategy to ensure that all of your abstractions and value judgments (main support sentences) are illustrated with one or more concrete statements of specific evidence (detail support sentences). The expanded paragraph structure is a good tool to rely on when you are writing timed papers or taking essay exams. Such a tool will help you flesh out content and produce fully developed paragraphs.

Point to Remember:

Whenever you write a sentence of value judgment, always follow it with one or more sentences of concrete evidence.

The following paragraph by Joe Kerkes uses the expanded paragraph structure to write about a form of entertainment: *using his personal computer.*

```
     Using my personal computer is entertainment at

its best. I have a copious collection of software

that I run on my computer. I write résumés and

reports using word-processing software. I also

create databases and spreadsheets using commercial

productivity programs and sometimes find myself

frittering away the hours playing one of the many

games I have acquired. A unique contrivance that

has been the object of my attention lately is a

gizmo known as a "mouse." I use it to draw and edit

in various programs. My favorite facet of "mousing"

is creating my own menus. Overall, I derive the

most satisfaction from writing programs using a

language like BASIC or Pascal. I have also written

a program that stores data to floppy disks and can

be recalled and edited as a file. Writing programs
```

```
allows me to create my own custom applications,

such as accounting modules and databases. I find

all aspects of computing fascinating.
```

The diagram below shows how Joe's paragraph is divided into the main and detail support structure.

Topic Sentence:	Using my personal computer is entertainment at its best.
Main Support 1:	I have a copious collection of software that I run on my computer.
Detail Support 1:	I write résumés and reports using word-processing software.
Detail Support 2:	I also create databases and spreadsheets using commercial productivity programs and sometimes find myself frittering away the hours playing one of the many games I have acquired.
Main Support 2:	A unique contrivance that has been the object of my attention lately is a gizmo known as the "mouse."
Detail Support 1:	I use it to draw and edit in various programs.
Detail Support 2:	My favorite facet of "mousing" is creating my own menus.
Main Support 3:	Overall, I derive the most satisfaction from programs using a language like BASIC or Pascal.
Detail Support 1:	I have also written a program that stores data to floppy disks and can be recalled and edited as a file.
Detail Support 2:	Writing programs allows me to create my own applications, such as accounting modules and databases.
Summary Sentence:	I find all aspects of computing fascinating.

EXERCISE

Earlier in this chapter, you created main support sentences for three of five different topic sentences:

1. *My college education will change my life.*
2. *Horror movies scare me to death!*
3. *Travelling is exciting.*

4. *My everyday activities cause me a lot of stress.*
5. *There is nothing more wonderful than falling in love.*

Now, take one of these topic sentences and the three main support sentences that you created and write an expanded paragraph. Remember, for every main support sentence, you should have one or more detail support sentences.

_____

_____

_____

_____

_____

_____

_____

_____

_____

_____

_____

_____

_____

_____

_____

_____

_____

_____

_____

_____

WRITING ASSIGNMENT

Write an expanded paragraph about your favorite form of entertainment: sports, movies, or music.

Step 1: Prewriting

Use the prewriting techniques mapping and listing to generate ideas about your favorite form of entertainment. Narrow your list to one topic on which you can write a paragraph. If you need help with narrowing the topic, see Chapter 2, "Organizing Your Ideas."

Step 2: Writing

Write your paragraph here.

_____

_____

_____

_____

_____

_____

_____

_____

_____

_____

_____

_____

_____

_____

_____

_____

_____

_____

Step 3: Revising, Editing, and Proofreading

After completing your paragraph, reread it. Check to see if any transitional devices are needed, and add them. Make sure that your topic sentence and summary sentence are focused. As always, check your spelling and punctuation.

Strategies for Paragraph Organization

In Chapter 2, "Organizing Your Ideas," we reviewed how to develop ideas and organize them into a logical order. In this chapter, you will learn additional organizational strategies. A writer who has carefully organized data, information, or ideas will already have a rough plan for the first draft of the paragraph. The following 12 organizational strategies will allow you to organize your thoughts in specific patterns while constructing your paragraph.

Degree of Importance

For this organizational strategy, your facts, events, or information should be listed from least important to most important. All that has to be considered is the relative importance of your data. If some points are less important, list them first, and save the more important facts for the end of your paragraph. You build from minor facts gradually to the most important fact or facts.

This organizational strategy can be used with any of the other strategies to arrange your facts better. In the following paragraph, Sheron LeGrant writes about Leonardo da Vinci (see Chapter 2 for the prewriting and organization explanations) using the organizational strategy of degree of importance to make her writing more effective.

```
    Leonardo da Vinci was a true Renaissance man,

excelling as an engineer, scientist, and artist.

Leonardo became an engineer as a result of his

interest in anything mechanical. He was among the

first to draw mechanical figures in an accurate,
```

precise manner. He designed such items as a parachute and a flying machine. After many studies, da Vinci wrote a book on mechanics. As his curiosity led him to investigate mechanical objects, it also made da Vinci, the scientist, interested in how the human body works. Leonardo studied anatomy to understand the structure of the human body. He furthered his knowledge of anatomy by doing dissections. He was among the first to document his studies by writing a book on anatomy. Da Vinci, the artist, used his artistic ability to record his observations. His pen-and-ink drawings of human anatomy were extremely accurate. His "divine proportions" of the human body came as a result of his anatomical studies. He developed a book on the theory of painting. Da Vinci then used his unique knowledge of human form and painting to create such famous works as the *Virgin of the Rocks, Mona Lisa,* and *The Last Supper.* Leonardo da Vinci was one of the most versatile men of all times and is admired even today for his engineering inventions, his scientific investigations, and his legacy of great art.

EXERCISE

In this exercise you will work on three topics. Use a prewriting technique (see Chapter 1) to generate ideas about each; write the generated ideas in the left-

hand column. In the right-hand column, rewrite your ideas in order of least important to most important.

Topic: Pollution

List of Ideas	*From Least to Most Important*
_____	_____
_____	_____
_____	_____
_____	_____
_____	_____
_____	_____
_____	_____
_____	_____

Topic: Reasons you need a college education

List of Ideas	*From Least to Most Important*
_____	_____
_____	_____
_____	_____
_____	_____
_____	_____
_____	_____
_____	_____
_____	_____

Topic: Reasons it is important to be able to write well

List of Ideas	*From Least to Most Important*
_____	_____
_____	_____
_____	_____
_____	_____
_____	_____
_____	_____
_____	_____
_____	_____
_____	_____

Illustration

With this strategy, you state your point and then provide examples to illustrate or prove it.

Example:

Topic: Computers

Hand-held computers

Personal computers

Minicomputers

Mainframe computers

Supercomputers

Carolyn Smith uses the illustration strategy in this paragraph about the different types of computers.

```
     If you ask the average person about computers,

he may visualize a keyboard and a monitor; however,
```

there are a variety of computers that do an infinite number of activities we often take for granted. Hand-held computers, such as calculators, TV remote controls, and cable boxes are found in nearly every home. Personal computers, such as the IBM PC, are used to do household budgets, keep books for small businesses, and even play video games. Minicomputers matching the DEC VAX are used to scan groceries at the checkout, do desktop publishing, and operate the rides at Disney World. Mainframes similar to the IBM 3090 series are used to process large volumes of data rapidly. These systems can be found in telephone companies and banks. Supercomputers such as those invented by Seymour Cray are used for government research and development by such organizations as National Aeronautics and Space Administration (NASA), the Internal Revenue Service (IRS), and the Central Intelligence Agency (CIA). It is amazing that such a variety of computers exist on the market today.

EXERCISE

Listed below are three topics. Choose one of these or create your own to write about, illustrating it with examples.

Topics: *How teenagers dress alike*
         How friends support each other in good and bad times
         What motion pictures I would like to make

Step 1: Use a prewriting technique (see Chapter 1) to generate examples that illustrate your topic statement. List your ideas on the lines below, and then organize them in order from least important to most important.

_____

_____

_____

_____

_____

_____

_____

_____

_____

_____

_____

_____

Step 2: Write your topic sentence on the line below. (If you need help formulating a topic sentence, refer to Chapter 22, "The Process of Writing a Paragraph.")

_____

Step 3: Use the space below to write your paragraph.

_____

_____

_____

_____

_____

_____

_____

_____

_____

_____

_____

_____

_____

_____

Step 4: After writing your paragraph, reread it. Make sure that you have used a variety of sentence patterns. As always, check your spelling and punctuation.

Description

This strategy allows your reader to see your topic as you describe it from top to bottom, front to back, outside to inside, or some other pattern.

Example:

Topic: Snowfall

Gray clouds hide the sun

Snow like soft down falls

God's fluffy blanket

No two flakes are alike

Kids catch flakes on their tongues

Air is fresh and crisp

Smoke from warm fires

James Ciaccio uses the descriptive method to organize his observations of a snowfall.

```
The sky is gray, and the air is bone-chilling

cold. The sun is hiding, withholding its brilliant
```

rays of warmth and happiness. Suddenly, from the sky, soft downy snow begins to fall. It is as though God has decided to bundle up the imperfections of the world in a fluffy blanket of purity. One by one, each snowflake falls. No two fall in the same place or are of the same size or shape. Some are stolen by tongues that snatch them from the sky, only to be analyzed by the taste buds as being cold and bitter. Each flake, with its shiny, diamondlike appearance, soon joins with the next to form a giant patchwork. As each flake falls, another stitch in the blanket is completed. Once the crafty needlework is finished, all that remains are the glistening white streets that illuminate the city, making up for the sun's hidden rays. The air is fresh, crisp, and clean, filled with the aroma of burning wood that is warming hearts and homes. The day has become cheery and bright.

EXERCISE

Listed below are three topics. Choose one of these or create your own to describe.

Topics: *The beach at sunset or midday*
Your dream car
A thunderstorm

Step 1: Use one of the prewriting techniques (see Chapter 1) to generate descriptive terms or phrases about your topic. Once you have generated a list of ideas, arrange them in a logical order of description: from top to bottom, from bottom to top, from front to back, or any other way that will give your reader a mental picture of the object or scene that you are describing. List your ideas in the left-

hand column, and arrange them in a logical spatial order in the right-hand column.

<table>
<tr><td align="center">*List of Ideas*</td><td align="center">*Logical Spatial Order*</td></tr>
<tr><td>_____</td><td>_____</td></tr>
<tr><td>_____</td><td>_____</td></tr>
<tr><td>_____</td><td>_____</td></tr>
<tr><td>_____</td><td>_____</td></tr>
<tr><td>_____</td><td>_____</td></tr>
<tr><td>_____</td><td>_____</td></tr>
<tr><td>_____</td><td>_____</td></tr>
<tr><td>_____</td><td>_____</td></tr>
<tr><td>_____</td><td>_____</td></tr>
</table>

Step 2: Write your topic sentence on the line below. (If you need help formulating a topic sentence, refer to Chapter 22, "The Process of Writing a Paragraph.")

_____

Step 3: Use the space below to write your paragraph.

_____

_____

_____

_____

_____

_____

_____

_____

_____

_____

_____

_____

_____

_____

Step 4: After you have finished writing your paragraph, reread it. Make sure that you have developed your description in a logical order. Again, check your spelling and punctuation.

Chronology

Events can be listed in a time sequence, or chronology. This organizational technique can also be called narrative.

Example:
Topic: August 12, 1988, fishing trip

Left Clearwater Beach

Developed some engine trouble

Arrived at the fishing spot

Fishing was great

Engine would not start

Battery dead

Radio dead

32 hours at sea

Prayed for good weather and help

Seasick

Hungry, ate raw fish

No water

Rescued by Coast Guard

Fred Astea uses the narrative method of organization in the following paragraph about his experience on the Gulf of Mexico.

On August 12, 1988, my father and I decided to take out the family boat for a short fishing trip to Clearwater Beach. On the way out, we began to experience engine trouble but decided to continue our trip. Upon arrival at our destination, which was approximately 40 miles west of Clearwater Beach, the fishing was excellent and we forgot all about the engine problems. Several hours later, we terminated our fishing expedition and found out that the engine would not start. Having depleted the battery of its energy, we discovered that the VHF radio would not transmit. We spent the next 32 hours at sea. During this time, we became very religious and began to pray for help and good weather. The second thing we did was ration the two remaining sodas as we did not know how long it would be before help arrived. During the evening hours, it was very dark and the wind began to pick up, rocking the boat up and down and making us seasick. The next morning, we were very hungry, so we decided to fillet thin slices of fish, which became our diet. We were finally rescued by the Coast Guard. Since that time, I've learned not to use the boat unless the engine is in good shape, to carry an extra battery, and to have sufficient food aboard.

EXERCISE

Listed below are three topics. Choose one of these or create your own to write a narrative/chronology about.

Topics: *A special surprise*
           An exciting adventure
           An award or prize you have won

Step 1: Use one of the prewriting techniques (see Chapter 1) to generate ideas for your topic. List them in chronological order to best narrate the topic that you have chosen.

_____

_____

_____

_____

_____

_____

_____

_____

_____

_____

_____

_____

_____

_____

Step 2: Write your topic sentence on the line below. (If you need help formulating a topic sentence, refer to Chapter 22, "The Process of Writing a Paragraph.")

_____

Step 3: Use the following space to write your paragraph.

_____

_____

_____

_____

_____

_____

_____

_____

_____

_____

_____

_____

_____

_____

_____

_____

Step 4: After you have completed your paragraph, reread it. Check to see if your facts are in chronological order. Check for subject-verb agreement, and correct any spelling or punctuation errors.

Process/Directional

Use this technique to describe how to do something—a process. Begin with the first step, and proceed logically to a conclusion. Recipes and directions for assembly are two common examples of process/directional writing.

Example:

Topic: How to fill an empty refrigerator

Step 1: Clean out the refrigerator.

Step 2: Get rid of all strange foods.

Step 3: Eat all the junk food.

Step 4: Don't buy groceries.

Step 5: Dress in loose-fitting clothes.

Step 6: Act poor.

Step 7: Call Mom or Dad, and act starved.

In the next example paragraph, Carolyn Smith humorously tells us how to fill an empty refrigerator.

How do you fill an empty refrigerator? These directions will not work for everyone, but if you are single, live alone, and have not yet reached executive status at your job, this method may work for you. First, you must clean out your refrigerator of all green or otherwise unrecognizable matter. Second, hide or give all those cans of beets and other strange foods that you bought for that weird diet and never planned to eat. Third, finish off all the potato chips, beer, chocolate chip cookies, and any other junk food that may be stored in your cupboards. Next, postpone buying groceries for two days. This whole process will give your kitchen an appearance of emptiness. The next step is to dress in loose-fitting clothes to give the impression that you have lost weight. You may also want to lend a trustworthy friend your television or stereo. The bareness of your apartment will give the appearance that your valuables have been pawned. The last crucial step depends on your gender. If you are a female, call your father, and in that "Daddy's girl" voice, invite him over. If you are a male, invite your mother over in your best "Momma's boy" voice. These very subtle hints will almost guarantee that the parent will return with a bag or two of groceries. Hence, you will have a full refrigerator. This method always worked for me; however, the only drawback is that moms and dads always seem to buy only the healthiest food.

EXERCISE

Listed below are three topics. Choose one of these or create your own to explain using the process/directional strategy.

Topics: How to trim a Christmas tree
How to bathe a cat
How to vote

Step 1: Use one of the prewriting techniques (see Chapter 1) to generate ideas for your subject. It is most important, in this type of organizational strategy, to start at the first step and continue step by step until the process is complete. Use the lines below to list your directions or process from the first step to the last step.

_____

_____

_____

_____

_____

_____

_____

_____

_____

_____

_____

_____

_____

_____

Step 2: Write your topic sentence on the line below. (If you need help formulating a topic sentence, refer to Chapter 22, "The Process of Writing a Paragraph.")

_____

Step 3: Use the space below to write your paragraph.

_____

_____

_____

_____

_____

_____

_____

_____

_____

_____

_____

_____

_____

Step 4: After you have finished writing your paragraph, reread it. Be sure that you have included all the logical steps in your instructions or process. Check for subject-verb agreement, and correct any spelling and punctuation errors.

Cause-and-Effect

In this strategy, you can either state an *effect* and then list its *causes,* or present the *causes* first and describe the *effect(s)* they have.

Example:

Topic: Cause: Parents ignore preschoolers

Effects:

1. Crying—Alerts parent

2. Aggression—Punishment instead of understanding

3. Withdrawal—Unnoticed by parent

The cause-and-effect organizational technique is used by Debbie Owen in the following paragraph about her experiences with her son.

Many times, a parent does not take the time to listen actively to her preschooler. This is an age of great emotional development for the child, and the effects of being ignored can be devastating. Children react in three different ways. Some will cry because their feelings are hurt. Fortunately, crying alerts the parent to the problem and gives her the opportunity to stop what she is doing and see what is wrong with her youngster. Other children become aggressive and try to demand the parent's attention. This behavior often backfires for the child; however, he usually ends up being disciplined for his unacceptable behavior rather than making the parent understand the reason for the outburst in the first place. The third type of reaction is often the most difficult to recognize. The child is so hurt that he quietly withdraws from the family. This withdrawal is usually so subtle that it can easily be mistaken by the parent as a long-awaited moment's peace, and the child's hurt goes on unnoticed. It is very important for the parent to look at herself objectively and to be aware of how she is interacting with her child. By taking the time to listen actively to what her child has to say, she is showing her child that she is interested in him, and her child's self-esteem will be given an important boost.

EXERCISE

Listed below are three topics. Choose one of these or create your own to write about using the cause-and-effect strategy.

Topics: *Improved study habits*
      Pollution
      Voter apathy

Step 1: Your topic will be the effect. *Use one of the prewriting techniques (see Chapter 1) to generate the possible* causes. *Organize your ideas in a logical order, such as from least important to most important.*

Step 2: Write your topic sentence on the line below. (If you need help formulating a topic sentence, refer to Chapter 22, "The Process of Writing a Paragraph.")

_____

Step 3: Use the space below to write your paragraph.

_____

_____

_____

_____

_____

_____

_____

_____

_____

_____

_____

_____

_____

_____

_____

Step 4: After you have finished your paragraph, reread it. Check to see if you have used sufficient main and detail support sentences. Be sure to check your spelling and punctuation.

Comparison and Contrast

This strategy focuses on how things are alike and different. Such an analysis can be developed in two ways: the alternating method and the block method.

With the ***alternating*** **method,** you make a direct, point-by-point argument, showing how two topics are either clearly alike or different. For instance, if you describe the size of one thing, you then describe the size of the other. The use of transitions is vital in this type of organizational strategy. The comparison may be bland and even confusing if the ideas are not presented coherently.

The alternating method is especially effective in comparing topics that are quite different, such as opposites.

Example:

Topic: Life in the city and life in the country

City	*Country*
covered with buildings	farms, fields, trees
traffic unbearable	very few cars on roads
streets rough and torn up	roads smooth and hilly
office-related jobs	farming-related jobs
buy most food	grow most food

Suzanne Brown uses this method of alternating subjects to contrast life in the city with life in the country.

The city and the country are two very different places to live. The city is mostly covered with buildings, both large and small, while the country consists mostly of farms, fields of crops and trees, and plenty of animals. Traffic is often unbearable in the city; it is all hustle and bustle. On the contrary, the country is quiet and relaxed. You see very few cars on the roads. The streets in the city are rough and often torn up; however, the country roads are smooth and hilly. The jobs in the city are mostly office related. In contrast, people in the country work on farms; they prepare and clean crops for sale. Families from the city buy most, if not all, of the food they eat. A lot of people in the country grow most of their own food. City life and country life both have their advantages and disadvantages.

With the **block method,** you discuss each topic separately, or in individual blocks. There is no going back and forth between topics, point by point; rather, you discuss the first topic in full before moving on to the second. In this case, a clear transition is needed at the point at which you end the discussion of the first topic and switch to the second.

The comparison made using the block method is much less direct than that made using the alternating method. Look again at the city life/country life comparison, restructured using the block method.

Example:

Topic: Life in the city and life in the country

City

covered with buildings

traffic unbearable

streets rough and torn up

office-related jobs

buy most food

Country

farms, fields, and trees

few cars

smooth, hilly roads

farming-related jobs

grow most food

Suzanne Brown rewrote her paragraph as follows:

The city and the country are two very different

places to live. The city is mostly covered with

buildings, both large and small. The buildings

mainly consist of food and clothing stores and

offices. Traffic is often unbearable in the city.

People are always in a hurry as they go about their

own business. The city is just hustle and bustle;

streets are often rough and torn up. Jobs in the

city are mostly office related. The people buy

their food in grocery stores. *On the other hand*, the country consists mostly of farms, fields of crops and trees, and animals. There are few cars on the smooth and hilly country roads. Living in the country is very peaceful and relaxing. The people are friendly to each other. Many of the jobs in the country consist of working on farms and preparing and cleaning the crops for sale. The farmers raise most of their own food. City life and country life have their advantages and disadvantages; however, I prefer living in the city.

EXERCISE

Listed below are three topics. Choose one of these or create your own to compare and contrast, using either the alternating method or the block method.

Topics: *Private colleges/Public colleges*
Foreign cars/Domestic cars
Vacationing at the beach/Vacationing in the mountains

Step 1: Use one of the prewriting techniques (see Chapter 1) to generate ideas about each of the compared/contrasted subjects. Organize your information on the lines below.

_____

_____

_____

_____

_____

_____

_____

_____

_____

_____

_____

_____

_____

_____

_____

Step 2: Write your topic sentence on the line below. (If you need help formulating a topic sentence, refer to Chapter 22, "The Process of Writing a Paragraph.")

_____

Step 3: Use the space below to write your paragraph.

_____

_____

_____

_____

_____

_____

_____

_____

_____

_____

_____

_____

_____

_____

_____

Step 4: After you have finished your paragraph, reread it. Check for misplaced or dangling modifiers. Also check your spelling and punctuation.

Classification

To *classify* means to place information into categories. To do so, you must first establish some sort of *criterion:* a rule to follow in deciding which information goes in which category. This is somewhat like comparison/contrast in that you look for likenesses among things; similar things obviously belong in the same category.

Some classifications are obvious, for instance, grouping people by age, sex, income, education, and so on. Demographics rely on this type of classification. In the following example, the large group *blood donors* is broken up into smaller groups, showing the types of people who give blood.

Example:

Topic: Blood donors

Students	5%
Elderly persons	10%
Professional businesspeople	65%

Sandra Bourget chose blood donors as her topic, using the classification strategy to illustrate her topic. She also arranges her different categories of blood donors in order from least to most important in terms of what percentage of the group they comprise.

    Many different types of people are blood donors.

Each and every one is vital to the health of our

country. High school students make up approximately

5 percent of our donor population. Any student 17

years of age with parents' permission may donate.

Research shows that many adults who began donating

as students have continued this life-saving

practice throughout their adult lives. Many retired

persons don't realize that in a state such as Florida, they can donate blood until their 86th birthday. Who says that just because your body ages that your blood does, too? Our elderly donors seem to be our safest donors. In their youth, promiscuous sex and illicit drug use were not common practices. Professional businesspeople with an eye on community involvement make up the largest group of donors. When a mobile unit is brought to their place of employment, they do not mind taking 20 minutes out of their schedule to help save a life. Allowing its employees to donate blood also puts the sponsoring company in the spotlight as a community-minded organization. Blood donors are a special breed. Only a small portion of the nation's population donates blood. Blood is the gift of life.

EXERCISE

Listed below are three topics. Choose one of these topics or create your own to classify.

Topics: *Spectator sports*
        Current fashion fads
        Occupations

Step 1: Use one of the prewriting techniques (see Chapter 1) to generate as many ideas about your topic as you can. Organize your data into categories on the lines below.

_____

_____

_____

_____

_____

_____

_____

_____

_____

_____

_____

_____

Step 2: Write your topic sentence on the line below. (If you need help formulating a topic sentence, refer to Chapter 22, "The Process of Writing a Paragraph.")

_____

Step 3: Use the space below to write your paragraph.

_____

_____

_____

_____

_____

_____

_____

_____

_____

_____

_____

_____

_____

Step 4: After you have completed writing your paragraph, reread it. Determine if you have a clear classification of facts. Revise your paragraph if you find any topic placed in an inappropriate classification. As always, check spelling and punctuation.

Division

In the division strategy, a single topic is broken into components. The idea is that you can understand the whole by looking at its parts. This is not only an effective means of explaining something to the reader; it also makes the writer's job easier. Rather than address one large topic, you can break it up and examine several smaller issues individually. For instance, in writing about an airplane, it would be useful to explain the function of each of its parts.

Example:

Topic: An airplane

Fuselage

Wings

Rudder

Elevator

Ken McBride uses the division strategy to describe the parts of an airplane in the following paragraph.

    An airplane is made up of several different
    parts. The long cylindrical body of the airplane is
    called the "fuselage." The fuselage acts as the
    main structure of the airplane and accommodates

many passengers. The "wings" are the structures that protrude out from both sides of the airplane. They give the airplane lift, which enables it to climb into the air. Located at the rear of the airplane is the "rudder." It helps to prevent rotation while it stabilizes the airplane and contributes to some of the turning. The "elevator," at the rear of the airplane keeps it aloft. When the airplane moves up or down, the elevator is the control surface doing the work. The elevator also helps while banking in a turn. These parts and many more enable the airplane to fly miles into the blue sky.

EXERCISE

Listed below are three topics. Choose one of these or create your own to explain using the division organizational strategy.

Topics: The branches of the United States government
          A football team
          An orchestra

Step 1: Use a prewriting technique (see Chapter 1) to generate ideas about your topic. List the components of your topics on the lines below.

_____

_____

_____

_____

_____

_____

_____

_____

_____

_____

_____

_____

_____

_____

Step 2: Write your topic sentence on the line below. (If you need help formulating a topic sentence, refer to Chapter 22, "The Process of Writing a Paragraph.")

_____

Step 3: Use the space below to write your paragraph.

_____

_____

_____

_____

_____

_____

_____

_____

_____

_____

_____

_____

_____

_____

_____

Step 4: After you have completed writing your paragraph, reread it. Determine if you have used the division strategy effectively. Revise your paragraph as needed for clarity. Check your spelling and punctuation.

Definition

To *define* something means to explain what it is. There are obviously many ways to do that. Think of what is included in a dictionary definition. It begins with a statement of general meaning; if there are alternate meanings, each is given, usually in order of importance. The definition may give examples of how the word can be used in a sentence, sometimes in its various forms. It may also give synonyms (like words) and antonyms (opposite words); the etymology (history) of the word may be outlined as well.

In using definition as an organizational strategy, follow the example set by the dictionary. Begin with a statement of general meaning, and then proceed to explain your topic using a variety of organizational strategies: illustration, comparison/contrast, classification, and so on.

You must decide which strategy will work best given your topic. In the following example, Beth Borgo decided that the best way to define *bouquet* was to give examples of the types and uses. Note that she begins with a two-part definition of the word *bouquet* and then lists examples for support material.

Example:

> Topic: Bouquet
> Definition: A cluster of flowers or a pleasant fragrance
>
> *Examples of bouquets*
>
> cluster of flowers
>
> wedding bouquets
>
> bouquets brought by suitors
>
> grocery stores sell them
>
> *Examples of pleasant fragrances*

In writing her paragraph, Beth chose to emphasize the first part of the definition of *bouquet,* "a cluster of flowers." She lists the different examples of bouquets; then she lists the second definition, that of a "pleasant fragrance," using the examples of liquor and wine.

The word "bouquet" is from the Old North French word "bosquet," meaning "clump." A bouquet of flowers is used for many purposes. Bouquets are one of the main parts of a wedding. All single girls gather, and the bride throws her bouquet. Whoever catches the bouquet is supposedly the next to be married. A bouquet can be a cluster of any type of flowers. During the holidays, thousands of arranged bouquets are sent to parents, grandparents, girlfriends, and special people. Bouquets are often given to a special person, just to let her know that she is being thought about or just to brighten up her day. In the past, and fortunately sometimes today, when the male picked up his date, it was proper to give the girl a bouquet of flowers at the time of greeting. Grocery stores sell bunches of bouquets that one can purchase to brighten up one's home or to purchase as a gift for someone. The word "bouquet" is also used to describe an aroma of a wine or a liqueur. These two examples are the best ways one can describe the word "bouquet."

EXERCISE

Listed below are three topics. Choose one of these or create your own to define.

Topics: *Crystal*
            Spice
            Gift

Step 1: Look up the definition of the word you chose in the dictionary. Keeping in mind the definition of your word, use one of the prewriting techniques (see Chapter 1) to generate material to further define your topic. Use the lines below to list your ideas and organize them in the order of least to most important.

_____

_____

_____

_____

_____

_____

_____

_____

_____

_____

_____

_____

_____

Step 2: Write your topic sentence on the line below. (If you need help formulating a topic sentence, refer to Chapter 22, "The Process of Writing a Paragraph.")

_____

Step 3: Use the space below to write your paragraph.

_____

_____

_____

_____

_____

_____

_____

_____

_____

_____

_____

_____

_____

_____

_____

Step 4: After you have completed writing your paragraph, reread it. Have you defined your topic clearly and completely? Consider if your information is presented in order from least to most important. As always, check your spelling and punctuation.

Persuasion/Argument

The persuasion/argument strategy is very straightforward: You state your position on an issue and back it up with points of proof, or supportive material. As with definition, that supportive material may be presented using other organizational strategies, depending on what suits your topic. In the following example, a cause-and-effect strategy is used, showing how heart disease can be prevented (effect) by altering certain lifestyle factors (causes).

Example:

Position: Heart disease can be prevented.

Points of proof: Reduce stress

Exercise

Stop smoking

Keep hypertension under control

Keep cholesterol level normal

Paramedic Ron Van Dyke uses this persuasion organizational strategy in the following paragraph to convince us that heart disease can be prevented.

Heart disease can be prevented by avoiding or reducing the risk factors. Stress is a risk factor that is sometimes easy to reduce. The work atmosphere or work schedule may need to be changed to lower stress. Most employers have the resources available to assist employees with stress management. Lack of exercise is a common risk factor. Sedentary jobs unfortunately promote sedentary lifestyles. Regular exercise is paramount to a healthy heart. Cigarettes, a significant risk factor, are consumed by approximately 30 percent of the adult population. Cigarette smoking makes the heart and lungs work harder, thus causing premature aging of these organs. High blood pressure is the leading cause of heart disease and often goes untreated. "Hypertension," another name for high blood pressure, is treatable with medication and diet. A high blood cholesterol level is by far the most common and most controllable risk factor. Consumption of fatty foods and lack of dietary fiber are causes of high cholesterol levels in the blood. Heart disease is one of the leading killers of mankind. Its risk factors can be as easy to avoid as taking a walk in the park and eating a proper diet.

EXERCISE

Listed below are three topics. Choose any of these topics or create one of your own to argue.

Topics: Abortion should be a matter of free choice.
Industry is the major cause of pollution.
Burning the U.S. flag should be illegal.

Step 1: Decide on an issue and determine which position you are going to take. Write your position statement on the line below.

_____

Use a prewriting technique (see Chapter 1) to generate data that will prove your position statement. Use the lines below to list your arguments; organize them in order from least to most important.

_____

_____

_____

_____

_____

_____

_____

_____

_____

_____

_____

_____

_____

_____

Step 2: Write your topic sentence on the line below. (If you need help formulating a topic sentence, refer to Chapter 22, "The Process of Writing a Paragraph.")

_____

Step 3: Use the space below to write your paragraph.

_____

_____

_____

_____

_____

_____

_____

_____

_____

_____

_____

_____

_____

_____

Step 4: After you have completed writing your paragraph, reread it. Evaluate whether your argument is convincing. Have you provided sufficient support material to prove your point? Check your spelling and punctuation.

Problem and Solution

The problem-and-solution strategy is also straightforward: You state a problem, and then list possible solutions to it. In recommending solutions, consider arranging them in order of importance (i.e., likelihood of success) or even chronologically, if appropriate.

Example:

Problem: I can't wake up in the morning.

Solutions: Go to bed early.

Get plenty of sleep.

Make lunch and get clothes ready the night before.

Shower in the morning.

Set alarm ahead.

Tanya Pereira has a serious problem that most of us have faced at one time or another: getting up in the morning. She uses the problem/solution organizational strategy to resolve her problem in the following paragraph.

Every work morning, without fail, I have a terrible time getting out of bed. When I hear the alarm, all sorts of thoughts go through my mind, such as calling in and saying I'll be late. However, I have found several solutions to ease my departure from bed. First, I go to bed early enough to get plenty of sleep each night. Most people only need six to eight hours of sleep, but I have found eight to nine is better for me. When I get enough sleep, I feel rested, and I'm even in a better mood. Second, I get things done the night before, such as making lunch and ironing what I'm going to wear that morning. However, I always leave my shower for the morning; it helps me wake up faster. Actually, the shower is the only thing I look forward to when getting up in the morning. Finally, I set the alarm clock 30 minutes ahead, so I'll have 30 minutes to snooze. When I snooze, it makes me feel as though I'm sleeping later than I should.

I have found that going to bed early, getting

things done the night before, and setting the alarm

clock ahead have helped me tremendously. I've even

made it to work on time for the last two weeks.

EXERCISE

Listed below are three topics. Choose one of these problems or create your own to resolve.

Topics: Overpopulation of urban areas
          Depletion of the world's mineral reserves
          Illiteracy

Step 1: Use one of the prewriting techniques (see Chapter 1) to generate ideas about your topic. List your ideas on the lines below, organizing them in order of importance.

_____

_____

_____

_____

_____

_____

_____

_____

_____

_____

_____

_____

_____

Step 2: Write your topic sentence on the line below. (If you need help formulating a topic sentence, refer to Chapter 22, "The Process of Writing a Paragraph.")

_____

Step 3: Use the space below to write your paragraph.

_____

_____

_____

_____

_____

_____

_____

_____

_____

_____

_____

_____

_____

_____

_____

Step 4: After you have completed writing your paragraph, reread it. Determine whether you have proposed legitimate solutions to the problem at hand. Have you ended with your best solution, namely, that which would most likely resolve the problem? Check your spelling and punctuation.

U|N|I|T F|I|V|E

Revising, Editing, and Proofreading

Arthur extracts Excalibur and is crowned king.

Luke Skywalker wields his Lightsaber in *Return of the Jedi.*

Time passes, but the role of the hero never changes. The hero, real or mythical, male or female, is ever on a quest to explore the unknown.

"Nothing you write, if you hope to be any good, will ever come out as you first hoped."

—Lillian Hellman

The third stage of the writing process is the revision stage, the time at which you polish your work. Revision is the difference between having confusing sentences that mislead your reader and having clear, concise sentences that convey your meaning. It is the difference between a paper so filled with grammar, punctuation, and spelling errors that it is incomprehensible and a paper carefully edited and proofread to contain few if any errors.

By revising your writing, you make it more effective, precise, and clear. During this stage, your inner critic is finally free to assert itself and become your editor by helping you to fine tune your writing. Revision includes checking overall development, including sentence order and variety. Editing includes checking for more specific grammar errors and confused wording. Proofreading means paying close attention to every word you have written; even one or two spelling or grammar errors can destroy the impact of everything you have tried to create. How seriously are people going to take you if you cannot spell? Should you trust a writer who makes mistakes in spelling, punctuation, subject-verb agreement, and so on? All of your hard work goes down the drain when you make a few common errors. Revising is your last chance to catch errors before the paper goes out with your name on it.

Unit Five will review how to revise, edit, and proofread in a *systematic* way. Your inner critic must learn how to locate and correct many common errors. Your goal is to develop a writing style that will allow your reader to move smoothly through your content.

Writing is a heroic act that requires patience, enthusiasm, and persistence. The writer is on a quest to explore the unknown and to communicate this new knowledge to the rest of the world.

24 Revising and Editing

Now that you have written your first draft, it is time to examine your paragraph closely. You become the editor to determine if your thoughts are arranged in a logical and clear manner, if you have made any errors in grammar, and if your spelling and punctuation are correct.

This chapter will lead you through the revision process in which you check for logical order, delete sentences that are not related to your topic, and add additional facts when needed. You will then examine the editing and proofreading process that will introduce you to the remaining chapters in this unit on sentence variety, punctuation, mechanics, spelling, commonly confused words, and common grammar errors.

Examining the Logical Arrangement of Ideas

Refer to the original prewriting techniques (Chapter 1) to check on the logical arrangement of your ideas. Have you followed one or more of the strategies for paragraph organization outlined in Chapter 23? Review your paragraph to see if that order has been duplicated. If your sequence of ideas has been changed, move the sentences around to reestablish your continuity of thought.

To show how this process works, examine the following paragraph written by Sheron LeGrant based on the organized list on Leonardo da Vinci formed in the prewriting chapter (Chapter 1). Sheron's list was logically organized according to the classification strategy. Once the subtopics were grouped within the broad, main topics, Sheron determined the order of her ideas from least to most important.

A. Engineer
    1. Mechanical drawing
    2. Parachute

        3. Flying machine
        4. Book on mechanics
    B. Scientist
        1. Studied anatomy
        2. Dissection
        3. Book on anatomy
    C. Artist
        1. Pen-and-ink sketches
        2. Divine proportions
        3. Theory on painting
        4. *Virgin of the Rocks*
        5. *Mona Lisa*
        6. *The Last Supper*

Example 1:
Main support sentences out of order

Leonardo da Vinci was a true Renaissance man, excelling as an engineer, scientist, and artist. [B]**As his curiosity led him to investigate mechanical objects, it also made da Vinci, the scientist, interested in how the human body works.** Leonardo wrote a book on anatomy. He studied anatomy to understand the structure of the human body. He furthered his knowledge of anatomy by doing dissections. [A]**Leonardo became an engineer as a result of his interest in anything mechanical.** He was among the first to draw mechanical figures in an accurate, precise manner. He wrote a book on mechanics. He designed such modern items as a parachute and a flying machine. [C]**Da Vinci, the artist, used his artistic ability to record his observations.** His pen-and-ink drawings of human

anatomy were extremely accurate. He developed a
book on the theory of painting. His "divine proportions" of the human body came as a result of his
anatomical studies. Da Vinci then used his unique
knowledge of the human form to create such famous
works as *Virgin of the Rocks, Mona Lisa,* and *The
Last Supper.* Leonardo da Vinci was one of the most
versatile men of all times and is admired even today
for his engineering inventions, his scientific
investigations, and especially for his legacy of
great art.

The bold-typed main support sentences *do not* follow the logical sequence of
ideas that Sheron developed as a result of the organization of her prewriting ideas.
Therefore, Sheron corrected her paragraph as follows:

Example 2:
Main support sentences in order;
Detail support sentences out of order

Leonardo da Vinci was a true Renaissance man,
excelling as an engineer, scientist, and artist.
[A]**Leonardo became an engineer as a result of his
interest in anything mechanical.** [1]He was among the
first to draw mechanical figures in an accurate,
precise manner. [4]He wrote a book on mechanics. He
designed such modern items as a [2]parachute and a
[3]flying machine. [B]**As his curiosity led him to
investigate mechanical objects, it also made da
Vinci, the scientist, interested in how the human**

body works. [7]Leonardo also wrote a book on anatomy. [5]He studied anatomy to understand the structure of the human body. [6]He furthered his knowledge of anatomy by doing dissections. [C]**Da Vinci, the artist, used his artistic ability to record his observations.** [8]His pen-and-ink drawings of human anatomy were extremely accurate. [10]He developed a book on the theory of painting. [9]His "divine proportions" of the human body came as a result of his anatomical studies. Da Vinci then used his unique knowledge of the human form to create such famous works as [11]*Virgin of the Rocks,* [12]*Mona Lisa,* and [13]*The Last Supper.* Leonardo da Vinci was one of the most versatile men of all times and is admired even today for his engineering inventions, his scientific investigations, and especially for his legacy of great art.

Sheron now has her main support sentences in the logical order from least to most important: (A) engineer, (B) scientist, and (C) painter. Look closely, however, at the numbered sentences in Example 2. The detail support sentences are not in the correct order. Sheron must do one more revision:

Example 3:
Correct paragraph with correct order

Leonardo da Vinci was a true Renaissance man, excelling as an engineer, scientist, and artist. [A]**Leonardo became an engineer as a result of his interest in anything mechanical.** [1]He was among the first to draw mechanical figures in an accurate, precise manner. He designed such items as a [2]parachute and a [3]flying machine. [4]After many studies, da Vinci wrote a book on mechanics. [B]**As his curiosity led him to investigate mechanical objects, it also made da Vinci, the scientist, interested in how the human body works.** [5]Leonardo studied anatomy to understand the structure of the human body. [6]He furthered his knowledge of anatomy by doing dissections. [7]He was among the first to document his studies by writing a book on anatomy. [C]**Da Vinci, the artist, used his artistic ability to record his observations.** [8]His pen-and-ink drawings of human anatomy were extremely accurate. [9]His "divine proportions" of the human body came as a result of his anatomical studies. [10]He developed a book on the theory of painting. Da Vinci then used his unique knowledge of human form and painting to create such famous works as [11]*Virgin of the Rocks,* [12]*Mona Lisa,* and [13]*The Last Supper.* Leonardo da Vinci was one of the most versatile men of all times and is admired even today for his engineering inventions, his scientific investigations, and especially for his legacy of great art.

Now Sheron's paragraph follows the logical organizational strategy she developed in Chapter 1 on prewriting and Chapter 22 on the process of writing a paragraph.

DELETING UNNECESSARY SUBTOPICS

During your inspection of the logical order of your thoughts, you may find that one of the facts or sentences does not fit the logical organization of your paragraph. Now is the time to delete that inappropriate sentence or fact. This revision will clarify the continuity of your paragraph. Refer to Chapter 2, "Organizing Your Ideas," for help in deleting subtopics.

EXERCISE

For each of the five topics below, circle the subtopic (a–d) that does not directly correspond.

1. Topic: English grammar
   a. Comma splice
   b. Character development
   c. Run-on sentence
   d. No end punctuation
2. Topic: My favorite movies
   a. *Star Wars*
   b. *Dead Poets Society*
   c. Plot analysis
   d. *The Ten Commandments*
3. Topic: One-on-one sports
   a. Football
   b. Boxing
   c. Tennis
   d. College wrestling
4. Topic: Value of a college education
   a. Better salary
   b. Job in your field of interest
   c. Knowledge
   d. A lot of homework
5. Topic: Great Renaissance artists
   a. Michelangelo
   b. Leonardo da Vinci
   c. Salvador Dali
   d. Botticelli

ADDING IDEAS TO AN INCOMPLETE TOPIC

As you reread your paragraph, you may find that you do not have enough ideas or facts to make it complete. Fill in the gaps by going back to Chapter 1 and using one of the prewriting techniques listed there to generate additional ideas or thoughts.

EXERCISE

For each of the five main support sentences listed below, use a prewriting technique to generate two concrete, specific facts; then, write one detail support sentence for each fact.

1. I have such a hard time learning to get along with difficult people. _____

   _____

   _____

   _____

2. The first day of school was a disaster. _____

   _____

   _____

   _____

3. My spring break was memorable. _____

   _____

   _____

   _____

4. The English grammar book really helped me in writing this paragraph. _____

   _____

   _____

   _____

5. Passing the driving test is not as easy as it looks. _____

   _____

   _____

   _____

Editing and Proofreading

Readers (and professors) expect a final copy that is correct in every way. Errors distract and confuse the reader and obscure the point you are attempting to make. Always allow time for a thorough editing and proofreading of your composition.

EDITING

Most people tend to repeat certain errors in their writing. A good way to remind yourself to look for these errors is to keep a checklist. Look at the last paper corrected by your professor. Make a list of the errors and the types of constructions in which they occurred.

Example:
Error Checklist

Error	*Type of Construction*
spelling	*their* instead of *they're*
missing comma	after an introductory clause
tense shift	an unnecessary shift from the past tense to the future tense in the same sentence
sentence fragment	missing verb

The editing session is also the time to review Chapter 29, "Commonly Confused Words," and Chapter 30, "Common Grammatical Errors." The errors are listed in order from those that appear most frequently (spelling) to those that are committed less frequently (incorrect pronoun shift).

My Personal Error Checklist

Error	*Type of Construction*
_____	_____
_____	_____
_____	_____
_____	_____
_____	_____
_____	_____
_____	_____
_____	_____
_____	_____
_____	_____
_____	_____

———————————   ———————————

———————————   ———————————

———————————   ———————————

———————————   ———————————

———————————   ———————————

———————————   ———————————

PROOFREADING

Many times, an error is simply an omission (leaving out an article) or a typographical error (*adn* for *and*). To catch errors, read your composition aloud. This approach slows you down and makes you concentrate on each word. You may also want to check Chapter 26, "Punctuation," Chapter 27, "Mechanics," and Chapter 28, "Spelling" for specific guidelines on these topics.

EXERCISE

Correct the grammatical and spelling errors in the paragraph below.[1]

I love to go to the health spa, working out
with all the equipment is revitalizing to my mind
and body. Although I cant quite keep up with the
aerobics instructor. I do get a good workout. All
of those thin women, at the front of the class, can
follow the aerobics instructer very good. My
friends and me, however, look like we is in slow
motion. I also work out with; free weights. working
out with the free weights are my favorite. Because
I can work out at my own pace. I use the Nautilus

[1]For the corrected paragraph, see Appendix D.

machines to augmented my free weight work out. I
like working out with the sophisticated machines
that help you with you're mussel tone. I prefer the
wieght lifting to aerobics; but I realize that I
need to improve my cardiovascular system as we'll
as my mussels, therefore, I split my week up into
airobic workouts, and weight lifting workouts.

_____

_____

_____

_____

_____

_____

_____

_____

_____

_____

_____

_____

25 *Sentence Variety*

Most students stop after Chapter 24, "Revising and Editing." That is unfortunate because the difference between an *adequate* writer and an *accomplished* writer is that the accomplished writer has learned one of the most important techniques of writing: sentence variety.

What is sentence variety, and why is it so important? **Sentence variety** characterizes writing in which a number of different sentence types are used. Namely, it is achieved by using a combination of the four sentence patterns: simple, compound, complex, and compound-complex. Sentence variety makes writing more interesting and pleasurable to read as it imitates the wide range of rhythms of speech.

Be assured, though, that sentence variety is rarely if ever achieved on the first draft. Rather, it is produced through careful editing and revising. For instance, some people tend to use only short, choppy, simple sentences; their writing sounds elementary, and their ideas seem fragmented and unrelated. Others write such long, convoluted sentences that it is difficult to figure out what they are saying; these individuals may also be prone to grammar and punctuation errors as their words are tangled up.

If you fall into either of these two categories of writers, working through this chapter will help you resolve your problem. We will begin with a review of the four sentence patterns (see also Chapter 16) and then consider techniques for achieving variety.

Review: The Four Sentence Patterns

1. The simple sentence is a single independent clause, which has both a subject and a complete verb and expresses a complete thought.

Example:
Marco Polo travelled to China.

2. A compound sentence is composed of two or more simple sentences (independent clauses) that can be joined in three ways:

   a. with a comma and a coordinating conjunction

   Example:
   My father is a brilliant biochemist, *and* my mother is a poet.

   b. with a semicolon

   Example:
   Marco Polo travelled to China; he also spent time in prison.

   c. with a semicolon and a conjunctive adverb followed by a comma

   Example:
   Don smiled at Mychelle; *however*, she pretended not to notice him.

3. A complex sentence is composed of one independent clause and at least one dependent (subordinate) clause. A complex sentence can be formed in two ways:

   a. independent clause/dependent clause

   Example:
   Our yard floods *after it rains.*
   Explanation:
   Do not put a comma before a dependent clause that is placed at the end of a sentence. Thus, no comma is necessary before *after.*

   b. dependent clause/independent clause

   Example:
   After it rains, our yard floods.
   Explanation:
   Place a comma after a dependent clause that comes first in the sentence. Thus, a comma is needed following *After it rains.*

4. A compound-complex sentence contains at least two independent clauses with at least one dependent clause connected to one of the independent clauses. Because of the complexity of this sentence pattern, it is often the most difficult to punctuate; however, its use adds diversity and complexity of thought to your writing. The following sentence is an example of a compound-complex sentence.

Example:

Before the dance was over, my friends and I left early; then, we went to a restaurant and talked for hours.

See the accompanying Quick Reference Chart for an overview of how to create and punctuate the different sentence types.

Quick Reference Chart:
Creating and Punctuating Sentences

1. Coordination Methods: Compound Sentences
   a. Independent Clause + comma + conjunction + Independent Clause
      Conjunctions: *and, but, for, nor, or, so, yet*
   b. Independent Clause + semicolon + conjunctive adverb + comma + Independent Clause
      Conjunctive adverbs: *consequently, furthermore, however, indeed, in fact, moreover, nevertheless, then, therefore*
   c. Independent Clause + semicolon + Independent Clause
2. Subordination Methods: Complex and Compound-Complex
   a. Independent Clause + Dependent Clause
      Dependent clause begins with: *after, although, as, as if, because, before, if, since, unless, until, when, whenever, whereas, while*
   b. Dependent Clause + comma + Independent Clause
      Dependent clause begins with: *after, although, as, as if, because, before, if, since, unless, until, when, whenever, whereas, while*

Achieving Sentence Variety

VARYING SENTENCE PATTERNS

Sheron's paragraph on Leonardo da Vinci from Chapter 24 is correct in grammar and organization but could still be improved. To remind you of the original structure, here is Sheron's original paragraph:

```
Leonardo da Vinci was a true Renaissance man,

excelling as an engineer, scientist, and artist.

Leonardo became an engineer as a result of his
```

interest in anything mechanical. He was among the
first to draw mechanical figures in an accurate,
precise manner. He designed such items as a
parachute and a flying machine. After many studies,
da Vinci wrote a book on mechanics. As his curiosity led him to investigate mechanical objects, it
also made da Vinci, the scientist, interested in
how the human body works. Leonardo studied anatomy
to understand the structure of the human body. He
furthered his knowledge of anatomy by doing dissections. He was among the first to document his studies by writing a book on anatomy. Da Vinci, the
artist, used his artistic ability to record his
observations. His pen-and-ink drawings of human
anatomy were extremely accurate. His "divine
proportions" of the human body came as a result of
his anatomical studies. He developed a book on the
theory of painting. Da Vinci then used his unique
knowledge of human form and painting to create such
famous works as *Virgin of the Rocks, Mona Lisa,* and
The Last Supper. Leonardo da Vinci was one of the
most versatile men of all times and is admired even
today for his engineering inventions, his scientific investigations, and especially for his legacy of
great art.

Sheron revised her paragraph as follows:

The *Virgin of the Rocks* by Leonardo da Vinci

Leonardo da Vinci was a true Renaissance man, excelling as an engineer, scientist, and artist. Leonardo became an engineer as a result of his interest in anything mechanical. To design such items as a parachute and a flying machine, da Vinci had to draw mechanical figures in an accurate, precise manner. Da Vinci combined his drawings and mechanical investigations in a book on mechanics. His curiosity about anything mechanical also resulted in his interest in the structure and func-

tion of the parts of the human body. Studying the
anatomy of the human body by doing dissections, da
Vinci, the scientist, became the first to document
his research by recording his observations in a
book on anatomy. Leonardo, the artist, used his
artistic ability to record his observations. His
pen-and-ink drawings of the "divine proportions" of
human anatomy were extremely accurate. After da
Vinci developed a book on the theory of painting,
he used his unique knowledge of human form and
painting to create such famous works as *Virgin of
the Rocks*, *Mona Lisa*, and *The Last Supper*. Leonardo
da Vinci was one of the most versatile men of all
times and is admired even today for his engineering
inventions, his scientific investigations, and his
legacy of great art.

This revision was accomplished by combining sentences and using different ways to begin sentences (see the next section, "Varying Sentence Beginnings").

Original Example:
> He was among the first to draw mechanical figures in an accurate, precise manner. He designed such items as a parachute and a flying machine.

Revised Example:
> To design such items as a parachute and a flying machine, da Vinci had to draw mechanical figures in an accurate, precise manner.

Explanation:
> The two original sentences were combined into one sentence by making the first sentence into an introductory modifier.

Original Example:
> Leonardo studied anatomy to understand the structure of the human body. He

furthered his knowledge of anatomy by doing dissections. He was among the first to document his studies by writing a book on anatomy.

Revised Example:

Studying the anatomy of the human body by doing dissections, da Vinci, the scientist, became the first to document his research by recording his observations in a book on anatomy.

Explanation:

The three original sentences were combined by rewording the first two and making the combined phrase an introductory modifier. The third sentence was reworded and became the independent clause.

Original Example:

His pen-and-ink drawings of human anatomy were extremely accurate. His "divine proportions" of the human body came as a result of his anatomical studies.

Revised Example:

His pen-and-ink drawings of the "divine proportions" of human anatomy were extremely accurate.

Explanation:

Both sentences state different aspects of the same topic: Leonardo's pen-and-ink drawings. The sentences were combined in the revision by a simple rewording to delete unnecessary words.

Original Example:

He developed a book on the theory of painting. Da Vinci then used his unique knowledge of human form and painting to create such famous works as *Virgin of the Rocks, Mona Lisa,* and *The Last Supper.*

Revised Example:

After da Vinci developed a book on the theory of painting, he used his unique knowledge of human form and painting to create such famous works as *Virgin of the Rocks, Mona Lisa,* and *The Last Supper.*

Explanation:

In the revision, the first sentence was combined with the second sentence by using the subordinating conjunction *after* and placing the new dependent clause at the beginning of the sentence followed by a comma.

EXERCISE

Turn to Chapter 23, "Strategies for Paragraph Organization," and choose one of the paragraphs that you wrote. Copy it in the space below. To determine if you are writing long enough sentences, count the number of words in each sentence. Above each sentence, identify the pattern that your sentence fits: S for simple, CD for compound, CX for complex, and C-C for compound-complex.

_____

_____

_____

_____

_____

_____

_____

_____

_____

_____

_____

_____

What did you discover? Are your sentences too short? Do you use a variety of sentence types or many of the same?

Revise your paragraph in the space below, correcting the problems you have found.

_____

_____

_____

_____

_____

_____

_____

_____

_____

_____

_____

_____

_____

_____

_____

_____

VARYING SENTENCE BEGINNINGS

Another way to create variety is to change the opening words by using infinitives, present participles, past participles, prepositional phrases, adverbs, dependent clauses, and transitional words.

Infinitive

Open a sentence by using an infinitive as a modifier.

Example:

> *To design* such items as a parachute and a flying machine, da Vinci had to draw mechanical figures in an accurate, precise manner.

An infinitive is formed by the word *to* and the simplest form of a verb: *to be, to draw, to eat, to go, to write.* These words, used at the beginning of the sentence, should be followed by a comma and act as a modifier for the next noun or pronoun that appears.

Present Participles

The present participle of a verb is the simplest form plus the *-ing* ending: *being, drawing, eating, going, writing.* A participle is a verb form used as an adjective. If a participle starts a phrase at the beginning of a sentence, it should be followed by a comma and will modify the next noun or pronoun in the sentence.

Example:

> *Studying the anatomy of the human body by doing dissections,* da Vinci, the scientist, became the first to document his research by recording his observations in a book on anatomy.

Past Participles

The past participle of the verb ends with *-ed* or has an irregular ending, such as the word *hidden*. If the past participle starts a phrase at the beginning of a sentence, it should be followed by a comma and will modify the next noun or pronoun in the sentence.

Example:

> *Hidden* away in his laboratory, Leonardo da Vinci studied the anatomy of the human body by doing dissections.

Prepositional Phrases

Use a prepositional phrase to open a sentence. Used at the beginning of a sentence, a prepositional phrase should be followed by a comma and will modify the next noun or pronoun in the sentence.

Examples:

> *By doing dissections,* da Vinci became the first to document his research on human anatomy.

> *After the dissections,* Leonardo documented his research in a book on anatomy.

Adverbs

Use an adverb (which usually ends with *-ly*) to open a sentence. Again, used in this way to begin a sentence, an adverb should be followed by a comma and will modify the next verb in the sentence.

Example:

> *Skillfully and carefully,* da Vinci drew the sketches of the first flying machine.

Dependent Clauses

Using a dependent clause at the beginning of the sentence will create one of the four sentence patterns: the complex sentence.

Example:

> *After da Vinci developed a book on the theory of painting,* he used his unique knowledge of human form and painting to create such works as *Virgin of the Rocks, Mona Lisa,* and *The Last Supper.*

Point to Remember:

When a dependent clause appears at the beginning of a sentence, it should be followed by a comma. But when it appears at the end of a sentence following the independent clause, it should not.

Transitional Words

Use the appropriate transitional word to open a sentence, namely, to show cause-and-effect, comparison, example, and so forth. (Refer to Chapter 22, "The Process of Writing a Paragraph," which includes a list of transitional devices.) Follow the transitional word or phrase with a comma.

Example:

Furthermore, Leonardo da Vinci was one of the greatest artists who ever lived.

EXERCISE

Look again at the paragraph you selected from Chapter 23. Do many of your sentences start with the same group of words or the same type of structure? Locate the problems and revise your paragraph by varying the openings of your sentences. Write your improved paragraph in the space below.

_____

_____

_____

_____

_____

_____

_____

_____

_____

_____

_____

_____

_____

_____

COMBINING SENTENCES

Combining sentences is a method used during the revision process to join short sentences to create more varied, interesting prose.

You can combine sentences by using coordination (creating compound sentences), subordination (creating complex sentences), or coordination and subordination (creating compound-complex sentences) or by combining different elements of sentences, as in the following example.

Original Example:

Admiral Robert Peary was the first to reach the North Pole.

Robert Peary was a great explorer.

Robert Peary was a courageous man.

Revised Example:

A great explorer and a courageous man, Admiral Robert Peary was the first to reach the North Pole.

Explanation:

The second and third sentences in the original were combined to make a modifier that describes Admiral Peary. Three short sentences were combined to make one longer, more fluid sentence.

Original Example:

Harriet Tubman was a fugitive slave and abolitionist.

She helped over 300 slaves escape to freedom.

She was active in the "Underground Railroad."

Revised Example:

Harriet Tubman, a fugitive slave and abolitionist, helped over 300 slaves escape to freedom through the "Underground Railroad."

Original Example:

King Arthur lived in Camelot.

His queen was Guinevere.

He ruled over the Knights of the Round Table.

Merlin the Magician and the enchanted sword, Excalibur, helped defeat his enemies.

Revised Example:

King Arthur and Queen Guinevere lived in Camelot, where he ruled over the Knights of the Round Table and defeated his enemies with the help of Merlin the Magician and the enchanted sword, Excalibur.

Look how these sets of sentences have been combined to create varied, interesting prose. The last example now takes only one sentence instead of four to deliver the message.

Point to Remember:

There is no right or wrong method for sentence combining as long as you punctuate correctly; create logical, understandable sentences; and do not write fragments. No one method of sentence combining is better than another, but do not use the same method for combining all your sentences. The objective is to achieve *variety*.

Sentence combining will teach you the different possibilities for exploring the English language, a supple language with great flexibility and an incredible syntax (word order). You will learn how to present information in a new form that will allow you to combine words in a more powerful way.

EXERCISE

In each of the following exercises, combine the set of sentences in two different ways.

1. Gandhi was an Indian.
   Gandhi was a nationalist leader.
   Gandhi practiced nonviolent civil disobedience.
   Gandhi freed his people from British rule.

   a. _____

   _____

   b. _____

   _____

2. Batman is a caped crusader.
   Batman is mysterious.
   Batman fights evil in Gotham City.
   Batman is handsome.

   a. _____

   _____

   b. _____

   _____

3. Obi Wan Kenobi taught Luke Skywalker about the Force.
   Luke Skywalker was a Jedi Knight.
   Luke Skywalker was the son of Darth Vader.

   a. _____

   _____

   b. _____

   _____

4. Amelia Earhart was a female pilot.
   She was the first woman to fly over the Atlantic.
   Amelia Earhart disappeared over the Pacific Ocean in 1937.

   a. _____

   _____

   b. _____

   _____

5. Sir Arthur Conan Doyle was a British writer.
   Doyle created Sherlock Holmes.
   Sherlock Holmes was a fictional character.
   Sherlock Holmes appeared in many short stories and four novels.

   a. _____

   _____

   b. _____

   _____

26 *Punctuation*

To *punctuate* is to break something up into units or intervals. In language, ***punctuation*** is the set of symbols we use to distinguish units of structure and meaning. When used according to standards, punctuation helps the reader follow and understand what you are trying to say. Moreover, punctuation helps you organize your ideas clearly and accurately, indicating where one thought ends and another thought begins.

In this chapter, we will cover the two types of punctuation: end punctuation and internal punctuation.

End Punctuation

End punctuation is used to end complete sentences. It indicates a major pause or break in thought. The period (.), question mark (?), and exclamation point (!) are each used to end a sentence of a particular type.

Examples:

That is what I said.   (statement)

That is what I said?   (question)

That is what I said!   (exclamation, strong emotion)

PERIODS

Points to Remember:

The period (.) has three uses.

1. **Use a period after a statement, command, or indirect question.**

Examples:

I feel fine.   (statement)

Call me tonight.   (command)

I wonder if I will finish my homework.   (indirect question)

2. **Use a period to separate elements in most abbreviations.**

Examples:

Dr.	r.s.v.p.	A.M.
etc.	B.C.	Ms.

3. **Use three periods as an *ellipsis*.**
   a. Use three dots (…) to indicate that one or more words have been left out in quoted material. (Note that there is a space before and after the ellipsis, as well as between each pair of dots.)
   b. Use four dots (….)—one as an actual period and three as an ellipsis—to indicate the end of an omitted sentence. (Note that the first dot, the period, is close to the preceding word. The other dots are all separated by spaces.)

Example:

"This book … renders scenes of the white, river rapids…."

EXERCISE

Provide the correct end punctuation for each of the following sentences.

1. What are the Dead Sea Scrolls ____

2. The Dead Sea Scrolls are some of the oldest copies of the Bible ____

3. Listen while I talk to you ____

4. Where were the Dead Sea Scrolls found ____

5. The Dead Sea Scrolls were found in Israel and Israeli-occupied

   territories ____

6. The Dead Sea Scrolls proved that modern Hebrew has not changed much in

   at least 2,000 years ____

7. Of what were the Dead Sea Scrolls made ____

8. The Dead Sea Scrolls were made of papyrus and leather, but one was made of

   copper ____

9. Did they find all the Dead Sea Scrolls ____

10. The Dead Sea Scrolls that have been found were not well preserved, and interpretation has been difficult ____

QUESTION MARKS

A question mark is used at the end of a sentence that asks a direct question.

Example:
Which topic shall I choose?

EXCLAMATION POINTS

An exclamation point adds strong emotion to a sentence, phrase, or single word, but in this book, we will concentrate on the complete sentence. Notice where the quotation marks are located in the example below.

Example:
Jim shouted, "Don't touch my albums!"

EXERCISE

Write five sentences using the end punctuation given.

1. (?) _____

2. (!) _____

3. (.) _____

4. (?) _____

5. (.) _____

Internal Punctuation

Internal punctuation is used to separate elements within a single sentence.

COMMAS

A comma (,) represents a short pause between words, phrases, or clauses.

Points to Remember:

1. Use a comma to separate two independent clauses joined by a coordinating conjunction (*and, but, for, nor, or, so, yet*) in a compound sentence.

Example:

I like the red car, *but* it costs too much.

EXERCISE

Add commas as needed to punctuate each of the following sentences correctly.

1. I like the microbiology class but I do not like the lab.

2. She will be a biology major or she will be an English major.

3. I would like to learn Old English but the college does not offer Old English in the spring.

4. I will take my chemistry over the summer so I will not have to take it this fall.

5. I would like to study Old English and I would also like to study Middle English.

2. Use a comma to set off introductory material (a word, a phrase, or a clause) at the beginning of a sentence.

Examples:

Nevertheless, you should have known better.   (word)

Without your help, we would be lost.   (phrase)

After I had come home, I noticed that the refrigerator was still open.   (clause)

EXERCISE

Add commas as needed to punctuate each of the following sentences correctly.

1. Although wood is the primary medium of African sculpture artists also use other media.

2. Indeed many sculptors use metal or terra cotta.

3. However some tribal artists use sculptures as bases for painting.

4. After forming a pot the artist will inscribe designs into the wet clay before firing.

5. Preparing for ritualistic ceremonies painters decorate the bodies of the dancers with brightly colored designs.

3. **Use commas to set off nonessential information. A *nonrestrictive clause* is a dependent clause that adds information but does not affect the basic meaning of the sentence.**

Example:
My neighbor, *who loves animals,* took in an abandoned kitten.

A *restrictive clause* is necessary to identify the subject of the sentence. Omit the commas before and after a restrictive clause.

Example:
The umbrella *that is lying in the corner* is mine.
Explanation:
The words *that is lying in the corner* are necessary to the meaning of the sentence. Without them, we would not know which umbrella was *mine.*

EXERCISE

Add commas as needed to punctuate each of the following sentences correctly.

1. Chinese art which is beautiful is based on the philosophy that sees a unifying pattern of life in all natural forms.

2. Chinese painting which is the oldest living art in the world is a celebration of nature.

3. The four seasons of the year which are also used by artists in other countries are the major themes of Chinese paintings.

4. Mrs. Susie Chang who was born in Taiwan is an excellent artist in the Chinese tradition of brush-and-ink painting.

5. Each of Susie's brush strokes that are executed with reverence for nature reflects an inner harmony.

4. **Use commas to separate most adjectives or adverbs describing the same noun or verb.**

Example:
It was a *cold, bleak* day.
Alternative Example:
It was a *bleak, cold* day.
Explanation:
If you cannot reverse the order of the adjectives (*bleak* and *cold*), they are not coordinate and do not require a comma.

Example:
They crept *slowly, quietly* down the basement stairs.
Alternative Example:
They crept *quietly, slowly* down the basement stairs.

Example:
It was a *low-hanging grape* vine.
Incorrect Alternative:
It was a *grape low-hanging* vine.
Explanation:
The adjectives (*low-hanging* and *grape*) are not equal and cannot be reversed.

Example:
They talked *very loudly* in class.
Incorrect Alternative:
They talked *loudly very* in class.
Explanation:
The adverbs (*very* and *loudly*) are not equal and cannot be reversed.

EXERCISE

Add commas as needed to punctuate each of the following sentences correctly.

1. Fiona wore a long black silk dress.

2. Adam wore a brown suit.

3. There is a huge ugly nasty creepy spider on the wall.

4. Susan Lee bought a reddish-brown coffee table.

5. The cute little white bear played in the water.

5. Use commas to separate items in a series of three or more items.

Example:
I have *a book, a pencil, and a pen.*

EXERCISE

Add commas as needed to punctuate each of the following sentences correctly.

1. My favorite provinces in Canada are Nova Scotia Quebec and Ontario.

2. To take the calculus test you need a pencil a calculator and two pieces of note-book paper.

3. The four lightest elements are hydrogen helium lithium and beryllium.

4. Australia has a lot of cattle major minerals cereals and fish.

5. Australia uses water power and major industrial power.

6. Use commas in dates and addresses and to separate cities and states or nations.

Examples:
I was born on *March 21, 1970,* and lived in *Toledo, Ohio,* most of my life.

I lived at *21 Oak Street, Seattle, Washington,* for 10 years.

Gina would like to visit *Paris, France,* and *Florence, Italy.*

EXERCISE

Add commas as needed to punctuate each of the following sentences correctly.

1. Have you ever been to Canton Ohio?

2. Babe Ruth was born in Baltimore Maryland on February 6 1895 and died in New York New York on August 16 1948.

3. The Dodgers were from Brooklyn New York in Babe Ruth's time.

4. The Braves were from Boston Massachusetts in Babe Ruth's time.

5. Have you ever been to Chicago Illinois?

7. **Use commas between units of numbers, sections, and subsections.**

Examples:

five feet, seven inches

Chapter 7, page 27, line 7

EXERCISE

Add commas as needed to punctuate each of the following sentences correctly.

1. There is a better explanation of electron distributions on page 12 paragraph 2.

2. I am only five feet four inches tall.

3. Actually I am five feet four inches tall in my shoes.

4. To be more specific, I am five feet four inches tall in my shoes while standing on my toes.

5. Look at Chapter 2 section 3 paragraph 7 line 4 for the answer to your question.

8. **Use a comma after the opening and in closing an informal letter.**

Example:

Dear Rob,

Love, Janet

SEMICOLONS

A semicolon represents a stronger separation than a comma but not as strong as a period or a colon (see following section). Semicolons separate independent clauses in special circumstances and serve to group items in a series when the series contains internal punctuation.

Points to Remember:

1. **Use a semicolon to separate independent clauses closely connected in meaning. (This construction forms a compound sentence without a conjunction. A semicolon must be used; however, if a comma were used, a comma splice would be formed.)**

Example:

We were happy with the sunny weather; the farmers were worried about the lack of rain.

2. Use a semicolon to separate two independent clauses joined by a conjunctive adverb. Place the semicolon before the conjunctive adverb (*therefore, however,* and *nevertheless*) and a comma after it. (The conjunctive adverbs are listed for you in Chapter 18, "Subordination.")

Example:
We were happy with the sunny weather; *however,* the farmers were worried about the lack of rain.

3. Use a semicolon to separate independent clauses when a coordinating conjunction is used and either of the clauses contain internal punctuation. (This construction forms a compound sentence; the semicolon has replaced the comma before the conjunction to clarify the significant pause needed here. This change is necessary because so many other commas are used to show smaller pauses.)

Example:
The chairman, a well-educated man, predicted a cost-of-living increase for next year; *but* his prediction, which seemed to be valid, proved to be incorrect.

4. Use semicolons to separate items in a series where a comma is insufficient because the list contains internal punctuation. (Again, the semicolon is needed for distinction.)

Example:
Guests include Lynda, the bride; Mychelle, the maid-of-honor; and Daryl, the bridegroom.

EXERCISE

Add semicolon(s) to punctuate each of the sentences correctly.

1. A beam of light travels at 186,000 miles in one second this distance is a long way to travel in one second.

2. Many galaxies are millions of light years away from the earth this distance is an incredibly long way to travel.

3. Our galaxy, the Milky Way, contains 400 billion stars and there are many millions of galaxies in our universe.

4. Our studies will include the Milky Way, our galaxy the sun, our star and the earth, our planet.

5. It is estimated that there are 10 thousand billion billion stars in our universe it makes me think that we are not alone.

6. A star that you see may not exist what you really see is the light from the star reaching you.

7. My favorite professors were Dr. Lockey, an immunologist Dr. Miles, a mathematician and Dr. Martin, a chemist.

8. If we could time travel, a topic about which many people are interested, we could reach other planets and Dr. Albert Einstein, a famous physicist, was fascinated by this idea.

9. The enormous size of the universe is inconceivable however, astronomers are fascinated by its possibilities.

10. Sally Ride was the first American woman astronaut other women have followed her into the space program.

COLONS

A colon represents a larger break than a semicolon but not as complete a break as a period or other end punctuation.

Points to Remember:

1. **Use a colon to introduce a list following a complete sentence.**

   Examples:
   Please send me the following supplies: *two pens, two pads of paper, and a pencil.*

   The following classes will be taught: *biology, chemistry, and physics.*

2. **Use a colon in expressions of time to separate hours, minutes, and seconds.**

   Example:
   It is 7:00 P.M.

3. **Use a colon following the salutation of a business letter.**

   Example:
   Dear Dr. Crook:

4. **Use a colon to separate parts of references.**

Examples:

He quoted from Chapter X: Section 12.

She quoted from Exodus 4: 6.

5. **Use a colon to separate the components of a ratio.**

Example:

It was 100:1 odds that our football team would win the game.

EXERCISE

Add a colon to punctuate each of the sentences correctly.

1. I enjoy writing at 2 00 A.M.

2. Bring the following with you to creative writing class a thesaurus, a dictionary, a pad of paper, and two pencils.

3. There is an important paragraph on dialog in Chapter 10 Section 2 in your creative writing book.

4. Look at Unit 4 section 3 of your music book.

5. When you freewrite, do not do the following worry, correct mistakes before you are finished writing, cry, throw temper tantrums, or frown.

HYPHENS

Hyphens connect things: pairs of words, multiple last names, compound numbers and fractions, continuous numbers, some prefixes and suffixes to nouns, and elements of words split at the end of a line.

Points to Remember:

1. **Use a hyphen with compound numbers and fractions. Hyphens are used with numbers written out and when fractions are used as adjectives.**

Examples:

A quart is *thirty-two* fluid ounces.

The quart is *three-fourths* full.

2. **Use a hyphen to show continuous numbers.**

Examples:

Read pages *24–48* in your literature book.

Albert Einstein (*1879–1955*)

3. **Use a hyphen with some prefixes and suffixes or to link words.**

Example:

The *secretary-elect* has a lot of *self-esteem.*

There is a trend in the English language, however, to eliminate the use of hyphens with many prefixes. For instance, most common prefixes—including *non, un, co, anti, pre, post,* and *pro*—are used without a hyphen, close to the word they modify: *nontraditional, unconventional, codependent, antinuclear, predetermine, postgraduate, prostudent.* Consult a current dictionary for guidelines on the use of suffixes.

4. **Use a hyphen to link compound adjectives that appear *directly before* the noun they modify.**

Examples:

Dr. Beaman is an important part of the *decision-making process.*

The oil company is involved in *deep-ocean* drilling.

5. **Use a hyphen to divide words at the end of a line to show that the rest of the word will follow on the next line. The word must be divided into syllables, and the hyphen placed at a syllabic break. To find out the correct syllabic division, look in your dictionary.**

Example:

I thought that you and I were going to sail down the Mississippi River.

6. **Use a hyphen to join multiple last names.**

Examples:

Mr. and Mrs. *Oliver-Smith* are going to speak at the convention.

Allison *Thomas-Rice* is the new division manager.

DASHES

Use a dash (—)[1] to indicate a sudden break in thought, an interruption, or an abrupt change in tone.

[1]A dash is usually created with two hyphens (--).

Examples:

My plans for this evening—so you won't bother to ask—are to see the movie *Hook.*

I had never been a good writer—at least, not until I took this class.

PARENTHESES

Point to Remember

Use parentheses to set off additional, illustrative, subordinate material.

Example:

George Washington (*1732–1799*) was our first president.

If the parenthetical information falls at the end of a sentence, the end punctuation is placed outside the closing parenthesis.

Examples:

We have provided a complete list of irregular verbs (*in the Appendix*).

Konrad Lorenz is considered the father of ethology (*the study of animal behavior*).

If the parenthetical information is a complete sentence, punctuate it appropriately. Put the end punctuation mark for the original sentence after the last word of that sentence, not just after the closing parenthesis.

Example:

We have provided a complete list of irregular *verbs*. (*See the Appendix.*)

EXERCISE

Add parentheses to make each sentence grammatically correct.

1. My friend took a class in etiology the study of the causes of disease.

2. Ethology the study of animal behavior is quite different from ethnology a branch of anthropology dealing with origins and characteristics of the races of man.

3. Kublai Khan 1215–1294 was an emperor of China.

4. When I studied advanced English grammar, we spent much time studying etymology the study of the historical change of a particular word.

5. Montezuma 1470–1520 was an Aztec emperor of Mexico.

BRACKETS

Use brackets to enclose subordinate material already within parentheses. In effect, brackets serve as a secondary level of parentheses.

Example:

> We visited my favorite place (EPCOT [Experimental Prototype Community of Tomorrow]) last summer.

Also use brackets to insert material within a quoted passage. This is sometimes necessary to clarify the meaning of a passage taken out of context.

Examples:

> "Sinclair Lewis is believed to have used his hometown, Sauk Centre [Minnesota], as a model in writing *Main Street,* the critical story of life in small-town America."

> "Mark Twain is most well known for his so-called 'boy's books' [*The Adventures of Tom Sawyer* and *The Adventures of Huckleberry Finn*], which recount some of the tales of his own boyhood."

Both of these uses of brackets are limited to formal writing, such as research papers and other scholarly or legal work.

APOSTROPHES

Points to Remember:

1. **Use an apostrophe to show the possessive form of a noun.**

   a. **Add -'s to form the possessive of singular nouns, including those singular nouns that end in -s.**[2]

   Examples:

   > *Jolly's new anklet* is an example of the intricate design of metalwork from India.

   > *Chris's notes* are excellent.

   b. **Add an apostrophe but *not* an -s to plural nouns ending in -s.**

   Example:

   > The *girls' favorite song* is "Under the Sea."

---

[2]A few singular nouns ending with an *s* or *z* sound require only an apostrophe in the possessive case to avoid creating an awkward sounding pronunciation. Examples: Ulysses', Achilles', Reynolds'.

c. Add *-'s* to plural nouns that do not end in *-s.*

Example:
The *children's toys* were strewn across the floor.

d. To show individual possession by two or more persons, make each noun or pronoun possessive.

Example:
Angelia's and *Corinna's* reports for their histology class were excellent.

e. To show joint ownership, make the last owner possessive.

Example:
Bill and Ted's journey was bogus.

f. In compound words, make the last word possessive.

Example:
Her *mother-in-law's pound cake* recipe was handed down from generation to generation.

2. Use apostrophes to form contractions.

Examples:
The lines were so long that we *weren't* (*were not*) able to see the movie *Robin Hood: Prince of Thieves.*

We'll (*we will*) try to see Arnold Schwarzenegger's film *Terminator 2: Judgment Day* instead.

3. Use a set of single marks (' ') to set off material already within quotation marks (also see next section).

Example:
Her mother said, "Clean all of this *'junk'* out of your room."

EXERCISE

Add an apostrophe(s) to punctuate each of the following sentences correctly.

1. I liked studying Geoffrey Chaucers *Canterbury Tales;* he was a medieval English poet.

2. Unfortunately, I didnt get to cover all of the tales because there were too many to cover in one semester.

3. I enjoyed looking at the pictures of Michelangelos sculptures; he was a Renaissance artist.

4. Its hard to believe that Botticelli painted *The Primavera*.

5. Im not an expert in the field of art history, but I love looking at the pictures in my humanities book.

6. We read some of Erasmus writings; he was a Dutch scholar and humanist.

7. Nostradamus predictions were read by many people; he was a French astrologer in the sixteenth century.

8. Titians art is fabulous; he was a sixteenth-century Italian artist.

9. Why arent there as many great painters today as there were during the Renaissance?

10. Who isnt fascinated with art and literature?

QUOTATION MARKS

Quotation marks are used to set off material representing someone's exact words, such as dialogue. Quotation marks are also used to highlight unfamiliar terms and identify the titles of poems, short stories, and TV shows.

Examples:

Mark Twain's *"The Man Who Corrupted Hadleyburg"* is considered by many to be a perfectly crafted short story.

Twain wrote the story in part to silence critics who said his work was *"uncontrolled and undisciplined."*

The man in the story, who is only revealed to the townspeople at the end, is an example of Twain's *"transcendent character."*

Mark Twain is famous for such sarcastic quips as, *"Man is the only animal that blushes—or needs to."*

EXERCISE

Add quotation marks as needed to punctuate each of the following sentences correctly.

1. The professor said softly, Write whatever comes to your mind for the next 20 minutes.

2. The student questioned, Should we write without checking what we have written?

3. The professor replied, Yes, this is why it's called freewriting; you want to write without interruptions.

4. The student mumbled, If I only knew what to write about.

5. The professor responded, Write about not having anything to write about; then, you will have something to write about.

27 *Mechanics*

Mechanics constitutes basic issues of style, including rules for capitalization and treatment of numbers and abbreviations. Many writers overlook these stylistic issues during revision when in fact they should be addressed in the last stages of fine-tuning. Some may pass off mechanics as nothing more than another set of picky rules. But good, careful writers know that consistent style shows attention to detail and concern for the quality of the finished product. Believe it or not, readers notice!

But often, the rules for capitalization, numbers, and abbreviations can be confusing because all grammar books do not agree on the same style. This chapter is based upon the most current usage; these guidelines will serve you well when you revise your writing. Consistency is the key.

Capitalization

Points to Remember:

1. **The first word in a sentence is always capitalized.**

   Examples:
   There are freshwater dolphins in South America.

   Sea turtles can get quite large.

2. **The pronoun *I* is always capitalized in English.**

   Example:
   Gina Lee said that I can paint well.

3. **Nouns or pronouns referring to God or Holy Scripture are capitalized.**

373

Examples:

God	the Torah
Our Father	the Koran
Jehovah	Allah
the Bible	the Old Testament
the Vedas	the Diamond Sutra

4. **The proper names of particular persons, places, or things are capitalized.**

Examples:

Shakespeare	Heinz ketchup
the Renaissance	the Chicago Bears
Congresswoman Smith	English
the Everglades	the Swiss Alps
Methodist	French
Chinese	Michael Jackson
Dr. Livingstone	Ms. Johnson
Los Angeles	the Missouri River

Deputy Foreign Minister Benjamin Netanyahu

Algebra 101 (if a number follows the course)

algebra (if no number follows it)

5. **The names of holidays are always capitalized.**

Examples:

Easter	Christmas
Labor Day	Yom Kippur
Ramadan	Passover
Thanksgiving	Rosh Hashanah
Mother's Day	New Year's Day

6. **Words used as essential parts of proper names are capitalized.**

Examples:

Tallahassee Community College (a specific college)

Lake Ontario (a specific lake)

Queen Elizabeth (a specific queen)

7. **Commonly used abbreviations of names of corporations, organizations, and some tests (acronyms) are always capitalized. (Note that periods are omitted in acronyms.)**

Examples:

AFL-CIO	ABC	CIA	ACT

AMA	AT&T	FBI	GRE
BBC	IBM	NASA	LSAT
NOW	TWA	NATO	SAT

8. **Days of the week and months of the year are capitalized, but names of seasons are not.**

Examples:
Monday, Tuesday, Wednesday
January, February, March
spring, summer, fall, winter

9. **Names of specific geographic locations are capitalized, but references to compass directions are not.**

Examples:
I live in the *Southeast,* but I'm moving to the *Midwest.*

The *northern* coast of California is spectacular.

Columbus sought to find Asia by sailing *west.*

10. **Names of planets, stars, constellations, and galaxies are capitalized. The words *earth, sun,* and *moon* are lower-case. Occasionally, when the earth is referred to as a celestial body, it is capitalized.**

Examples:

the Milky Way	Mars
Andromeda	Alpha Centauri
Venus	Saturn
the Big Dipper	Sirius

11. **The first word and all other words except articles (*a, an, the*) and prepositions under five letters (*with, by, in, to*) in the title of a book, essay, movie, play, poem, chapter, short story, and other publications are capitalized.**

Examples:
Umberto Eco Wrote *The Name of the Rose* in 1980.

My favorite movie is *Star Wars.*

Carl's favorite short story is "A Clean Well Lighted Place" by Ernest Hemingway.

I subscribe to *The New York Times.*

My favorite play is *Death of a Salesman* by Arthur Miller.

12. The salutation of a business or formal letter and only the first word in the close of a letter are capitalized.

Examples:

Dear Sir:	Dear Ms. Smith:
Sincerely,	Best wishes,

EXERCISE

Circle the letter(s) in each of the following sentences that should be capitalized.

1. many great artists emerged during the renaissance.

2. some of my favorite artists are michelangelo buonarroti, sandro botticelli, and raphael.

3. i wish i had their talent.

4. the *david* by michelangelo is in florence, italy.

5. A friend of mine spent last march and april in italy.

6. the first three planets of our solar system are mercury, venus, and earth.

7. the closest star to our sun is alpha centauri.

8. the milky way is the name of our galaxy.

9. nasa stands for National Aeronautics and Space Administration.

10. nasa was founded in 1958 by president eisenhower.

NUMBERS

Again, the rules for handling numbers vary. Often, a number is spelled out or in figures depending on whether the context is personal, business, scholarly, or scientific. Namely, it is more acceptable to use numbers in scientific or technical writing than in personal or narrative writing.

Points to Remember:

1. **Numbers from one to ten are written as words; numbers 11 and above are written as figures. In a series of numbers, some under and some above ten, digits are used throughout.**

Examples:

There are *four* birds.

The children ranged in age from *6* to *16*.

There are *9,000* species of birds and *18,000* species of fish but only *3,500* species of mammals.

2. **Fractions are normally written out except in technical and scientific papers. When numbers are written out, they are hyphenated.**

Examples:

three-fourths, one-third, one-half

ABBREVIATIONS

Abbreviations must be used consistently to make sense.

Points to Remember:

1. **Use a period after most abbreviations, including:**

   a. **Titles followed by names**

   Examples:

Capt. Robert Apodaca	*Dr.* Azzura Givens
Gen. H. Norman Schwarzkopf	*Hon.* Justice Sandra Day O'Connor
O. B. Hardison, *Jr.*	*1st Lt.* Christopher T. Vaughan
Maj. Marie Rossi	*Mr.* Paul Rossi
Mrs. Henrietta Delk	*Ms.* Kristina M. Diecidue
Pfc. Frank Bradish	*Rev. Dr.* Martin Luther King, *Jr.*
Sgt. Daniel Stamaris	Robert J. Morgan, M.A.

   b. **Expressions of time or eras**

   Examples:

A.M.	(ante meridiem)
P.M.	(post meridiem)
B.P.	(before present)
B.C.	(before Christ)[1]
B.C.E.	(before the Christian Era)
A.D.	(*anno Domini,* in the year of the Lord)[2]

2. **Common abbreviations, or acronyms, usually appear without periods.**

---

[1]B.C. appears after the year: 27 B.C.
[2]A.D. appears before the year: A.D. 1453.

Examples:

NBC	UN	TV
FCC	USSR	AM/FM (radio)
IRS	UK	APB (all points bulletin)

3. **Foreign phrases, scholarly abbreviations, and less familiar acronyms are often abbreviated (and use periods).**

Examples:

R.S.V.P.	P.S.	etc.
H.U.D.	i.e.	e.g.

4. **The names of the states of the United States can be abbreviated (no periods).**

Examples:

NY	NJ	FL
CA	GA	PA

5. **Scientific terms, such as units of measurement, are often abbreviated (no periods).**

Examples:

mph (miles per hour)
km (kilometer)
cm (centimeter)

6. **As a general rule but particularly with uncommon abbreviations, use the full name of the group or term the first time it appears, and include the abbreviation in parentheses following it. After this introduction, use the abbreviation consistently.**

Examples:

The *National Organization for Women* (*NOW*), a feminist organization, was founded in the mid-1960s after the *Equal Employment Opportunity Commission* (*EEOC*) failed to enforce parts of civil rights legislation. *NOW* has continued to promote occupational opportunities for women, sometimes at odds with the *EEOC.*

EXERCISE

Give the correct abbreviation for each of the following words.

1. mister _____   2. junior _____

3. doctor _____   4. reverend _____

5. captain _____   6. California _____

7. centimeter _____   8. before Christ _____

9. your own state _____   10. television _____

28 *Spelling*

One of the most important parts of step 3 of the writing process is to check for spelling errors. This should be a regular part of your proofreading. Spelling errors distract the reader from the meaning of your message and also give the impression that your work has been prepared carelessly.

Spelling is one of the most difficult aspects of written English. There are many rules and unfortunately, many exceptions to the rules. Practice is the only way to improve your spelling.

Using a Dictionary

A dictionary may be the most important tool for any writer. It contains much more information than many students realize. An **abridged** dictionary is the most common type used, but because it is abbreviated, it does not contain as much information as an **unabridged** dictionary. Although it is not necessary to own one, students should have access to an unabridged dictionary; there is usually one located in every library.

The word you look up in the dictionary is called the **main entry word,** or simply the **entry.** You should note that not all entries are single words. Moreover, the dictionary also includes prefixes and suffixes, as well as abbreviations.

Points to Remember:
   What information is usually included in a dictionary entry?

1. **Spelling and syllable division**
2. **Pronunciation**
3. **Etymology (the origin or development of a word, such as the language from which it came)**
4. **Definition(s)**
5. **Part of speech**
6. **Alternative parts of speech**

7. **Four principal parts of the verb**
8. **Antonyms**
9. **Synonyms**

Note that not every entry contains all of this information. Nonetheless, the information given most often appears in this order.

Look at the following examples of dictionary entries, and note the information that each contains:

Example:

serious[1]

Spelling and syllable division

Pronunciation — Part of speech — Etymology — Definitions

sē · ri · ous (sir′ē əs) *adj.* [ME. *seryows* < ML. *seriosus* < L. *serius,* grave, orig., prob. weighty, heavy < ? IE. base **swer-,* whence OE. *swær,* heavy, sad. Goth. *swers,* important, orig., heavy] **1.** of, showing, having, or caused by earnestness or deep thought; earnest, grave, sober, or solemn *[a serious man]* **2.** *a)* meaning what one says or does; not joking or trifling; sincere *b)* meant in earnestness; not said or done in play **3.** concerned with grave, important, or complex matters, problems, etc.; weighty *[a serious novel]* **4.** requiring careful consideration or thought; involving difficulty, effort, or considered action *[a serious problem]* **5.** giving cause for concern; dangerous *[a serious wound]* —**se′ri · ous · ly** *adv.* —**se′ri · ous · ness** *n.*

SYN. —**serious** implies absorption in deep thought or involvement in something really important as distinguished from something frivolous or merely amusing *[he takes a serious interest in the theater]*; **grave** implies the dignified weightiness of heavy responsibilities or cares *[a grave expression on his face]*; **solemn** suggests an impressive or awe-inspiring seriousness *[a solemn ceremony]*; **sedate** implies a dignified, proper, sometimes even prim seriousness *[a sedate clergyman]*; **earnest** suggests a seriousness of purpose marked by sincerity and enthusiasm *[an earnest desire to help]*; **sober** implies a seriousness marked by temperance, self-control, emotional balance, etc. *[a sober criticism]* —***ANT.*** **frivolous, flippant**

Synonyms   Antonyms —   Alternative parts of speech

Example:

abracadabra[2]

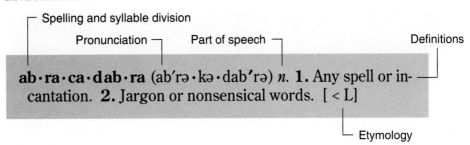

Spelling and syllable division

Pronunciation — Part of speech — Definitions

ab·ra·ca·dab·ra (ab′rə·kə·dab′rə) *n.* **1.** Any spell or in-cantation. **2.** Jargon or nonsensical words. [< L]

Etymology

Example:

dive[3]

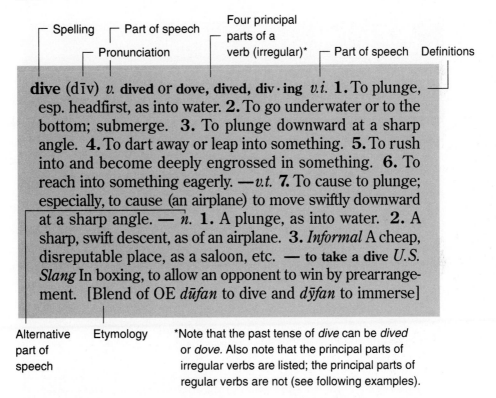

Spelling — Part of speech

Pronunciation

Four principal parts of a verb (irregular)* — Part of speech Definitions

dive (dīv) *v.* **dived** or **dove, dived, div·ing** *v.i.* **1.** To plunge, esp. headfirst, as into water. **2.** To go underwater or to the bottom; submerge. **3.** To plunge downward at a sharp angle. **4.** To dart away or leap into something. **5.** To rush into and become deeply engrossed in something. **6.** To reach into something eagerly. —*v.t.* **7.** To cause to plunge; especially, to cause (an airplane) to move swiftly downward at a sharp angle. — *n.* **1.** A plunge, as into water. **2.** A sharp, swift descent, as of an airplane. **3.** *Informal* A cheap, disreputable place, as a saloon, etc. — **to take a dive** *U.S. Slang* In boxing, to allow an opponent to win by prearrangement. [Blend of OE *dūfan* to dive and *dȳfan* to immerse]

Alternative part of speech

Etymology

*Note that the past tense of *dive* can be *dived* or *dove*. Also note that the principal parts of irregular verbs are listed; the principal parts of regular verbs are not (see following examples).

Example:

Eiffel Tower[4]

[2]"Abracadabra," pg. 2 from *Funk & Wagnalls Standard Desk Dictionary.* Copyright © 1980 by Harper & Row, Publishers, Inc. Reprinted by permission of HarperCollins Publishers.

[3]"Dive," pg. 187 from *Funk & Wagnalls Standard Desk Dictionary.* Copyright © 1980 by Harper & Row, Publishers, Inc. Reprinted by permission of HarperCollins Publishers.

[4]Entry of "Eiffel Tower" from the book *Webster's New World Dictionary,* Second College Edition, by David B. Guralnik, pg. 447. Copyright © 1986 by Simon & Schuster, Inc. Used by permission of the publisher, New World Dictionaries/A division of Simon & Schuster, Inc., New York, N.Y. 10023.

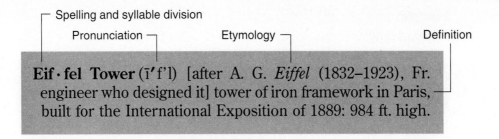

Spelling and syllable division

Pronunciation ⌐   Etymology ⌐   Definition

Eif·fel Tower (ī′f′l) [after A. G. *Eiffel* (1832–1923), Fr. engineer who designed it] tower of iron framework in Paris, built for the International Exposition of 1889: 984 ft. high.

Example:

explore[5]

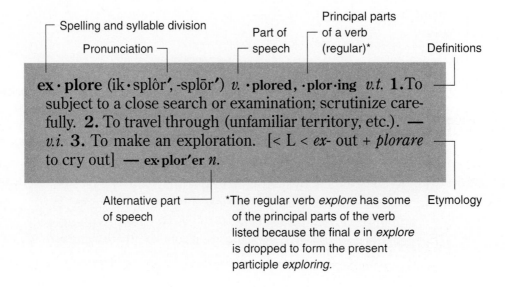

Spelling and syllable division

Part of   Principal parts
speech   of a verb
(regular)*   Definitions

Pronunciation ⌐

ex·plore (ik·splôr′, -splōr′) *v.* ·**plored, ·plor·ing** *v.t.* **1.**To subject to a close search or examination; scrutinize carefully. **2.** To travel through (unfamiliar territory, etc.). — *v.i.* **3.** To make an exploration. [< L < *ex-* out + *plorare* to cry out] — **ex·plor′er** *n.*

Alternative part   *The regular verb *explore* has some   Etymology
of speech   of the principal parts of the verb
listed because the final *e* in *explore*
is dropped to form the present
participle *exploring*.

Example:

discover [6]

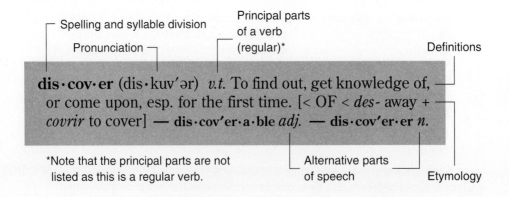

Spelling and syllable division   Principal parts
of a verb
(regular)*   Definitions

Pronunciation ⌐

dis·cov·er (dis·kuv′ər) *v.t.* To find out, get knowledge of, or come upon, esp. for the first time. [< OF < *des-* away + *covrir* to cover] — **dis·cov′er·a·ble** *adj.* — **dis·cov′er·er** *n.*

*Note that the principal parts are not   Alternative parts
listed as this is a regular verb.   of speech   Etymology

SPELLING VIA COMPUTER

In this age of computers, many people do all of their writing via word processors or typewriters with memory capabilities. A valuable feature of such technology is the spelling assistance it offers. Most word-processing programs include spell-checking functions in which your text will be scanned for spelling errors; some programs even suggest what the correct word might be. Specialized writing software may also provide sophisticated functions, such as dictionaries, synonym finders, outlining, and grammar checkers.

If you write on a computer of some sort and have access to spell-checking and other functions, certainly use them. Take advantage of all of the tools available to help improve your writing. But don't forego using the dictionary and other conventional aids. There is some basic knowledge that technology cannot and should not supplant.

Spelling Guidelines

As we stated in the introduction to this chapter, spelling in the English language is complicated by the number of inconsistencies in what rules do exist. In short, there are rules that can be followed *most* but not all of the time. If you can remember these rules, you will at least have a foundation on which to build your knowledge of spelling.

PREFIXES AND SUFFIXES

A **prefix** is one or more syllables added to the beginning of a root word to modify its meaning and form a new word. The spelling of the root word does not change when you add a prefix.

Examples:

operate → cooperate   guide → misguide

entry → reentry   visible → invisible

A **suffix** is one or more syllables placed after a root word to modify its meaning and form a new word. The spelling of the root word does not *generally* change when a suffix is added, but there are some exceptions. Consider the suffixes *-ness* and *-ly*.

Examples:

kind → kindness   kindly

keen → keenness   keenly

Exceptions:

happy → happiness   happily

ready → readiness   readily

The following guidelines offer some assistance regarding spelling changes when adding suffixes. To be absolutely sure of spelling, consult the root word in the dictionary.

Points to Remember:

1. **Whether or not to double the last letter of the root word can be a problem. Remember the following:**

   a. **In words of one syllable—Double the last consonant to add a suffix (such as *-er, -est, -ing, -ed, -ance,* and *-ence*) when the last three letters of the word end in a consonant-vowel-consonant (CVC) pattern and the suffix begins with a vowel. This rule is called the *CVC rule*.**

   Example:
   swim → swimmer   swimming

   Explanation:
   The last three letters of *swim* are *-wim,* which fits the CVC pattern; therefore, double the last consonant when adding the suffixes *-er* and *-ing*.

   Example:
   wet → wetter, wettest, wetting, wetted

   Explanation:
   The last and only three letters of *wet* are *wet*. It does fit the CVC pattern, so double the last consonant before adding the suffix.

   Do *not* double the consonant if it is preceded by two or more vowels or another consonant.

   Examples:
   sleep + -ing = sleeping

   leap + -ing = leaping

   cool + -er = cooler

   Do *not* double the consonant if the suffix begins with a consonant.

   Examples:
   fit + -ness = fitness

   ship + -ment = shipment

   red + -ness = redness

   There is an exception: If the word ends with the same letter with which the suffix begins, keep both letters.

Examples:

room + -mate = roommate

mortal + -ly = mortally

usual + -ly = usually

EXERCISE

Add the suffix shown to each of the following words; double the final consonant if necessary.

1. sit   (-ing) _____   (-er) _____

2. ship   (-ment) _____   (-ing) _____

3. read   (-er) _____   (-ing) _____

4. dial   (-ing) _____   (-ed) _____

5. run   (-er) _____   (-ing) _____

b. **Words of more than one syllable**—The CVC rule also applies with one more condition: If the accent is on the *last* syllable, *double* the consonant.

Example:

admit → admitted, admitting

Do *not* double the last consonant to add a suffix if the multisyllabic word has the CVC structure but is not accented on the last syllable.

Examples:

answer → answered, answering

benefit → benefited, benefiting

Do not double the last consonant if, when the suffix is added, the accent shifts from the last syllable to the first syllable.

Examples:

pre-*férr* + -ence = *préf*-er-ence

in-*férr* + -ence = *ín*-fer-ence

EXERCISE

Add the suffix shown to each of the following words; double the final consonant if necessary.

1. begin   (-ing) _____   (-er) _____

2. pardon   (-er) _____   (-ing) _____

3. admit   (-ed) _____   (-ing) _____

4. travel   (-er) _____   (-ed) _____

5. prefer   (-ence) _____   (-ing) _____

EXERCISE

Add an -ed and an -ing to each of the following words; double the final consonant if necessary.

	-ed	*-ing*
1. hop	_____	_____
2. recommend	_____	_____
3. transfer	_____	_____
4. annihilate	_____	_____
5. compel	_____	_____
6. boil	_____	_____
7. rip	_____	_____
8. forfeit	_____	_____
9. peel	_____	_____
10. wrap	_____	_____
11. sail	_____	_____
12. spray	_____	_____
13. fish	_____	_____
14. delegate	_____	_____
15. analyze	_____	_____

	-ed	-ing
16. whip	_____	_____
17. negotiate	_____	_____
18. reminisce	_____	_____
19. shift	_____	_____
20. fatigue	_____	_____

2. **Changing the *y* to *i*—When adding a suffix to a word that ends with a *y*, change the *y* to *i* if the letter before the *y* is a consonant.**

Example:
happy + -ness = happiness

Keep the final *y* if the letter before the *y* is a vowel.

Example:
delay + ed = delayed

EXERCISE

Add -er and -est to each of the following words; double the final consonant if necessary.

	-er	-est
1. happy	_____	_____
2. pretty	_____	_____
3. ugly	_____	_____
4. merry	_____	_____
5. silly	_____	_____

3. **Keeping the final *e*—For words that end in *-e*, drop the final *-e* if the suffix being added begins with a vowel.**

Examples:
love + -ing = loving

love + -able = lovable

If the suffix being added begins with a consonant, keep the final *-e*.

Examples:

love + -ly = lovely

love + -less = loveless

Again, there are exceptions: Memorize the spellings of the following words because they **do not** follow the rules for keeping the final *-e*.

argument	awful	courageous
judgment	manageable	noticeable
truly		

EXERCISE

Add the suffix shown to each of the following words; drop or keep the final -e as necessary.

1. hope   (-ing) _____   (-ful) _____

2. time   (-er) _____   (-less) _____

3. pure   (-ly) _____   (-ity) _____

4. argue   (-able) _____   (-ment)_____

5. sincere   (-ly) _____   (-ity) _____

PLURALS

Another set of guidelines will help you remember how to spell the plural forms of most nouns.

Points to Remember:

1. **To form the plurals of most singular nouns, add *-s*.**

    Examples:

    cat → cats   dog → dogs

    course → courses   maze → mazes

2. **To form the plural of a noun ending in *-s, -ch, -sh, -x,* or *-z,* add *-es*.**

    Examples:

    atlas → atlases   sandwich → sandwiches

    ash → ashes   reflex → reflexes

3. To form the plural of a noun ending in *y* preceded by a vowel, add *-s*. For a noun ending in *y* preceded by a consonant, change the *y* to *i* and add *-es*.

Examples:

birthday → birthdays   boy → boys

toy → toys   valley → valleys

body→ bodies   charity → charities

fantasy → fantasies   story → stories

4. To form the plural of a noun ending in *f,* change the *f* to *v* and add *-s* or *-es.*

Examples:

half → halves   loaf → loaves

self → selves   wife → wives

wolf → wolves

EXERCISE

Add -s *or* -es *to form the plural of each of the following words.*

1. echo _____
2. delivery _____

3. alley _____
4. tax _____

5. match _____
6. company _____

7. baby _____
8. tomato _____

9. potato _____
10. radio _____

11. wolf _____
12. delay _____

13. study _____
14. fee _____

15. enemy _____
16. fry _____

17. cello _____
18. church _____

19. nephew _____
20. eagle _____

SPECIFIC SPELLING RULES

The following specific rules will help you in certain situations.

Points to Remember:

1. Words with *ei* or *ie*—Generally, put the *i* before the *e*.

   Examples:

   believe, brief, niece, yield

   But put *e* before *i* after the letter *c*.

   Examples:

   ceiling, conceit, deceive, receipt

   Put *e* before *i* when the sound is a "long *a*" (*ā*).

   Examples:

   freight, vein, feign, veil

2. Words with the "seed" sound—Only one word ends with *-sede:*

   Example:

   supersede

   Only three words end with *-ceed:*

   Examples:

   exceed, proceed, and succeed

   All the other words that have the "seed" sound end with *-cede.*

   Examples:

   accede, concede, precede, recede, secede

3. Exceptions to the rules above—You will just have to memorize the following words as there is no logic for their spelling:

   Examples:

ancient	conscience	either	foreign
forfeit	height	leisure	protein
seize	sovereign	their	weird

EXERCISE

Complete each of the following words correctly by adding either ei *or* ie *in the space provided.*

1. c____ling

2. rec____ving

3. br____f

4. ____ther

5. rel____ve

6. w____ght

7. p____rce

8. y____ld

9. dec____ve

10. prot____n

Commonly Misspelled Words

Keep this list handy when you write. Are any of these words particular problems for you? (See the next section.)

accessory	acknowledgment	acquittal	address
analysis	annihilate	anxious	argument
athlete			
barbecue	beginning	behavior	biscuit
breathe			
cafeteria	calendar	carburetor	chaperon
comparison	compel	conscience	conscientious
consensus			
definite	delegate	desperate	disappoint
disapprove			
efficient	enthusiastic	environment	especially
exaggerate			
familiar	fatigue	financial	forfeit
genius	government	grammar	
illegal	illegible	integration	intelligent
jeopardy	jewelry		
knowledge			
limousine	losing	luxurious	
maintain	mathematics	matinee	meant
minimum	misspell	monotonous	municipal
necessary	negotiate	noticeable	
occasion	opinion	opportunity	optimist
optimistic	outrageous		

paralysis	parliament	pastime	perform
perseverance	personally	personnel	physics
possess	prefer	prejudice	privilege
prominent	prophecy	psychology	pursue
reference	referred	reminisce	representative
rhythm	ridiculous		
semester	separate	since	sovereign
success	sufficient	synonym	
tariff	taught	temperature	thorough
transferred	treacherous		
unanimous	until		
weight	wrath	written	

Your Personal List of Misspelled Words

Keep a personal list of words that you commonly misspell. Review it as you revise your writing.

1. _____   2. _____

3. _____   4. _____

5. _____   6. _____

7. _____   8. _____

9. _____   10. _____

11. _____   12. _____

13. _____   14. _____

15. _____   16. _____

17. _____   18. _____

19. _____   20. _____

21. _____   22. _____

23. _____   24. _____

25. _____   26. _____

27. _____   28. _____

29. _____   30. _____

Commonly Confused Words

Many words in the English language have similar spellings but very different meanings (*principle/principal*). Other words have similar meanings but not similar spellings (*which/that, among/between*). To use these words correctly, you must learn what they mean as well as how to spell them.

A/AN/AND

The words *a* and *an* are used as articles, but *and* is a conjunction.
Use the article *a* before a word that begins with a consonant sound.

Examples:
  a book, *a* pencil, *a* union, *a* unicorn
Explanation:
  The words *book* and *pencil* begin with consonant sounds. The words *union* and *unicorn* also begin with a consonant sound, even though they do not begin with consonants.

Use the article *an* before a word that begins with a vowel sound.

Examples:
  an empire, *an* orange, *an* hour, *an* honest man
Explanation:
  The words *empire* and *orange* begin with vowel sound, as do the words *hour* and *honest*. Note that the form of the article depends upon the word directly after it and not the noun or pronoun being referred to, as in *an honest man*.

ACCEPT/EXCEPT

The word *accept* means "to receive or agree to" while *except* means "but" or "to exclude."

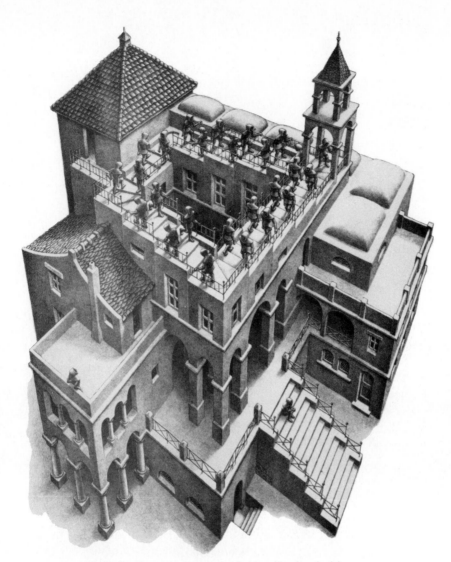

M. C. Escher creates a confusing illusion in his
lithograph *Ascending and Descending.*

Examples:

Bob will *accept* Bill's offer of $100.

Everyone received a B on the test *except* Marina, who got an A.

ADVICE/ADVISE

The word *advice* is a noun which means "a suggestion or opinion." *Advise* is a
verb meaning "to counsel."

Examples:

If Whitney had taken my *advice,* she would not have crawled out the window.

Please *advise* her that I will not tell her mother.

AFFECT/EFFECT

Affect is a verb that means "to influence or change." *Effect* used as a noun means "a result"; *effect* used as a verb means "to cause something to happen."

Examples:

Changes in the economy *affect* the way we live.

The *effect* of the drug has not been proven.

The invention of this new computer will *effect* a complete change in how businesses are run.

AISLE/ISLE

An *aisle* is a narrow passage. *Isle* is a poetic term for island.

Examples:

The father of the bride led his daughter down the *aisle* of the church.

Come escape with me and live on a deserted *isle.*

ALL READY/ALREADY

All ready is two words meaning that "all are prepared." *Already* means "previously."

Examples:

We are *all ready* to go out to dinner.

I *already* wrote my paragraph.

ALLUDE/ELUDE

Allude means "to refer" while *elude* means "to avoid."

Examples:

Bob *alluded* to his fascinating past.

The criminal *eluded* the police.

ALLUSION/ILLUSION

An *allusion* is a reference. An *illusion* is a false appearance.

Examples:

The professor made an *allusion* to the Bible in his lecture.

The magician performed an *illusion* in his act.

ALTAR/ALTER

An *altar* (noun) is a sacred platform. To *alter* (verb) means "to change."

Examples:

The priest lit the candle on the *altar*.

Please *alter* this skirt so that it is shorter.

AMONG/BETWEEN

Among is a preposition that refers to groups of more than two things. *Between,* another preposition, refers to just two things.

Examples:

The friendship *among* the three sisters is a close one.

The friendship *between* Adam and Alisa is a close one.

ANTONYM/HOMONYM/SYNONYM

Antonyms are words that have opposite meanings, such as *good* and *bad*. *Homonyms* are words that sound alike but are spelled differently (*hear* and *here*). *Synonyms* are words with similar meanings, such as *sweet* and *sugary.*

ANY ONE/ANYONE

Any one is two adjectives or a pronoun (*one*) modified by an adjective (*any*). *Anyone,* an indefinite pronoun, means "anybody."

Examples:

Please do not carry too many packages at *any one* time.

Anyone can learn to play the piano.

APPRAISE/APPRISE

Appraise means "to make an estimate." *Apprise* means "to inform."

Examples:

The agent was asked to *appraise* the jewelry for its value.

Please *apprise* me of your whereabouts.

ARE/OUR

The verb *are* is a form of the verb *to be*. The pronoun *our* means "belonging to us."

Examples:

We *are* ready to go on vacation.

Our house needs painting.

BARE/BEAR

Bare is an adjective that means "uncovered or empty." As a noun, a *bear* is an animal; as a verb, *bear* means "to carry or endure."

Examples:

The cupboards are *bare.*

Sometimes I don't think I can *bear* any more problems.

The baby *bear* likes honey.

BOARD/BORED

A *board* (noun) is a piece of lumber or a committee. *Bored* (verb) is the past tense of *bore,* which means "to be uninterested."

Examples:

The *board* of trustees will meet today.

I am very *bored* with weeknight television.

BRAKE/BREAK

A *brake* (noun) is a device for stopping a moving part. A *break* (noun) is a fracture, fragment, or pause. *Break* used as a verb means "to fracture, burst, or crack."

Examples:

My car's *brakes* need repairing.

We will take a *break* every hour.

Be careful not to *break* the window while cleaning it.

BY/BUY/BYE

The word *by* is a preposition meaning "beside." The word *buy* is a verb meaning "to purchase." The word *bye* is an informal interjection meaning "goodbye."

Examples:

By the clear, bubbling stream, the weeping willow branches swayed in the breeze.

The college will *buy* new computers for the data-processing classes.

She said, "*Bye,* Stacy!"

CAN/MAY

Can implies ability. *May* denotes permission.

Examples:

Carl *can* bench press 325 pounds even though he does not do it often.

May I go to the movies?

CAPITAL/CAPITOL

A *capital* is a city that is the official seat of the government or an upper-case letter. A *capitol* is a legislative building.

Examples:

Austin is the *capital* of Texas.

The *Capitol* building in Washington, D.C., is beautiful.

CHOOSE/CHOSE

Choose means "to select." *Chose* is the past tense of *to choose.*

Examples:

Choose a dress to wear to the party tonight.

Yesterday, Tracey *chose* the restaurant for lunch.

CITE/SIGHT/SITE

Cite (verb) means "to refer to." *Sight* (noun) means "to have the ability to see." A *site* (noun) is a location.

Examples:

Please *cite* the correct pages for your reference.

Sight is one of the most complicated senses.

On this *site*, the worst battle of the Civil War took place.

COARSE/COURSE

Coarse (adjective) means "rough." A *course* (noun) is a path or a class.

Examples:

You need *coarse* sandpaper to sand the first layer of wood on that old chair.

This physics *course* is too difficult.

COMMON/MUTUAL

Common means "shared by two or more people or things." *Mutual* means "reciprocal."

Examples:

In *Thelma and Louise,* Geena Davis and Susan Sarandon have a lot in *common.*

It is to our *mutual* interest to work together.

COMPARE/CONTRAST

Compare means "to examine similarities." *Contrast* means "to examine differences."

Examples:

When we *compare* the prices, this stereo is more expensive than yours.

Living in Alaska and living in Mississippi are quite a *contrast.*

COMPLEMENT/COMPLIMENT

A *complement* (noun) is something that completes. To *compliment* (verb) is to praise. *Compliment* (noun) is a statement of praise or admiration.

Examples:

The new sofa *complements* the rest of the living room.

Please *compliment* Stacy on her speech.

The *compliment* caused Angelia to blush.

CONNOTATION/DENOTATION

Connotation is the secondary or suggested meaning of a word or expression. *Denotation* is the specific association that the word expresses.

Examples:

The *denotation* of the word "home" is "a structure in which people reside."

The *connotation* of "home" includes feelings of family, security, love, and happiness.

CONSCIENCE/CONSCIOUS

Conscience (noun) is the inner sense of right and wrong. *Conscious* (adjective) means being mentally aware.

Examples:

Listen to your *conscience* when you have to make a moral choice.

COUNCIL/COUNSEL/CONSUL

A *council* (noun) is a group chosen to give advice. *Counsel* means "advice" (noun) or "to advise" (verb). A *consul* (noun) is a government agent who lives in a foreign country and serves to protect the interests of the citizens of his own country.

Examples:

The *council* recommended that our city should open a new recreation area.

Neil's father tried to *counsel* him about women.

The American *consul* to Kuwait was evacuated during the Gulf War.

DAIRY/DIARY

A *dairy* is a farm concerned with the production of milk products. A *diary* is a journal.

Examples:

The grocery store receives a daily shipment of *dairy* products.

Gina writes an entry in her *diary* every night.

DESERT/DESSERT

A *desert* (noun) is a dry, sandy piece of land; as a verb *desert* means "to abandon." A *dessert* (noun) is the final course of a meal.

Examples:

Of all places, the car broke down in the *desert.*

You should never *desert* a friend.

The *dessert* bar featured over 25 types of ice cream.

DEVICE/DEVISE

A *device* (noun) is an invention or plan. *Devise* (verb) means "to plan or invent."

Examples:

The *device* used to measure miles is called an "odometer."

The committee *devised* a plan to decrease its spending.

DIE/DYE

Die (verb) means "to cease to exist." As a verb, *dye* means "to color" or as a noun, "the substance used to produce a color."

Examples:

> Many ancient heroes *died* defending their people.
>
> Indigo *dye* was used by the ancient Egyptians.

DUAL/DUEL

Dual (adjective) means "double." A *duel* (noun or verb) is a confrontation or battle between two people.

Examples:

> The actress played a *dual* role in the movie.
>
> Valmont fought a *duel* with the young music teacher.
>
> Valmont and the young music teacher *duel* in the movie.

ELICIT/ILLICIT

Elicit (verb) means "to draw forth." *Illicit* (adjective) means "illegal."

Examples:

> The attorney tried to *elicit* information from her clients.
>
> All of the *illicit* items were confiscated by the police.

EMIGRANT/IMMIGRANT

An *emigrant* is a person who leaves a country. An *immigrant* is a person who comes into a country.

Examples:

> The *emigrants* left Europe in hope of finding more freedom.
>
> Ellis Island, once a landing port for *immigrants,* has become a museum in honor of them.

EMINENT/IMMANENT/IMMINENT

Eminent means "distinguished." *Immanent* means "inherent, living, or remaining." *Imminent* means "expected in the near future."

Examples:

> The *eminent* literature professor was well liked by many students.
>
> God's presence is *immanent* throughout the universe.
>
> The building is expected to open in the *imminent* future.

FAIR/FARE

As an adjective, *fair* means "just or right," or "a light complexion." As a noun, *fair* means "carnival." A *fare* (noun) is a transportation fee; as a verb, *fare* means "to go through an experience."

Examples:

Most people rated the restaurant's food and service as *fair*.

The bus *fare* has risen drastically over the years.

FORMALLY/FORMERLY

Formally means "done in a correct manner." *Formerly* means "at an earlier time."

Examples:

The staff *formally* welcomed the new administrator with an afternoon tea.

Tonya *formerly* appeared on another television show.

FORTH/FOURTH

Forth (preposition) means "forward, out into view." *Fourth* means "one-quarter (1/4)" used as a noun and "in the number-four position" used as an adjective.

Examples:

My sister went *forth* armed with confidence to find a new job.

Only a *fourth* of the construction has been completed on the stadium.

The *fourth* applicant withdrew from consideration.

GORILLA/GUERRILLA

A *gorilla* is an ape. A *guerrilla* is a member of a small defensive team of soldiers, who are often volunteers.

Examples:

Jane Goodall studied *gorilla* life for many years.

Moshe Dayan studied *guerrilla* warfare for many years.

HEAR/HERE

Hear (verb) means to perceive or sense sounds. *Here* (adverb) means "in this place."

Examples:

Can you actually *hear* a pin drop?

The new mall will be located *here*.

HEARD/HERD

Heard is the past tense of the verb *to hear.* A *herd* (noun) is a group of animals.

Examples:

I *heard* Beethoven's *Ninth Symphony* on the radio today.

The *herd* of wild horses moved across the meadow, grazing on the new spring grass.

HOARSE/HORSE

Hoarse is an adjective that describes a rough sound. A *horse* (noun) is an animal.

Examples:

My voice is *hoarse* from talking all day.

I love riding *horses.*

IMPLY/INFER

To *imply* is to hint or make a suggestion. To *infer* is to receive or draw a conclusion.

Examples:

She *implied* that she would be interested in taking the job.

I *inferred* from their conversation that something was wrong.

ITS/IT'S

Its is a possessive pronoun. *It's* is the contraction of *it is* or *it has.*

Examples:

The dog chased *its* tail.

It's too late to go out now.

KNOW/NO

Know (verb) means "to understand, to perceive, or to learn." *No* is the antonym of *yes.*

Examples:

I *know* exactly how you feel.

There are *no* more cookies left.

LAY/LIE

Lay is a transitive verb (takes an object) that means "to put" or "to place." *Lie* is an intransitive verb (no object) that means "to recline."

Examples:

Shelly *lay* the magazine on the table.

Lie down and take a nap for a while.

LEAD/LED

Lead, as a noun, is a type of metal; as a verb it means "to guide or direct." *Led* is the past tense of the verb *to lead.*

Examples:

Tracey *will lead* the Girl Scouts down the path.

Lead is a heavy metal.

Moses *led* the Israelites through the desert for forty years.

LOOSE/LOSE/LOSS

Loose (adjective) means "not tight." *Lose* (verb) means "to fail to win" or "to misplace something." *Loss* (noun) means "failure."

Examples:

She always wears *loose* clothing.

I hope we don't *lose* to the other team.

Our *loss* of the football game upset the team.

MINER/MINOR

A *miner* (noun) is a person who extracts minerals from the earth. *Minor* (adjective) means "unimportant," while *minor* (noun) means an under-aged person.

Examples:

The *miner* discovered a new coal deposit.

Bob and Helen realize that they have only *minor* problems.

A *minor* cannot enter the nightclub.

MORAL/MORALE

Moral (adjective) means "pertaining to accepted customs of society as right or wrong." *Morale* (noun) means "state of well-being."

Examples:

Without a *moral* code, a society would be destroyed.

We must keep our *morale* high by being cheerful.

PAIL/PALE

A *pail* (noun) is a cylindrical container for holding things. *Pale* (adjective) means "lacking intensity of color."

Examples:

Fill the *pail* with water.

Her face looks *pale.*

PAIN/PANE

Pain (noun) is bodily suffering or distress. A *pane* (noun) is a single plate of glass.

Examples:

A broken arm causes great *pain.*

Amber broke the *pane* in the garage door window with her baseball.

PASSED/PAST

Passed (verb) means "gone by" or "to receive a passing grade." *Past* as a noun means "a time gone by"; as an adjective, "that which has already occurred"; and as a preposition, "beyond."

Examples:

I *passed* both classes with A's.

You cannot change events in your *past.*

You can, however, learn from *past* mistakes.

It was *past* noon when they arrived.

PATIENCE/PATIENTS

Patience is the quality of being calm under trying circumstances. *Patients* are those persons under medical care.

Examples:

Some people lack the *patience* to finish a long task.

The doctor has many *patients* waiting in his office.

PEACE/PIECE

Peace (noun) is the absence of war. A *piece* (noun) is a part or section.

Examples:

Give *peace* a chance.

Can I have a *piece* of your cake?

PERSONAL/PERSONNEL

Personal (adjective) means "private." *Personnel* (noun) are employees.

Examples:

I do not feel like discussing my *personal* life.

The *personnel* in our office were pleased with their Christmas presents.

PLAIN/PLANE

Plain (adjective) means "simple, not fancy," or (noun) "an area of flat land." A *plane* (noun) is a flat surface, a short term for *airplane,* or a surface generated by a straight line on any two points in geometry.

Examples:

Vicky's clothes are never *plain* looking.

The African *plain* is very dry.

We watched the *planes* land at the airport.

Many students enjoy studying *plane* geometry.

PRESENCE/PRESENTS

Presence (noun) is the condition of being. As a noun, *presents* means "gifts"; as a verb, *present* means "to give."

Examples:

His *presence* is necessary at the convention.

You may *present* the award to Stephanie.

Your *presents* are under the Christmas tree.

PRINCIPAL/PRINCIPLE

As a noun, *principal* means "the head of a school." As an adjective, *principal* means "most important." A *principle* (noun) is a fundamental truth.

Examples:

> The *principal* of the high school spoke at commencement.
>
> The *principal* reason you came to college is to learn.
>
> People must live their lives by moral *principles*.

PROCEED/PRECEDE

Proceed (verb) means "to go forward" or "carry on or continue any action." *Precede* (verb) means "to go or come before."

Examples:

> The climbers will *proceed* with their plans to scale the cliff face by noon.
>
> The guide will *precede* the rest of the climbing party up the cliff face.

QUIET/QUITE

Quiet (adjective) means "free of noise" or (noun) "the condition of being free of noise." *Quite* (adverb) means "to a considerable extent."

Examples:

> The library is a *quiet* place to study.
>
> We enjoyed the *quiet* of the lake.
>
> Shelly is *quite* happy to go to Notre Dame University.

RAIN/REIN/REIGN

Rain (noun) is precipitation from the clouds. A *rein* (noun) is a strap used to control a horse. A *reign* (noun) is a period of rule.

Examples:

> It will *rain* today according to the meteorologist.
>
> Remember to hold onto the horse's *reins* when you ride.
>
> Queen Elizabeth's *reign* has been a long one.

RIGHT/RITE/WRITE

The word *right* can be used in many forms and has many meanings. As an adjective, *right* means "correct or accurate," "suitable or proper," or "opposite of left." As a noun, a *right* is something to which you are entitled, such as privileges and ownership. The verb *right* means "to correct or avenge" or "to restore to an upright position." As an adverb, *right* means "directly," "immediately," "correctly," "extremely," or "precisely." Consult the dictionary to be sure of the use that's appropriate for your work.

A *rite* (noun) is a ceremony. *Write* (verb) means "to form letters and words on a surface."

Examples:

She knew the *right* answer but hesitated to speak up.

It is important for aspiring politicians to associate with the *right* people.

State laws differ regarding to what mineral *rights* property owners are entitled.

Robin Hood sought to *right* the wrongs created by economic injustice.

My house is on the *right* side of the street.

The pitch went *right* over home plate.

Marriage is a sacred *rite* of the church.

Write to me when you have the time.

ROAD/RODE

A *road* (noun) is a street. *Rode* (verb) is the past tense of ride.

Examples:

She lives on a small country *road.*

Indiana Jones *rode* into the desert in search of the Holy Grail.

SCENE/SEEN

A *scene* (noun) is a setting or a view. *Seen* (verb) is the past participle of the verb *to see.*

Examples:

The *scene* of the Pacific Ocean is breathtaking.

I have *seen* Mel Gibson in many movies.

SENSE/SINCE

Sense as a noun is the ability to perceive; *sense* can also be used as a verb to mean "perceive." *Since* means "because" or "from the time that."

Examples:

Humans have five major *senses;* unfortunately common *sense* is not one of them.

I *sense* that you are angry with me.

Since he has been gone, I have really missed him.

STATIONARY/STATIONERY

Stationary (adjective) means "not moving." *Stationery* (noun) means "writing materials and office supplies."

Examples:

A *stationary* weather front meant that it would rain all weekend.

I went to the *stationery* store to buy some office supplies.

THAN/THEN

Than (preposition) means "as compared with." As an adverb, *then* means "at that time" or "therefore"; as a noun, *then* refers to a particular time.

Examples:

David is more handsome *than* Steve.

The audience started cheering; *then,* Billy Joel came out on stage.

By *then,* we were too tired to care.

THEIR/THERE/THEY'RE

Their (adjective) is the possessive form of *they. There* (adverb) means "in that place." *They're* is the contraction of *they are.*

Examples:

Their fortunes are waiting for them.

Look over *there.*

They're planning to study tonight.

TO/TOO/TWO

To (preposition) means "in the direction of." *Too* (adverb) means "also" or (adjective) "excessive." *Two* (adjective) denotes a number greater than one.

Examples:

Please go *to* the store.

Anne wants to go, *too.*

That is *too* large to fit in my car.

I want *two* hamburgers.

THREW/THOROUGH/THROUGH

Threw (verb) is the past tense of *throw*. *Thorough* (adjective) means "complete." *Through* (preposition) means "in one side and out the other" or "by means of."

Examples:

Joe Namath *threw* the ball many times in Superbowl III.

The police have made a *thorough* search.

Let's walk *through* the park.

She got the job *through* her mother, the company president.

WAIST/WASTE

The *waist* (noun) is the part of the body around the torso. To *waste* (verb) means "to squander."

Examples:

Her *waist* is small.

Please do not *waste* money.

WEAK/WEAK

Weak (adjective) means "feeble" or "the opposite of strong." A *week* (noun) is seven days.

Examples:

Every chain has a *weak* link.

I have to hand in my report in a *week*.

WEAR/WERE/WHERE

Wear (verb) means "to put onto the body" or "to tire or diminish." *Were* (verb) is the past tense of *to be*. *Where* (adverb) means "in what place" or (noun) "a particular place."

Examples:

People tend to *wear* the latest fashions.

We *were* trapped in the elevator for a few minutes.

Where is Superman when you need him?

Where I grew up, people wanted to know their neighbors.

WEATHER/WHETHER

The *weather* (noun) is the daily climate conditions. *Whether* (conjunction) means "if."

Examples:

The *weather* calls for rain all weekend.

I'm not sure *whether* to buy the shoes today or tomorrow.

WHICH/THAT

Which is a nonrestrictive pronoun that refers to animals and things. *That* is a restrictive pronoun that refers to people, animals, and things. *Who* can be used as both types and refers only to people.

Examples:

The report, *which* I forgot to hand in, was due today.

The book *that* I finished yesterday was intriguing.

Professor Morgan, *who* is the best earth science teacher, is teaching biology this fall.

The students *who* interrupted the speaker were protesting against the destruction of tropical rain forests.

WHO/WHOM

Who is used as the subject of a sentence or clause but never an object. *Whom* is always used as an object of the verb or preposition; it can never be used as the subject.

Examples:

Who is at my door?

The student *who* had the highest GPA won the scholarship.

Whom did you choose as the winner of the contest?

The woman about *whom* the newspaper wrote is suing for libel.

WHO'S/WHOSE

Who's is the contraction of *who is* or *who has*. *Whose* is a possessive pronoun.

Examples:

Who's knocking on my door?

Whose literature book is this?

YOUR/YOU'RE

Your is the possessive form of *you*. *You're* is the contraction of *you are*.

Examples:

Don't forget to take *your* coat.

You're going to be cold tonight.

EXERCISE

Circle the correct word(s) to complete each of the following sentences.

1. Louis Comfort Tiffany (1848–1933) was (a, an) wonderful artist.

2. Louis' father, Charles Tiffany, was (a, and) jeweler and retailer.

3. Louis Tiffany was (a, an) artist and designer (an, and) a leader in the Art Nouveau movement.

4. I would gladly (accept, except) a free original of any one of Louis Tiffany's works.

5. All of my friends (accept, except) Traci have seen an original of Tiffany's stained glass windows in a museum.

6. Aunt Mary always has good (advice, advise) to give me whenever I need her help.

7. Whitney had (all ready, already) finished writing the essay when the professor told the class to turn in the papers.

8. We are (all ready, already) to spend the day at EPCOT and Disney-MGM Studios to celebrate completing the writing of our book.

9. Lynda stood at the (altar, alter) with her husband-to-be.

10. I would like to give you some (advice, advise) on your paragraph.

11. I would (advice, advise) you to proofread your writing several times before handing it in.

12. Ask your uncle for (advice, advise).

13. Studying grammar has (affected, effected) my writing by improving it.

14. The (affects, effects) of the new medicine were beneficial.

15. The bride walked down the (aisle, isle) with her proud father beside her.

16. The criminal tried to (allude, elude) the undercover detective.

17. The professor made an (allusion, illusion) to a passage in the Bible.

18. (Any one, Anyone) can improve his or her writing skills.

19. The professor should (appraise, apprise) the students of what is covered in the (course, coarse).

20. When you have questions, ask (our, are) professor.

EXERCISE

Circle the correct word(s) to complete each of the following sentences.

1. If a (bear, bare) has no clothes on, then it is (bear, bare).

2. There will be a (board, bored) meeting today at 3:00 P.M.

3. If you are tired, take a (brake, break).

4. Rob went (by, buy, bye) the bookstore today to (by, buy, bye) a book by Stephen King.

5. (Can, May) I borrow your thesaurus?

6. Always start off a sentence with a (capital, capitol).

7. You must think before you (choose, chose).

8. The pastor will (cite, sight, site) an important passage from the Bible.

9. You have to buy (coarse, course) sandpaper when first sanding wood.

10. We made a (common, mutual) agreement to see one another again.

11. You will have to (compare, contrast) the similarities and (compare, contrast) the differences between the two computer programs before purchasing one.

12. I would like to pay you a (complement, compliment) on your wonderful essay.

13. The word "dog" has a negative (connotation, denotation) when it is used to describe a man or a woman.

14. Although Mohammed Ali was knocked down by Joe Frazier, he still remained (conscience, conscious).

15. My uncle used to be a (council, counsel, consul) in Europe.

16. I write in my (dairy, diary) every day.

17. Carl's favorite (desert, dessert) is apple pie.

18. I am going to (device, devise) a scheme to study all the vocabulary words in one hour.

19. I will not (die, dye) my hair.

20. The air filter that I bought has a (dual, duel) fan.

EXERCISE

Circle the correct word(s) to complete each of the following sentences.

1. The (elicit, illicit) items are stored in the police station's property room.

2. A lot of (emigrants, immigrants) come to the United States every year in search of a better life.

3. You had better leave at once; you are in (eminent, immanent, imminent) danger.

4. You have to pay a (fair, fare) to get onto the ferry.

5. You should always be (fair, fare) with people.

6. When you go to a business convention, you must dress and act (formally, formerly).

7. Let Jayne have a (forth, fourth) of your candy bar, Symone.

8. (Gorilla, Guerrilla) warfare is a serious problem in the Middle East and South America.

9. (Here, Hear) is the book about Louis Tiffany's most famous works for Aunt Henrietta.

10. Have you ever (heard, herd) of the word "hermeneutics"?

11. She has the flu, and her voice sounds (hoarse, horse).

12. Are you (implying, inferring) that I don't know what I am doing?

13. (Its, It's) a good idea to purchase a dictionary and a thesaurus before taking Freshman English.

14. I (know, no) what you mean.

15. (Lead, led) is a heavy metal.

16. I am going to (lay, lie) down.

17. This large shirt is too (loose, lose, loss).

18. The team suffered its second (loose, lose, loss).

19. It was difficult for him to (loose, lose, loss) weight.

20. A coal (miner, minor) works very hard.

EXERCISE

Circle the correct word(s) to complete each of the following sentences.

1. We are all faced with making (moral, morale) choices.

2. She almost fainted, and her face looked (pail, pale).

3. The window (pain, pane) in your living room is huge.

4. We (passed, past) the French bakery on the way home.

5. My (patience, patients) wears thin when I am given a deadline.

6. May I have a (peace, piece) of your banana nut bread?

7. After my interview, I had to fill out some forms in the (personal, personnel) department.

8. (Plain, Plane) geometry is not my favorite subject.

9. Jackie received a lot of Christmas (presence, presents).

10. We have to learn some basic (principals, principles) in physics.

11. This is (quiet, quite) a lovely apartment you have.

12. Grab the (rains, reins, reigns) of the horse!

13. I (right, rite, write) with my (right, rite, write) hand.

14. I have the (right, rite, write) to vote.

15. Indiana Jones (road, rode) a beautiful brown stallion into the sunset in his third motion picture.

16. My favorite (scene, seen) in *Dead Poets Society* is when the students stand on top of their desks at the end of the movie.

17. Thomas Paine had good common (sense, since).

18. I have a (stationary, stationery) bicycle.

19. Steve's computer has more memory (than, then) Naomi's does.

20. (Their, There, They're) coming over to show you how to use your new computer.

EXERCISE

Circle the correct word(s) to complete each of the following sentences.

1. There are (to, too, two) many people enrolled in this class.

2. You must do a (threw, thorough, through) job of cleaning.

3. The children ran (threw, thorough, through) the park laughing and playing.

4. Scarlett O'Hara had a thin (waist, waste).

5. I will send you the check sometime next (weak, week).

6. If it (wear, were, where) up to me, we'd go.

7. My sister Susan is going to (wear, were, where) a velvet dress to dinner tonight.

8. I want to watch the (weather, whether) report.

9. It's not (weather, whether) you win or lose but how you play the game that's important.

10. The football game (which, that) we saw last night was great.

11. The book (which, that) the professor recommended was rather boring.

12. The book, (which, that) I personally found boring, was on the best-seller list.

13. A number of the women (who, whom) belonged to the group decided to boycott the convention.

14. (Who, Whom) is coming to the meeting this afternoon?

15. (Who, Whom) did the committee nominate for president?

16. After (who, whom) did they name the baby?

17. (Who's, Whose) book is this?

18. (Who's, Whose) the French Impressionist painter (who, whom) likes to paint men and women dancing?

19. (Your, You're) in charge of addressing the invitations.

20. (Your, You're) reprint of Dali's *The Persistence of Memory* is at my house.

30 *Common Grammatical Errors*

This chapter presents the most common grammar errors students make. You will see that many of the mistakes you make are common errors, and you will learn how to detect and correct them. This chapter was created by taking hundreds of student papers and performing the statistical analysis needed to determine the most common errors. You should find the results interesting, familiar, and helpful in revising your own writing.

1. Incorrect spelling
2. Missing comma after introductory element
3. Superfluous commas
4. Missing or misplaced apostrophe
5. Vague pronoun reference
6. Fused (run-on) sentence
7. Lack of subject-verb agreement
8. Sentence fragment
9. Wrong verb form
10. Incorrect word choice
11. Missing comma(s) in nonrestrictive element
12. Wrong or missing preposition or article
13. Missing comma in series
14. Comma splice
15. Incorrect capitalization
16. Choppy sentences
17. Errors in italics (underlining)
18. Superfluous semicolons
19. Dangling or misplaced modifiers
20. Unnecessary or incorrect pronoun shift

We will address each in turn.

INCORRECT SPELLING

Incorrect spelling is by far the most common student error. Students become upset when they type *nda* and are marked off for spelling *and* incorrectly. Nonetheless, typographical errors (typos) are still spelling mistakes. For more hints on spelling, refer to Chapter 28, "Spelling."

MISSING COMMA AFTER INTRODUCTORY ELEMENT

A comma is needed following an introductory word.

Examples:

Frankly, I don't like green cars.

However, Sara does teach swimming on the weekends.

A comma is also needed following an introductory phrase or clause.

Examples:

Because of the blackout, we were not able to watch our favorite TV program.

Without the telephone, my niece could not survive.

Although I bought my own car, my parents helped me out with my insurance.

Even if an editor reads over your content, you should still reread it.

SUPERFLUOUS COMMAS

Superfluous commas are those that are not needed. Many students sprinkle commas over a paragraph like salt over a batch of french fries. There are many different types of writing situations in which students use superfluous commas.

Example:

I sit in the living room, and watch the television.

Explanation:

A comma is not needed after *room.* Some students feel the need to add an extra comma when they see two verbs in a sentence or *and* anywhere in the sentence. This is not a compound sentence.

CORRECTED EXAMPLE:

I sit in the living room and watch the television.

Example:

I will go to the store now, even though I will be late for work.

Explanation:

A comma is not needed after *now.* You do not need a comma before the subordinating conjunction *even though.* Do not add a comma before a subordinating conjunction when the subordinating conjunction is in the middle of the sentence.

CORRECTED EXAMPLE:

I will go to the store now even though I will be late for work.

Example:

The book, that is on the table, is mine.

Explanation:

Commas are not needed around a restrictive element such as the phrase *that is on the table*. Something is restrictive if it restricts the meaning of the sentence or is essential to the meaning of the sentence. It is not added information; it is necessary to tell which book is being talked about.

CORRECTED EXAMPLE:

The book that is on the table is mine.

MISSING OR MISPLACED POSSESSIVE APOSTROPHE

A possessive apostrophe shows that something belongs to something or someone else. Students have trouble with words that end in -*s*. The most common mistake is confusing the words *its* and *it's*.

Example:

I think that *it's* time to reread my paragraph.

Explanation:

The word *it's* is a contraction for *it is*.

Example:

I saw a bacteria under the microscope, and *its* flagella were moving.

Explanation:

The word *its* shows possession, namely, the flagella belonging to the bacteria.

Example:

Be careful not to break the *books* binding.

Explanation:

A possessive apostrophe is needed for the word *book*.

CORRECTED EXAMPLE:

Be careful not to break the *book's* binding.

Example:

Chris' notes were impeccable.

Explanation:

When the word that shows possession ends in -*s,* add -'*s* unless the addition of -*s* would cause an awkward-sounding pronunciation.

CORRECTED EXAMPLE:

Chris's notes were impeccable.

VAGUE PRONOUN REFERENCE

Always make sure that your audience knows to which noun or pronoun your pronoun is referring.

Example:

I saw my friends Sara and Holly in the store, and when I waved to *her,* she spilled *her* soda.

Explanation:

Who? Who spilled her soda? The pronoun *her* is vague; there is no clear referent.

CORRECTED EXAMPLE:

I saw my friends Sara and Holly in the store, and when I waved to *Sara,* she spilled *her* soda.

Example:

I went to the zoo, and I saw a dog show and a bird show; *it* was great.

Explanation:

What was great? The pronoun *it* is vague.

CORRECTED EXAMPLE:

I went to the zoo, and I saw a dog show and a bird show; the *dog show* was great.

FUSED (RUN-ON) SENTENCE

A fused sentence is two or more independent clauses written as a single sentence with no punctuation.

Example:

Gina likes to go to the movies but Marina likes to go to the beach.

Explanation:

There is no punctuation between the two independent clauses. Add a comma before the coordinating conjunction *but* to correct the fused sentence.

CORRECTED EXAMPLE:

Gina likes to go to the movies, but Marina likes to go to the beach.

Example:

I need to study for a physics exam and I also need to write a paragraph for English class.

Explanation:

There is no punctuation between the two independent clauses. You need to add a comma before the coordinating conjunction *and* to correct the fused sentence.

CORRECTED EXAMPLE:

I need to study for a physics exam, and I also need to write a paragraph for English class.

SUBJECT-VERB AGREEMENT

The subject must agree with the verb.

Example:

My brother and his friend *is* doing well.

Explanation:

Sometimes, students look at only the subject before the verb and choose a verb form that is singular. The compound subject *brother* and *friend* is plural.

CORRECTED EXAMPLE:

My *brother* and his *friend are* doing well.

Example:

My brother who is playing with building blocks *are* only five years old.

Explanation:

The plural noun *blocks* is part of a restrictive element. The subject of the sentence is *brother.*

CORRECTED EXAMPLE:

My *brother* who is playing with building blocks *is* only five years old.

Example:

The tires on the car *is* radials.

Explanation:

The subject of the sentence is *tires* not *car; car* is the object of the preposition.

CORRECTED EXAMPLE:

The *tires* on the car *are* radials.

SENTENCE FRAGMENT

A sentence fragment is a group of words that do not make a complete sentence.

Example:

When I am happy.

Explanation:

The thought is not complete. *When I am happy* is a dependent clause. The sentence fragment is caused by the subordinating conjunction *when.*

CORRECTED EXAMPLE:

When I am happy, I smile.

Example:

After midnight.

Explanation:

Often, a response to a question is a sentence fragment.

CORRECTED EXAMPLE:

Whitney went to the party *after midnight.*

WRONG VERB FORM

Wrong verb form can be caused by the wrong tense, a shift in verb tense, or a wrong form, which usually occurs when using irregular verbs.

Example:

I *use* to be good at mathematics.

Explanation:

The past tense of *use* is *used.* This mistake is a very common error.

CORRECTED EXAMPLE:

I *used* to be good at mathematics.

Example:

I like *jumping* rope and *to play* basketball.

Explanation:

The verbals *jumping* and *to play* are not parallel; *jumping* is a gerund and *to play* is an infinitive. The verbals must be parallel.

CORRECTED EXAMPLE:

I like *jumping* rope and *playing* basketball.

Example:

My brother *singed* a nice song.

Explanation:

The past tense of the verb *sing* is *sang.*

CORRECTED EXAMPLE:

My brother *sang* a nice song.

INCORRECT WORD CHOICE

Incorrect word choice occurs when the writer is confused by words that are similar. (For more help with this problem, see Chapter 29, "Commonly Confused Words.")

Example:

Everyone is going to the baseball game *accept* me.

Explanation:

The word that is needed is *except,* which means "but." The word *accept* means "to receive."

CORRECTED EXAMPLE:

Everyone is going to the baseball game *except* me.

Example:

You should limit eating *diary* products.

Explanation:

The word that is needed is *dairy,* which means "milk products." The word *diary* means "journal."

CORRECTED EXAMPLE:

You should limit eating *dairy* products.

MISSING COMMA(S) IN NONRESTRICTIVE ELEMENT

Commas are needed around a nonrestrictive element. A nonrestrictive element gives additional information, but it does not restrict the meaning of the sentence; therefore, a nonrestrictive element should be enclosed within commas.

Example:

Holly *who was in the art club last year* was first to speak.

Explanation:

The nonrestrictive element *who was in the art club last year* provides nonessential information. It must be enclosed within commas.

CORRECTED EXAMPLE:

Holly, *who was in the art club last year,* was first to speak.

Example:

Kim was forced to write a paragraph *which she does not like doing.*

Explanation:

The nonrestrictive element is *which she does not like doing.* It is nonessential and must be set off by a comma.

CORRECTED EXAMPLE:

Kim was forced to write a paragraph, *which she does not like doing.*

WRONG OR MISSING PREPOSITION OR ARTICLE

Students sometimes just simply do not notice that they have forgotten to add an article or preposition, and sometimes they use the wrong preposition or article.

Example:

I think that you should play *a* instrument.

Explanation:

The word *a* is an incorrect article. The word *instrument* takes the article *an*, not *a*.

CORRECTED EXAMPLE:

I think that you should play *an* instrument.

Example:

I agree *to* your brother that writing a paragraph is not too difficult.

Explanation:

You agree *with* a person, not *to* a person.

CORRECTED EXAMPLE:

I agree *with* your brother that writing a paragraph is not too difficult.

MISSING COMMA IN SERIES

Students seem to forget to add the final comma in a series; it should precede the conjunction. Sometimes, students neglect to add extra commas in a sentence that has more than three items.

Example:

My favorite groups are the Beatles, the Eagles and UB40.

Explanation:

A comma is needed after the second item in the series, *the Eagles,* before the word *and.*

CORRECTED EXAMPLE:

My favorite groups are the Beatles, the Eagles, and UB40.

Example:

The parts of speech are nouns, pronouns, adjectives, adverbs verbs propositions conjunctions, and interjections.

Explanation:

Several commas are missing. A comma is needed after each part of speech in the series. (Obviously, a period goes at the end.)

CORRECTED EXAMPLE:

The parts of speech are nouns, pronouns, adjectives, adverbs, verbs, prepositions, conjunctions, and interjections.

COMMA SPLICE

A comma splice occurs when two independent clauses are joined with a comma; "stronger" punctuation is needed, such as a semicolon or a period.

Example:

Van Gogh was a great Dutch artist, Bach was a great German composer.

Explanation:

Two independent clauses are joined with only a comma. Either add a coordinating conjunction and a comma or a semicolon but not both a coordinating conjunction and a semicolon.

CORRECTED EXAMPLE:

Van Gogh was a great Dutch artist, and Bach was a great German composer.

Alternative Example:

Van Gogh was a great Dutch artist; Bach was a great German composer.

INCORRECT CAPITALIZATION

Review the rules for capitalization in Chapter 27, "Mechanics."

Example:

I live at 1225 west oak street, seattle, washington.

Explanation:

The names of streets, cities, and states need to be capitalized.

CORRECTED EXAMPLE:

I live at 1225 *West Oak Street, Seattle, Washington.*

Example:

william shakespeare, an english writer, wrote during the renaissance.

Explanation:

In addition to names, eras and nationalities should also be capitalized.

CORRECTED EXAMPLE:

William Shakespeare, an *English* writer, wrote during the *Renaissance.*

CHOPPY SENTENCES

Choppy sentences do not flow easily, but they can still be grammatically correct.

Example:

I don't like school. I like mathematics. I only like to study mathematics with my best friend.

Explanation:

These sentences are short and choppy. The information is presented in small parts without joining them together. It sounds as if a robot is speaking.

CORRECTED EXAMPLE:

I don't like school, but I do like to study mathematics with my best friend.

ERRORS IN ITALICS (UNDERLINING)

Because you can't *italicize* words while handwriting, you <u>underline</u> instead. Underline the titles of books, movies, plays, major works of poetry, ships, spacecraft, and works of art.

Example:

I loved the movie Back to School.

Explanation:

The movie title *Back to School* needs to be underlined.

CORRECTED EXAMPLE:

I loved the movie <u>Back to School</u>.

Example:

We enjoyed reading the Iliad and the Odyssey.

Explanation:

The titles of the epics the *Iliad* and the *Odyssey* should be underlined.

CORRECTED EXAMPLE:

We enjoyed reading the <u>Iliad</u> and the <u>Odyssey</u>.

SUPERFLUOUS SEMICOLONS

Superfluous semicolons occur when you add semicolons where they do not belong. This error usually occurs when you use a semicolon where a comma should go; this mistake is also known as *overpunctuation*.

Example:

Holly*; who was in the art club last year;* was first to speak.

Explanation:

The semicolons around the nonrestrictive element are incorrect. The nonrestrictive element *who was in the art club last year* should be set off by commas.

CORRECTED EXAMPLE:

Holly*, who was in the art club last year,* was first to speak.

Example:

Van Gogh was a great Dutch artist; *and* Bach was a great German composer.

Explanation:

There are two independent clauses joined by a semicolon and a coordinating conjunction. This error is an example of overpunctuation, or using a semicolon where a comma should be.

CORRECTED EXAMPLE:

Van Gogh was a great Dutch artist, *and* Bach was a great German composer.

DANGLING OR MISPLACED MODIFIERS

A misplaced modifier can be corrected by changing the word order. A dangling modifier is a participle or other modifier that does not logically describe the noun or pronoun closest to it in the sentence.

Example:

Drinking from the birdbath, my grandmother saw a robin.

Explanation:

The participial phrase *drinking from the birdbath* is used as an adjective and must be moved to the end of the sentence (unless, of course, my grandmother has been drinking from the birdbath).

CORRECTED EXAMPLE:

My grandmother saw *a robin drinking from the birdbath.*

Example:

Walking down the street, the curb tripped me.

Explanation:

Curbs do not *walk down the street.* The sentence should be revised to include a noun that the participial phrase *walking down the street* can modify.

CORRECTED EXAMPLE:

Walking down the street, I tripped over the curb.

UNNECESSARY OR INCORRECT PRONOUN SHIFT

An unnecessary pronoun shift occurs when the writer shifts from one kind of pronoun to another. Sometimes, the pronouns do not agree in number.

Example:

When *you are* writing a paragraph, *one* should keep in mind not to shift pronouns unnecessarily.

Explanation:

The pronoun shifts from *you* to *one* in the sentence, which is a common error.

CORRECTED EXAMPLE:

When *one is* writing a paragraph, *one* should keep in mind not to shift pronouns unnecessarily.

Example:

A student may take *their* book to class.

Explanation:

The pronoun *their* does not agree in number with *a student.* Choose either *his* or *her.*

CORRECTED EXAMPLE:

A student may take *her* book to class.

Appendixes

A. Complete Conjugation of the Regular Verb *To Move*
B. Most Common Irregular Verbs
C. Conjugation of Four Irregular Verbs
D. Uncorrected Paragraph and Corrected Paragraph (from Chapter 24)

Appendix A: Complete Conjugation of the Regular Verb To Move

Four Principal Parts

Infinitive—to move
Past—moved
Past Participle—moved
Present Participle—moving

Present Tense

	Singular	*Plural*
First Person	I move	We move
Second Person	You move	You move
Third Person	He, she, it moves	They move

Past Tense

(base form of the verb + -*d* or -*ed*)

	Singular	*Plural*
First Person	I moved	We moved
Second Person	You moved	You moved
Third Person	He, she, it moved	They moved

Future Tense

(*will* or *shall* + the base form of the verb)

	Singular	Plural
First Person	I will (shall) move	We will (shall) move
Second Person	You will move	You will move
Third Person	He, she, it will move	They will move

Present Perfect Tense

(*have* or *has* + the past participle)

	Singular	Plural
First Person	I have moved	We have moved
Second Person	You have moved	You have moved
Third Person	He, she, it *has* moved	They have moved

Past Perfect Tense

(*had* + the past participle)

	Singular	Plural
First Person	I had moved	We had moved
Second Person	You had moved	You had moved
Third Person	He, she, it had moved	They had moved

Future Perfect Tense

(*will have* or *shall have* + the past participle)

	Singular	Plural
First Person	I will (shall) have moved	We will (shall) have moved
Second Person	You will have moved	You will have moved
Third Person	He, she, it will have moved	They will have moved

Present Progressive Tense

(*am, is, are* + present participle)

	Singular	Plural
First Person	I am moving	We are moving
Second Person	You are moving	You are moving
Third Person	He, she, it is moving	They are moving

Past Progressive Tense

(*was, were* + present participle)

	Singular	Plural
First Person	I was moving	We were moving

Second Person	You were moving	You were moving
Third Person	He, she, it was moving	They were moving

Future Progressive Tense

(*will* or *shall* + *be* + present participle)

	Singular	*Plural*
First Person	I will (shall) be moving	We will (shall) be moving
Second Person	You will be moving	You will be moving
Third Person	He, she, it will be moving	They will be moving

Present Perfect Progressive Tense

(*has* or *have* + *been* + present participle)

	Singular	*Plural*
First Person	I have been moving	We have been moving
Second Person	You have been moving	You have been moving
Third Person	He, she, it has been moving	They have been moving

Past Perfect Progressive Tense

(*had* + *been* + present participle)

	Singular	*Plural*
First Person	I had been moving	We had been moving
Second Person	You had been moving	You had been moving
Third Person	He, she, it had been moving	They had been moving

Future Perfect Progressive Tense

(*will* or *shall* + *have* + *been* + present participle)

	Singular	*Plural*
First Person	I will have been moving	We will have been moving
Second Person	You will have been moving	You will have been moving
Third Person	He, she, it will have been moving	They will have been moving

Appendix B:
Most Common Irregular Verbs

Base Form	*Past Tense*	*Past Participle*
arise	arose	arisen
awake	awoke	awakened, awoken
be	was, were	been

Base Form	*Past Tense*	*Past Participle*
bear	bore	borne, born
beat	beat	beaten
become	became	become
befall	befell	befallen
begin	began	begun
bend	bent	bent
bet	bet	bet
bid (offer)	bid	bid
bid (command)	bade	bidden
bind	bound	bound
bite	bit	bitten
bleed	bled	bled
blow	blew	blown
break	broke	broken
bring	brought	brought
build	built	built
burn	burned, burnt	burned, burnt
burst	burst	burst
buy	bought	bought
cast	cast	cast
catch	caught	caught
choose	chose	chosen
cling	clung	clung
clothe	clothed, clad	clothed, clad
come	came	come
cost	cost	cost
creep	crept	crept
cut	cut	cut
deal	dealt	dealt
dig	dug	dug
dive	dived, dove	dived
do	did	done
draw	drew	drawn
dream	dreamed, dreamt	dreamed, dreamt
drink	drank	drunk
drive	drove	driven
eat	ate	eaten
fall	fell	fallen
feed	fed	fed
feel	felt	felt
fight	fought	fought
find	found	found
flee	fled	fled

Base Form	Past Tense	Past Participle
fling	flung	flung
fit	fitted, fit	fitted, fit
fly	flew	flown
forbid	forbade, forbad	forbidden
forget	forgot	forgotten, forgot
forecast	forecast, forecasted	forecast, forecasted
forgive	forgave	forgiven
forsake	forsook	forsaken
freeze	froze	frozen
get	got	gotten, got
give	gave	given
go	went	gone
grind	ground	ground
grow	grew	grown
hang (an object)	hung	hung
hang (a person)	hanged	hanged
have	had	had
hear	heard	heard
hide	hid	hidden
hit	hit	hit
hold	held	held
hurt	hurt	hurt
inlay	inlaid	inlaid
keep	kept	kept
kneel	knelt, kneeled	knelt, kneeled
knit	knit, knitted	knit, knitted
know	knew	known
lay (put)	laid	laid
lead	led	led
lean	leaned, leant	leaned, leant
leap	leaped, leapt	leaped, leapt
leave	left	left
lend	lent	lent
let	let	let
lie (recline)	lay	lain
light	lighted, lit	lighted, lit
lose	lost	lost
make	made	made
mean	meant	meant
meet	met	met
mow	mowed	mowed, mown
pay	paid	paid
prove	proved	proved, proven

Base Form	*Past Tense*	*Past Participle*
put	put	put
quit	quit, quitted	quit, quitted
read	read	read
rid	rid, ridded	rid, ridded
ride	rode	ridden
ring	rang	rung
rise	rose	risen
run	ran	run
say	said	said
see	saw	seen
seek	sought	sought
sell	sold	sold
send	sent	sent
set	set	set
sew	sewed	sewn, sewed
shake	shook	shaken
shave	shaved	shaved, shaven
shear	sheared	sheared, shorn
shed	shed	shed
shine ("to give light")	shone	shone
shine ("to polish")	shined	shined
shoot	shot	shot
show	showed	showed, shown
shrink	shrank	shrunk
shut	shut	shut
sing	sang	sung
sink	sank	sunk
sit	sat	sat
slay	slew	slain
sleep	slept	slept
slide	slid	slid, slidden
sling	slung	slung
slink	slunk	slunk
slit	slit	slit
sow	sowed	sown, sowed
speak	spoke	spoken
speed	sped, speeded	sped, speeded
spell	spelled, spelt	spelled, spelt
spend	spent	spent
spill	spilled, spilt	spilled, spilt
spin	spun	spun
split	split	split
spread	spread	spread
spring	sprang	sprung

Base Form	Past Tense	Past Participle
stand	stood	stood
steal	stole	stolen
stick	stuck	stuck
sting	stung	stung
stink	stank, stunk	stunk
stride	strode	stridden
strike	struck	struck, stricken
string	strung	strung
strive	strove	striven
swear	swore	sworn
sweep	swept	swept
swell	swelled	swollen, swelled
swim	swam	swum
swing	swung	swung
take	took	taken
teach	taught	taught
tear	tore	torn
tell	told	told
think	thought	thought
throw	threw	thrown
understand	understood	understood
wake	woke, waked	waked, woken
wear	wore	worn
weave	wove	woven
weep	wept	wept
win	won	won
wind	wound	wound
withdraw	withdrew	withdrawn
withhold	withheld	withheld
wring	wrung	wrung
write	wrote	written

Appendix C:
Conjugation of Four Irregular Verbs

TO BEGIN

Four Principal Parts

Infinitive—to begin
Past—began
Past Participle—begun
Present Participle—beginning

Present Tense

	Singular	Plural
First Person	I begin	We begin
Second Person	You begin	You begin
Third Person	He, she, it *begins*	They begin

Past Tense

	Singular	Plural
First Person	I began	We began
Second Person	You began	You began
Third Person	He, she, it began	They began

Future Tense

(*will* or *shall* + the base form of the verb)

	Singular	Plural
First Person	I will (shall) begin	We will (shall) begin
Second Person	You will begin	You will begin
Third Person	He, she, it will begin	They will begin

Present Perfect Tense

(*have* or *has* + the past participle)

	Singular	Plural
First Person	I have begun	We have begun
Second Person	You have begun	You have begun
Third Person	He, she, it *has* begun	They have begun

Past Perfect Tense

(*had* + the past participle)

	Singular	Plural
First Person	I had begun	We had begun
Second Person	You had begun	You had begun
Third Person	He, she, it had begun	They had begun

Future Perfect Tense

(*will have* or *shall have* + the past participle)

	Singular	Plural
First Person	I will (shall) have begun	We will (shall) have begun

Second Person	You will have begun	You will have begun
Third Person	He, she, it will have begun	They will have begun

TO BE

The most important and most irregular verb in the English language is *to be*. It is not only the primary state of being verb, but it is also the helping verb for all of the progressive tenses and for all of the verbs in the passive voice.

Four Principal Parts

Infinitive—to be
Past—was/were
Past Participle—been
Present Participle—being

Present Tense

	Singular	Plural
First Person	I am	We are
Second Person	You are	You are
Third Person	He, she, it *is*	They are

Past Tense

	Singular	Plural
First Person	I was	We were
Second Person	You were	You were
Third Person	He, she, it *was*	They were

Future Tense

(*will* or *shall* + the base form of the verb)

	Singular	Plural
First Person	I will (shall) be	We will (shall) be
Second Person	You will be	You will be
Third Person	He, she, it will be	They will be

Present Perfect Tense

(*have* or *has* + the past participle)

	Singular	Plural
First Person	I have been	We have been
Second Person	You have been	You have been
Third Person	He, she, it *has* been	They have been

Past Perfect Tense

(*had* + the past participle)

	Singular	Plural
First Person	I had been	We had been
Second Person	You had been	You had been
Third Person	He, she, it had been	They had been

Future Perfect Tense

(*will have* or *shall have* + the past participle)

	Singular	Plural
First Person	I will (shall) have been	We will (shall) have been
Second Person	You will have been	You will have been
Third Person	He, she, it will have been	They will have been

TO HAVE

To have is another important irregular verb. It shows possession or ownership and is also used as a helping verb with the past participle of other verbs to form the perfect tenses.

Four Principal Parts

Infinitive—to have
Past—had
Past Participle—had
Present Participle—having

Present Tense

	Singular	Plural
First Person	I have	We have
Second Person	You have	You have
Third Person	He, she, it *has*	They have

Past Tense

	Singular	Plural
First Person	I had	We had
Second Person	You had	You had
Third Person	He, she, it had	They had

Future Tense

(*will* or *shall* + the base form of the verb)

	Singular	Plural
First Person	I will (shall) have	We will (shall) have
Second Person	You will have	You will have
Third Person	He, she, it will have	They will have

Present Perfect Tense

(*have* or *has* + the past participle)

	Singular	Plural
First Person	I have had	We have had
Second Person	You have had	You have had
Third Person	He, she, it *has* had	They have had

Past Perfect Tense

(*had* + the past participle)

	Singular	Plural
First Person	I had had	We had had
Second Person	You had had	You had had
Third Person	He, she, it had had	They had had

Future Perfect Tense

(*will have* or *shall have* + the past participle)

	Singular	Plural
First Person	I will (shall) have had	We will (shall) have had
Second Person	You will have had	You will have had
Third Person	He, she, it will have had	They will have had

TO DO

To do is an irregular verb frequently used because it has so many different meanings.

Four Principal Parts

Infinitive—to do
Past—done
Past Participle—done
Present Participle—doing

Present Tense

	Singular	Plural
First Person	I do	We do
Second Person	You do	You do
Third Person	He, she, it *does*	They do

Past Tense

	Singular	Plural
First Person	I did	We did
Second Person	You did	You did
Third Person	He, she, it did	They did

Future Tense

(*will* or *shall* + the base form of the verb)

	Singular	Plural
First Person	I will (shall) do	We will (shall) do
Second Person	You will do	You will do
Third Person	He, she, it will do	They will do

Present Perfect Tense

(*have* or *has* + the past participle)

	Singular	Plural
First Person	I have done	We have done
Second Person	You have done	You have done
Third Person	He, she, it *has* done	They have done

Past Perfect Tense

(*had* + the past participle)

	Singular	Plural
First Person	I had done	We had done
Second Person	You had done	You had done
Third Person	He, she, it had done	They had done

Future Perfect Tense

(*will have* or *shall have* + the past participle)

	Singular	Plural
First Person	I will (shall) have done	We will (shall) have done
Second Person	You will have done	You will have done
Third Person	He, she, it will have done	They will have done

Appendix D:
Uncorrected Paragraph
and Corrected Paragraph

(from Chapter 24)

Uncorrected

I love to go to the health spa, working out with all the equipment is revitalizing to my mind and body. Although I cant quite keep up with the aerobics instructor. I do get a good workout. All of those thin women, at the front of the class, can follow the aerobics instructer very good. My friends and me, however, look like we is in slow motion. I also work out with; free weights. working out with the free weights are my favorite. Because I can work out at my own pace. I use the Nautilus machines to augmented my free weight work out. I like working out with the sophisticated machines that help you with you're mussel tone. I prefer the wieght lifting to aerobics; but I realize that I need to improve my cardiovascular system as we'll as my mussels, therefore, I split my week up into airobic workouts, and weight lifting workouts.

Corrected

I love to go to the health spa; working out with all the equipment is revitalizing to my mind and body. Although I can't quite keep up with the aerobics instructor, I do get a good workout. All of those thin women at the front of the class can follow the aerobics instructor very well. My friends and I, however, look like we are in slow motion. I also work out with free weights. Working out with the free weights is my favorite because I can work out at my own pace. I use the Nautilus machines to augment my free-weight workout. I like working out with the sophisticated machines that help you with your muscle tone. I prefer the weight lifting to aerobics, but I realize that I need to improve my cardiovascular system as well as my muscles; therefore, I split my week up into aerobic workouts and weight-lifting workouts.

Index